Bank Management

Bank Management

Edited by
Brie Forester

Larsen & Keller
www.larsen-keller.com

Bank Management
Edited by Brie Forester
ISBN: 978-1-63549-655-0 (Hardback)

Larsen & Keller

Published by Larsen and Keller Education,
5 Penn Plaza,
19th Floor,
New York, NY 10001, USA

Cataloging-in-Publication Data

Bank management / edited by Brie Forester.
p. cm.
Includes bibliographical references and index.
ISBN 978-1-63549-655-0
1. Bank management. 2. Banks and banking. 3. Management.
I. Forester, Brie.
HG1615 .B36 2018
332.1--dc23

Printed and bound in China.

For more information regarding Larsen and Keller Education and its products, please visit the publisher's website www.larsen-keller.com

Table of Contents

Preface

Bank management focuses on the systematic administration of the bank. It is associated with various concerns like asset management, liability management, liquidity management and capital management. Issuing loans, credit intermediation, maturity transformation, netting and settlement of payments, etc. are some of the key functions of a bank. Different approaches, evaluations and methodologies on bank management have been included in this book. As this field is emerging at a rapid pace, the contents of this textbook will help the readers understand the modern concepts and applications of the subject.

A detailed account of the significant topics covered in this book is provided below:

Chapter 1- Banks are institutions which receive deposits. These deposits are further converted into credit. There are various types of banks; some of these are commercial banks, community banks, land development banks, postal savings banks, private banks and offshore banks. This is an introductory chapter which will introduce briefly all the significant aspects of bank management.

Chapter 2- Asset and liability management is the supervision of the risks that can arise due to discrepancy between assets and liabilities. Wholesale funding, gap analysis, duration analysis, and hedge funds are some of the topics discussed in the section. This chapter elucidates the crucial theories and principles of asset liability management.

Chapter 3- Credit risk is the failure of the borrower to not be able to make the required payments. The different types of credit risks are credit default risk, country risk and concentration risk. This chapter has been carefully written to provide an easy understanding of the varied facets of credit risk.

Chapter 4- Operational risk is the risk that is incurred by and is inherent in, the institutional structure, staff and internal processes of any recognized company or organization. Operational risk is unavoidable and is suffered unwillingly. Bank management is best understood in confluence with the major topics listed in the following chapter.

I would like to make a special mention of my publisher who considered me worthy of this opportunity and also supported me throughout the process. I would also like to thank the editing team at the back-end who extended their help whenever required.

Editor

1

An Introduction to Banking Industry

Banks are institutions which receive deposits. These deposits are further converted into credit. There are various types of banks; some of these are commercial banks, community banks, land development banks, postal savings banks, private banks and offshore banks. This is an introductory chapter which will introduce briefly all the significant aspects of bank management.

Bank

A bank is a financial institution that accepts deposits from the public and creates credit. Lending activities can be performed either directly or indirectly through capital markets. Due to their importance in the financial stability of a country, banks are highly regulated in most countries. Most nations have institutionalized a system known as fractional reserve banking under which banks hold liquid assets equal to only a portion of their current liabilities. In addition to other regulations intended to ensure liquidity, banks are generally subject to minimum capital requirements based on an international set of capital standards, known as the Basel Accords.

Banking in its modern sense evolved in the 14th century in the prosperous cities of Renaissance Italy but in many ways was a continuation of ideas and concepts of credit and lending that had their roots in the ancient world. In the history of banking, a number of banking dynasties — notably, the Medicis, the Fuggers, the Welsers, the Berenbergs and the Rothschilds — have played a central role over many centuries. The oldest existing retail bank is Banca Monte dei Paschi di Siena, while the oldest existing merchant bank is Berenberg Bank.

History

Banking began with the first prototype banks of merchants of the ancient world, which made grain loans to farmers and traders who carried goods between cities. This began around 2000 BC in Assyria and Babylonia. Later, in ancient Greece and during the Roman Empire, lenders based in temples made loans and added two important innovations: they accepted deposits and changed money. Archaeology from this period in ancient China and India also shows evidence of money lending activity.

The origins of modern banking can be traced to medieval and early Renaissance Italy, to the rich cities in the centre and north like Florence, Lucca, Siena, Venice and Genoa.

The Bardi and Peruzzi families dominated banking in 14th-century Florence, establishing branches in many other parts of Europe. One of the most famous Italian banks was the Medici Bank, set up by Giovanni di Bicci de' Medici in 1397. The earliest known state deposit bank, Banco di San Giorgio (Bank of St. George), was founded in 1407 at Genoa, Italy.

Among many other things, the Code of Hammurabi from 1754 BC recorded interest-bearing loans.

Modern banking practices, including fractional reserve banking and the issue of banknotes, emerged in the 17th and 18th centuries. Merchants started to store their gold with the goldsmiths of London, who possessed private vaults, and charged a fee for that service. In exchange for each deposit of precious metal, the goldsmiths issued receipts certifying the quantity and purity of the metal they held as a bailee; these receipts could not be assigned, only the original depositor could collect the stored goods.

The sealing of the Bank of England Charter (1694).

Gradually the goldsmiths began to lend the money out on behalf of the depositor, which led to the development of modern banking practices; promissory notes (which evolved into banknotes) were issued for money deposited as a loan to the goldsmith. The goldsmith paid interest on these deposits. Since the promissory notes were payable on demand, and the advances (loans) to the goldsmith's customers were repayable over a longer time period, this was an early form of fractional reserve banking. The promissory notes developed into an assignable instrument which could circulate as a safe and convenient form of money backed by the goldsmith's promise to pay, allowing goldsmiths to advance loans with little risk of default. Thus, the goldsmiths of London became the forerunners of banking by creating new money based on credit.

The Bank of England was the first to begin the permanent issue of banknotes, in 1695. The Royal Bank of Scotland established the first overdraft facility in 1728. By the beginning of the 19th century a bankers' clearing house was established in London to allow multiple banks to clear transactions. The Rothschilds pioneered international finance on a large scale, financing the purchase of the Suez canal for the British government.

A 640 BC one-third stater electrum coin from Lydia, where gold and silver coins were used for the first time

Etymology

The word *bank* was borrowed in Middle English from Middle French *banque*, from Old Italian *banca*, meaning "table", from Old High German *banc, bank* "bench, counter". Benches were used as makeshift desks or exchange counters during the Renaissance by Jewish Florentine bankers, who used to make their transactions atop desks covered by green tablecloths.

Definition

The definition of a bank varies from country to country.

Under English common law, a banker is defined as a person who carries on the business of banking, which is specified as:

- conducting current accounts for his customers,
- paying cheques drawn on him/her, and
- collecting cheques for his/her customers.

In most common law jurisdictions there is a Bills of Exchange Act that codifies the law in relation to negotiable instruments, including cheques, and this Act contains a statutory definition of the term *banker*: *banker* includes a body of persons, whether incorporated or not, who carry on the business of banking' (Section 2, Interpretation).

Although this definition seems circular, it is actually functional, because it ensures that the legal basis for bank transactions such as cheques does not depend on how the bank is structured or regulated.

Banco de Venezuela in Coro.

Branch of Nepal Bank in Pokhara, Western Nepal.

The business of banking is in many English common law countries not defined by statute but by common law, the definition above. In other English common law jurisdictions there are statutory definitions of the *business of banking* or *banking business*. When looking at these definitions it is important to keep in mind that they are defining the business of banking for the purposes of the legislation, and not necessarily in general. In particular, most of the definitions are from legislation that has the purpose of regulating and supervising banks rather than regulating the actual business of banking. However, in many cases the statutory definition closely mirrors the common law one. Examples of statutory definitions:

- "banking business" means the business of receiving money on current or deposit account, paying and collecting cheques drawn by or paid in by customers, the making of advances to customers, and includes such other business as the Authority may prescribe for the purposes of this Act; (Banking Act (Singapore), Section 2, Interpretation).
- "banking business" means the business of either or both of the following:

1. receiving from the general public money on current, deposit, savings or other similar account repayable on demand or within less than [3 months] ... or with a period of call or notice of less than that period;
2. paying or collecting cheques drawn by or paid in by customers.

Since the advent of EFTPOS (Electronic Funds Transfer at Point Of Sale), direct credit, direct debit and internet banking, the cheque has lost its primacy in most banking systems as a payment instrument. This has led legal theorists to suggest that the cheque based definition should be broadened to include financial institutions that conduct current accounts for customers and enable customers to pay and be paid by third parties, even if they do not pay and collect cheques .

Standard Business

Large door to an old bank vault.

Banks act as payment agents by conducting checking or current accounts for customers, paying cheques drawn by customers on the bank, and collecting cheques deposited to customers' current accounts. Banks also enable customer payments via other payment methods such as Automated Clearing House (ACH), Wire transfers or telegraphic transfer, EFTPOS, and automated teller machines (ATMs).

Banks borrow money by accepting funds deposited on current accounts, by accepting term deposits, and by issuing debt securities such as banknotes and bonds. Banks lend money by making advances to customers on current accounts, by making installment loans, and by investing in marketable debt securities and other forms of money lending.

Banks provide different payment services, and a bank account is considered indispensable by most businesses and individuals. Non-banks that provide payment services such as remittance companies are normally not considered as an adequate substitute for a bank account.

Banks can create new money when they make a loan. New loans throughout the banking system generate new deposits elsewhere in the system. The money supply is usually increased by the act of lending, and reduced when loans are repaid faster than new ones are generated. In the United Kingdom between 1997 and 2007, there was an increase in the money supply, largely caused by much more bank lending, which served to push up property prices and increase private debt. The amount of money in the economy as measured by M4 in the UK went from £750 billion to £1700 billion between 1997 and 2007, much of the increase caused by bank lending. If all the banks increase their lending together, then they can expect new deposits to return to them and the amount of money in the economy will increase. Excessive or risky lending can cause borrowers to default, the banks then become more cautious, so there is less lending and therefore less money so that the economy can go from boom to bust as happened in the UK and many other Western economies after 2007.

Range of Activities

Activities undertaken by banks include personal banking, corporate banking, investment banking, private banking, transaction banking, insurance, consumer finance, foreign exchange trading, commodity trading, trading in equities, futures and options trading and money market trading.

Channels

An American bank in Maryland

Banks offer many different channels to access their banking and other services:

- Automated teller machines
- A branch in a retail location
- Call centre
- Mail: most banks accept cheque deposits via mail and use mail to communicate to their customers, e.g. by sending out statements
- Mobile banking is a method of using one's mobile phone to conduct banking transactions

- Online banking is a term used for performing multiple transactions, payments etc. over the Internet
- Relationship managers, mostly for private banking or business banking, often visiting customers at their homes or businesses
- Telephone banking is a service which allows its customers to conduct transactions over the telephone with automated attendant, or when requested, with telephone operator
- Video banking is a term used for performing banking transactions or professional banking consultations via a remote video and audio connection. Video banking can be performed via purpose built banking transaction machines (similar to an Automated teller machine), or via a video conference enabled bank branch clarification
- DSA is a Direct Selling Agent, who works for the bank based on a contract. Its main job is to increase the customer base for the bank.

Business Models

A bank can generate revenue in a variety of different ways including interest, transaction fees and financial advice. Traditionally, the most significant method is via charging interest on the capital it lends out to customers. The bank profits from the difference between the level of interest it pays for deposits and other sources of funds, and the level of interest it charges in its lending activities.

This difference is referred to as the spread between highly the cost of funds and the loan interest rate. Historically, profitability from lending activities has been cyclical and dependent on the needs and strengths of loan customers and the stage of the economic cycle. Fees and financial advice constitute a more stable revenue stream and banks have therefore placed more emphasis on these revenue lines to smooth their financial performance.

In the past 20 years, American banks have taken many measures to ensure that they remain profitable while responding to increasingly changing market conditions.

- First, this includes the Gramm–Leach–Bliley Act, which allows banks again to merge with investment and insurance houses. Merging banking, investment, and insurance functions allows traditional banks to respond to increasing consumer demands for "one-stop shopping" by enabling cross-selling of products (which, the banks hope, will also increase profitability).
- Second, they have expanded the use of risk-based pricing from business lending to consumer lending, which means charging higher interest rates to those customers that are considered to be a higher credit risk and thus increased chance

of default on loans. This helps to offset the losses from bad loans, lowers the price of loans to those who have better credit histories, and offers credit products to high risk customers who would otherwise be denied credit.

- Third, they have sought to increase the methods of payment processing available to the general public and business clients. These products include debit cards, prepaid cards, smart cards, and credit cards. They make it easier for consumers to conveniently make transactions and smooth their consumption over time (in some countries with underdeveloped financial systems, it is still common to deal strictly in cash, including carrying suitcases filled with cash to purchase a home).

  However, with the convenience of easy credit, there is also increased risk that consumers will mismanage their financial resources and accumulate excessive debt. Banks make money from card products through interest charges and fees charged to cardholders, and transaction fees to retailers who accept the bank's credit and/or debit cards for payments.

This helps in making a profit and facilitates economic development as a whole.

Products

A former building society, now a modern retail bank in Leeds, West Yorkshire.

An interior of a branch of National Westminster Bank on Castle Street, Liverpool

Retail

- Savings account
- Recurring deposit account
- Fixed deposit account
- Money market account
- Certificate of deposit (CD)
- Individual retirement account (IRA)
- Credit card
- Debit card
- Mortgage
- Mutual fund
- Personal loan
- Time deposits
- ATM card
- Current accounts
- Cheque books
- Automated Teller Machine (ATM)

Business (or Commercial/investment) Banking

- Business loan
- Capital raising (equity / debt / hybrids)
- Revolving credit
- Risk management (foreign exchange (FX)), interest rates, commodities, derivatives)
- Term loan
- Cash management services (lock box, remote deposit capture, merchant processing)
- Credit services

Capital and Risk

Banks face a number of risks in order to conduct their business, and how well these risks are managed and understood is a key driver behind profitability, and how much capital a bank is required to hold. Bank capital consists principally of equity, retained earnings and subordinated debt.

After the 2007-2009 financial crisis, regulators force banks to issue *Contingent convertible bonds* (CoCos).These are hybrid capital securities that absorb losses in accordance with their contractual terms when the capital of the issuing bank falls below a certain level. Then debt is reduced and bank capitalization gets a boost. Owing to their capacity to absorb losses, CoCos have the potential to satisfy regulatory capital requirement.

Some of the main risks faced by banks include:

- Credit risk: risk of loss arising from a borrower who does not make payments as promised.
- Liquidity risk: risk that a given security or asset cannot be traded quickly enough in the market to prevent a loss (or make the required profit).
- Market risk: risk that the value of a portfolio, either an investment portfolio or a trading portfolio, will decrease due to the change in value of the market risk factors.
- Operational risk: risk arising from execution of a company's business functions.
- Reputational risk: a type of risk related to the trustworthiness of business.
- Macroeconomic risk: risks related to the aggregate economy the bank is operating in.

The capital requirement is a bank regulation, which sets a framework within which a bank or depository institution must manage its balance sheet. The categorization of assets and capital is highly standardized so that it can be risk weighted.

Banks in the Economy

SEB main building in Tallinn, Estonia

Economic Functions

The economic functions of banks include:

1. Issue of money, in the form of banknotes and current accounts subject to cheque or payment at the customer's order. These claims on banks can act as money because they are negotiable or repayable on demand, and hence valued at par. They are effectively transferable by mere delivery, in the case of banknotes, or by drawing a cheque that the payee may bank or cash.

2. Netting and settlement of payments – banks act as both collection and paying agents for customers, participating in interbank clearing and settlement systems to collect, present, be presented with, and pay payment instruments. This enables banks to economize on reserves held for settlement of payments, since inward and outward payments offset each other. It also enables the offsetting of payment flows between geographical areas, reducing the cost of settlement between them.

3. Credit intermediation – banks borrow and lend back-to-back on their own account as middle men.

4. Credit quality improvement – banks lend money to ordinary commercial and personal borrowers (ordinary credit quality), but are high quality borrowers. The improvement comes from diversification of the bank's assets and capital which provides a buffer to absorb losses without defaulting on its obligations. However, banknotes and deposits are generally unsecured; if the bank gets into difficulty and pledges assets as security, to raise the funding it needs to continue to operate, this puts the note holders and depositors in an economically subordinated position.

5. Asset liability mismatch/Maturity transformation – banks borrow more on demand debt and short term debt, but provide more long term loans. In other words, they borrow short and lend long. With a stronger credit quality than most other borrowers, banks can do this by aggregating issues (e.g. accepting deposits and issuing banknotes) and redemptions (e.g. withdrawals and redemption of banknotes), maintaining reserves of cash, investing in marketable securities that can be readily converted to cash if needed, and raising replacement funding as needed from various sources (e.g. wholesale cash markets and securities markets).

6. Money creation/destruction – whenever a bank gives out a loan in a fractional-reserve banking system, a new sum of money is created and conversely, whenever the principal on that loan is repaid money is destroyed.

Bank Crisis

Banks are susceptible to many forms of risk which have triggered occasional systemic crises. These include liquidity risk (where many depositors may request withdrawals in excess of available funds), credit risk (the chance that those who owe money to the bank will not repay it), and interest rate risk (the possibility that the bank will become unprofitable, if rising interest rates force it to pay relatively more on its deposits than it receives on its loans).

OTP Bank in Prešov (Slovakia)

Banking crises have developed many times throughout history, when one or more risks have emerged for a banking sector as a whole. Prominent examples include the bank run that occurred during the Great Depression, the U.S. Savings and Loan crisis in the 1980s and early 1990s, the Japanese banking crisis during the 1990s, and the subprime mortgage crisis in the 2000s.

Size of Global Banking Industry

Assets of the largest 1,000 banks in the world grew by 6.8% in the 2008/2009 financial year to a record US$96.4 trillion while profits declined by 85% to US$115 billion. Growth in assets in adverse market conditions was largely a result of recapitalization. EU banks held the largest share of the total, 56% in 2008/2009, down from 61% in the previous year. Asian banks' share increased from 12% to 14% during the year, while the share of US banks increased from 11% to 13%. Fee revenue generated by global investment banking totalled US$66.3 billion in 2009, up 12% on the previous year.

The United States has the most banks in the world in terms of institutions (5,330 as of 2015) and possibly branches (81,607 as of 2015). This is an indicator of the geography and regulatory structure of the USA, resulting in a large number of small to medium-sized institutions in its banking system. As of Nov 2009, China's top 4 banks have in excess of 67,000 branches (ICBC:18000+, BOC:12000+, CCB:13000+,

ABC:24000+) with an additional 140 smaller banks with an undetermined number of branches. Japan had 129 banks and 12,000 branches. In 2004, Germany, France, and Italy each had more than 30,000 branches—more than double the 15,000 branches in the UK.

Regulation

Currently commercial banks are regulated in most jurisdictions by government entities and require a special bank license to operate.

Usually the definition of the business of banking for the purposes of regulation is extended to include acceptance of deposits, even if they are not repayable to the customer's order—although money lending, by itself, is generally not included in the definition.

Unlike most other regulated industries, the regulator is typically also a participant in the market, being either a publicly or privately governed central bank. Central banks also typically have a monopoly on the business of issuing banknotes. However, in some countries this is not the case. In the UK, for example, the Financial Services Authority licenses banks, and some commercial banks (such as the Bank of Scotland) issue their own banknotes in addition to those issued by the Bank of England, the UK government's central bank.

Banking law is based on a contractual analysis of the relationship between the *bank* (defined above) and the *customer*—defined as any entity for which the bank agrees to conduct an account.

The law implies rights and obligations into this relationship as follows:

1. The bank account balance is the financial position between the bank and the customer: when the account is in credit, the bank owes the balance to the customer; when the account is overdrawn, the customer owes the balance to the bank.

2. The bank agrees to pay the customer's checks up to the amount standing to the credit of the customer's account, plus any agreed overdraft limit.

3. The bank may not pay from the customer's account without a mandate from the customer, e.g. a cheque drawn by the customer.

4. The bank agrees to promptly collect the cheques deposited to the customer's account as the customer's agent, and to credit the proceeds to the customer's account.

5. The bank has a right to combine the customer's accounts, since each account is just an aspect of the same credit relationship.

6. The bank has a lien on cheques deposited to the customer's account, to the extent that the customer is indebted to the bank.

7. The bank must not disclose details of transactions through the customer's account—unless the customer consents, there is a public duty to disclose, the bank's interests require it, or the law demands it.

8. The bank must not close a customer's account without reasonable notice, since cheques are outstanding in the ordinary course of business for several days.

These implied contractual terms may be modified by express agreement between the customer and the bank. The statutes and regulations in force within a particular jurisdiction may also modify the above terms and/or create new rights, obligations or limitations relevant to the bank-customer relationship.

Some types of financial institution, such as building societies and credit unions, may be partly or wholly exempt from bank license requirements, and therefore regulated under separate rules.

The requirements for the issue of a bank license vary between jurisdictions but typically include:

1. Minimum capital

2. Minimum capital ratio

3. 'Fit and Proper' requirements for the bank's controllers, owners, directors, or senior officers

4. Approval of the bank's business plan as being sufficiently prudent and plausible.

Types of Banks

Banks' activities can be divided into:

- retail banking, dealing directly with individuals and small businesses;
- business banking, providing services to mid-market business;
- corporate banking, directed at large business entities;
- private banking, providing wealth management services to high-net-worth individuals and families;
- investment banking, relating to activities on the financial markets.

Most banks are profit-making, private enterprises. However, some are owned by government, or are non-profit organizations.

Types of Banks

National Bank of the Republic, Salt Lake City 1908

ATM Al-Rajhi Bank

A branch of Union Bank in, Visakhapatnam

- Commercial banks: the term used for a normal bank to distinguish it from an investment bank. After the Great Depression, the U.S. Congress required that banks only engage in banking activities, whereas investment banks were limited to capital market activities. Since the two no longer have to be under separate ownership, some use the term "commercial bank" to refer to a bank or a division of a bank that mostly deals with deposits and loans from corporations or large businesses.
- Community banks: locally operated financial institutions that empower employees to make local decisions to serve their customers and the partners.
- Community development banks: regulated banks that provide financial services and credit to under-served markets or populations.
- Land development banks: The special banks providing long-term loans are called land development banks (LDB). The history of LDB is quite old. The first LDB was started at Jhang in Punjab in 1920. The main objective of the LDBs are to promote the development of land, agriculture and increase the agricultural production. The LDBs provide long-term finance to members directly through their branches.
- Credit unions or co-operative banks: not-for-profit cooperatives owned by the depositors and often offering rates more favourable than for-profit banks. Typically, membership is restricted to employees of a particular company, residents of a defined area, members of a certain union or religious organizations, and their immediate families.
- Postal savings banks: savings banks associated with national postal systems.
- Private banks: banks that manage the assets of high-net-worth individuals. Historically a minimum of USD 1 million was required to open an account, however, over the last years many private banks have lowered their entry hurdles to USD 350,000 for private investors.
- Offshore banks: banks located in jurisdictions with low taxation and regulation. Many offshore banks are essentially private banks.

- Savings bank: in Europe, savings banks took their roots in the 19th or sometimes even in the 18th century. Their original objective was to provide easily accessible savings products to all strata of the population. In some countries, savings banks were created on public initiative; in others, socially committed individuals created foundations to put in place the necessary infrastructure. Nowadays, European savings banks have kept their focus on retail banking: payments, savings products, credits and insurances for individuals or small and medium-sized enterprises. Apart from this retail focus, they also differ from commercial banks by their broadly decentralized distribution network, providing local and regional outreach—and by their socially responsible approach to business and society.
- Building societies and Landesbanks: institutions that conduct retail banking.
- Ethical banks: banks that prioritize the transparency of all operations and make only what they consider to be socially responsible investments.
- A direct or internet-only bank is a banking operation without any physical bank branches, conceived and implemented wholly with networked computers.

Types of Investment Banks

- Investment banks "underwrite" (guarantee the sale of) stock and bond issues, trade for their own accounts, make markets, provide investment management, and advise corporations on capital market activities such as mergers and acquisitions.
- Merchant banks were traditionally banks which engaged in trade finance. The modern definition, however, refers to banks which provide capital to firms in the form of shares rather than loans. Unlike venture caps, they tend not to invest in new companies.

Both Combined

A branch of BDO Unibank in SM Aura Premier, BGC

- Universal banks, more commonly known as financial services companies, engage in several of these activities. These big banks are very diversified groups that, among other services, also distribute insurance— hence the term bancassurance, a portmanteau word combining "banque or bank" and "assurance", signifying that both banking and insurance are provided by the same corporate entity.

Other Types of Banks

- Central banks are normally government-owned and charged with quasi-regulatory responsibilities, such as supervising commercial banks, or controlling the cash interest rate. They generally provide liquidity to the banking system and act as the lender of last resort in event of a crisis.
- Islamic banks adhere to the concepts of Islamic law. This form of banking revolves around several well-established principles based on Islamic canons. All banking activities must avoid interest, a concept that is forbidden in Islam. Instead, the bank earns profit (markup) and fees on the financing facilities that it extends to customers.

Challenges within the Banking Industry

United States

Citibank, The People's Trust Company Building, Brooklyn.

The United States banking industry is one of the most heavily regulated and guarded in the world, with multiple specialized and focused regulators. All banks with FDIC-insured deposits have the Federal Deposit Insurance Corporation (FDIC) as a regulator. However, for soundness examinations (i.e., whether a bank is operating in a sound manner), the Federal Reserve is the primary federal regulator for Fed-member state banks; the Office of the Comptroller of the Currency (OCC) is the primary federal regulator for national banks; and the Office of Thrift Supervision, or OTS, is the primary federal regulator for thrifts. State non-member banks are examined by the state agencies as well as the FDIC. National banks have one primary regulator—the OCC.

Each regulatory agency has their own set of rules and regulations to which banks and thrifts must adhere. The Federal Financial Institutions Examination Council (FFIEC) was established in 1979 as a formal inter-agency body empowered to prescribe uniform principles, standards, and report forms for the federal examination of financial institutions. Although the FFIEC has resulted in a greater degree of regulatory consistency between the agencies, the rules and regulations are constantly changing.

In addition to changing regulations, changes in the industry have led to consolidations within the Federal Reserve, FDIC, OTS, and OCC. Offices have been closed, supervisory regions have been merged, staff levels have been reduced and budgets have been cut. The remaining regulators face an increased burden with increased workload and more banks per regulator. While banks struggle to keep up with the changes in the regulatory environment, regulators struggle to manage their workload and effectively regulate their banks. The impact of these changes is that banks are receiving less hands-on assessment by the regulators, less time spent with each institution, and the potential for more problems slipping through the cracks, potentially resulting in an overall increase in bank failures across the United States.

Safra National Bank, New York

The changing economic environment has a significant impact on banks and thrifts as they struggle to effectively manage their interest rate spread in the face of low rates on loans, rate competition for deposits and the general market changes, industry trends and economic fluctuations. It has been a challenge for banks to effectively set their growth strategies with the recent economic market. A rising interest rate environment may seem to help financial institutions, but the effect of the changes on consumers and businesses is not predictable and the challenge remains for banks to grow and effectively manage the spread to generate a return to their shareholders.

The management of the banks' asset portfolios also remains a challenge in today's economic environment. Loans are a bank's primary asset category and when loan quality becomes suspect, the foundation of a bank is shaken to the core. While always an issue for banks, declining asset quality has become a big problem for financial institutions.

There are several reasons for this, one of which is the lax attitude some banks have adopted because of the years of "good times." The potential for this is exacerbated by the reduction in the regulatory oversight of banks and in some cases depth of management. Problems are more likely to go undetected, resulting in a significant impact on the bank when they are discovered. In addition, banks, like any business, struggle to cut costs and have consequently eliminated certain expenses, such as adequate employee training programs.

Banks also face a host of other challenges such as ageing ownership groups. Across the country, many banks' management teams and board of directors are ageing. Banks also face ongoing pressure by shareholders, both public and private, to achieve earnings and growth projections. Regulators place added pressure on banks to manage the various categories of risk. Banking is also an extremely competitive industry. Competing in the financial services industry has become tougher with the entrance of such players as insurance agencies, credit unions, cheque cashing services, credit card companies, etc.

As a reaction, banks have developed their activities in financial instruments, through financial market operations such as brokerage and have become big players in such activities.

Loan Activities of Banks

To be able to provide home buyers and builders with the funds needed, banks must compete for deposits. The phenomenon of disintermediation had to dollars moving from savings accounts and into direct market instruments such as U.S. Department of Treasury obligations, agency securities, and corporate debt. One of the greatest factors in recent years in the movement of deposits was the tremendous growth of money market funds whose higher interest rates attracted consumer deposits.

To compete for deposits, US savings institutions offer many different types of plans:

- Passbook or ordinary deposit accounts – permit any amount to be added to or withdrawn from the account at any time.
- NOW and Super NOW accounts – function like checking accounts but earn interest. A minimum balance may be required on Super NOW accounts.

- Money market accounts — carry a monthly limit of preauthorized transfers to other accounts or persons and may require a minimum or average balance.
- Certificate accounts — subject to loss of some or all interest on withdrawals before maturity.
- Notice accounts — the equivalent of certificate accounts with an indefinite term. Savers agree to notify the institution a specified time before withdrawal.
- Individual retirement accounts (IRAs) and Keogh plans — a form of retirement savings in which the funds deposited and interest earned are exempt from income tax until after withdrawal.
- Checking accounts — offered by some institutions under definite restrictions.
- All withdrawals and deposits are completely the sole decision and responsibility of the account owner unless the parent or guardian is required to do otherwise for legal reasons.
- Club accounts and other savings accounts — designed to help people save regularly to meet certain goals.

Type of Accounts

Suburban bank branch

Bank statements are accounting records produced by banks under the various accounting standards of the world. Under GAAP there are two kinds of accounts: debit and credit. Credit accounts are Revenue, Equity and Liabilities. Debit Accounts are Assets and Expenses. The bank credits a *credit account* to increase its balance, and debits a *credit account* to decrease its balance.

The customer debits his or her savings/bank (asset) account in his ledger when making a deposit (and the account is normally in debit), while the customer credits a credit card (liability) account in his ledger every time he spends money (and the account is normally in credit). When the customer reads his bank statement, the statement will show a credit to the account for deposits, and debits for withdrawals of funds. The customer with a positive balance will see this balance reflected as a credit balance on the bank statement. If the customer is overdrawn, he will have a negative balance, reflected as a debit balance on the bank statement.

Brokered Deposits

One source of deposits for banks is brokers who deposit large sums of money on behalf of investors through trust corporations. This money will generally go to the banks which offer the most favourable terms, often better than those offered local depositors. It is possible for a bank to engage in business with no local deposits at all, all funds being brokered deposits. Accepting a significant quantity of such deposits, or "hot money" as it is sometimes called, puts a bank in a difficult and sometimes risky position, as the funds must be lent or invested in a way that yields a return sufficient to pay the high interest being paid on the brokered deposits. This may result in risky decisions and even in eventual failure of the bank. Banks which failed during 2008 and 2009 in the United States during the global financial crisis had, on average, four times more brokered deposits as a percent of their deposits than the average bank. Such deposits, combined with risky real estate investments, factored into the savings and loan crisis of the 1980s. Regulation of brokered deposits is opposed by banks on the grounds that the practice can be a source of external funding to growing communities with insufficient local deposits. There are different types of accounts: saving, recurring and current accounts.

Globalization in the Banking Industry

In modern time there has been huge reductions to the barriers of global competition in the banking industry. Increases in telecommunications and other financial technologies, such as Bloomberg, have allowed banks to extend their reach all over the world, since they no longer have to be near customers to manage both their finances and their risk. The growth in cross-border activities has also increased the demand for banks that can provide various services across borders to different nationalities. However, despite these reductions in barriers and growth in cross-border activities, the banking industry is nowhere near as globalized as some other industries. In the USA, for instance, very few banks even worry about the Riegle–Neal Act, which promotes more efficient interstate banking. In the vast majority of nations around the globe the market share for foreign owned banks is currently less than a tenth of all market shares for banks in a particular nation. One reason the banking industry has not been fully globalized is that it is more convenient to have local banks provide loans to small business and individuals. On the other hand, for large corporations, it is not as important in what nation the bank is in, since the corporation's financial information is available around the globe.

Private Bank

Private banks are the banks owned by either the individual or a general partner(s) with limited partner(s). Private banks are not incorporated. In any such case, the creditors can look to both the "entirety of the bank's assets" as well as the entirety of the sole-proprietor's/general-partners' assets.

These banks have a long tradition in Switzerland, dating back to at least the Revocation of the Edict of Nantes (1685). Private banks also have a long tradition in the UK where C. Hoare & Co. has been in business since 1672.

There were many private banks in Europe, but most have now become incorporated companies, so the term is rarely true any more. Today, the term "private bank" can also refer to the financial institution specializing in financial advice and services for high-net-worth individuals (private banking).

"Private banks" can also refer to non-government owned banks in general, in contrast to government-owned (or nationalized) banks, which were prevalent in communist, socialist and some social democratic states in the 20th century.

Notable Private Banks

This list contains two types of banks:

- Unincorporated banks owned by either an individual or a general partner(s) with limited partner(s).
- Incorporated banks specialized in wealth management for high-net-worth individuals.

Public Bank

A public bank is a bank, a financial institution, in which a state or public actors are the owners. It is a company under state control.

Public or 'state-owned' banks proliferated globally in the late 19th and early 20th centuries as vital agents of industrialisation in capitalist and socialist countries alike; as late as 2012, state banks still owned and controlled up to 25 per cent of total global banking assets.

History of Banking

The history of banking refers to the development of banks and banking throughout history, with banking defined by contemporary sources as an organization which provides facilities for acceptance of deposits and provision of loans.

The history begins with the first prototype banks of merchants of the ancient world, which made grain loans to farmers and traders who carried goods between cities. This began around 2000 BC in Assyria and Babylonia. Later, in ancient Greece and during the Roman Empire, lenders based in temples made loans and added two important innovations: they accepted deposits and changed money. Archaeology from this period in ancient China and India also shows evidence of money lending activity.

Many histories position the crucial historical development of a banking system to medieval and Renaissance Italy and particularly the affluent cities of Florence, Venice and Genoa. The Bardi and Peruzzi families dominated banking in 14th century Florence, establishing branches in many other parts of Europe. The most famous Italian bank was the Medici bank, established by Giovanni Medici in 1397. The oldest bank still in existence is Banca Monte dei Paschi di Siena, headquartered in Siena, Italy, which has been operating continuously since 1472.

The development of banking spread from northern Italy throughout the Holy Roman Empire, and in the 15th and 16th century to northern Europe. This was followed by a number of important innovations that took place in Amsterdam during the Dutch Republic in the 17th century, and in London in the 18th century. During the 20th century, developments in telecommunications and computing caused major changes to banks' operations and let banks dramatically increase in size and geographic spread. The financial crisis of 2007–2008 caused many bank failures, including some of the world's largest banks, and provoked much debate about bank regulation.

Ancient Precedents

More stable economic relations were brought about with a change in socio-economic conditions from a reliance on hunting and gathering of foods to agricultural practice, during periods beginning sometime after 12,000 BC, at approximately 10,000 years ago in the Fertile Crescent, in northern China about 9,500 years ago, about 5,500 years ago in Mexico and approximately 4,500 in the eastern parts of the United States.

Monetary

The history of banking is intertwined with the history of money. Ancient types of money known as grain-money and food cattle-money were used from a time of around at least 9000 BC, as two of the earliest things understood as things to be made use of for the purposes of barter (Davies).

Anatolian obsidian as a raw material for Stone Age tools was being distributed from as early as about 12,500 B.C., the occurrence of an organized trade was current during the 9th millennium (Cauvin;Chataigner 1989). Within Sardinia, which was the location of one of the four main sites for sourcing the material deposits of obsidian within the Mediterranean, trade using obsidian was replaced during the 3rd millennia by trade instead of copper and silver.

Record-keeping

Detailed account of raw materials and workdays for a basketry workshop. Clay, ca. 2040 BC (Ur III)

History of Accounting

Objects used for record keeping, "bulla" and *tokens*, have been recovered from within Near East excavations, dated to a period beginning 8000 B.C.E and ending 1500 B.C.E., as records of the counting of agricultural produce. Commencing in the late fourth millennia mnemonic symbols were in use by members of temples and palaces to serve to record stocks of produce. Types of records accounting for trade exchanges of payments were being made firstly about 3200. A very early writing on clay tablet called the *Code of Hammurabi*, refers to the regulation of a banking activity of sorts within the civilization (Armstrong) of an era which dates to ca. 1700 BCE, banking was well enough developed to justify laws governing banking operations. Later during the Achaemenid Empire (after 646 BC.), further evidence is found of banking practices in the Mesopotamia region.

Structural

By the 5th millennium B.C. the settlements of Sumer, such as Eridu, were formed around a central temple. In the fifth millennium, people began to build and live in the civilization of cities, providing a structure for the construction of institutions and establishments. Tell Brak and Uruk were two early urban settlements.

Earliest Forms of Banking

Mesopotamia and Persia

Banking as an archaic activity (or quasi-banking) is thought to have begun at various times, during a period as early as the latter part of the 4th millennia B.C., to within the 4th to 3rd millennia B.C.

Prior to the reign of Sargon I of Akkad (2335–2280 B.C.) the occurrence of trade was limited to the internal boundaries of each city-state of Babylon and the temple located at the centre of economic activity there-in; trade at the time for citizens external to the city was forbidden.

In Babylonia of 2000 B.C., people depositing gold were required to pay amounts as much as one sixtieth of the total deposited. Both the palaces and temple are known to have provided lending and issuing from the wealth they held—the palaces to a lesser extent. Such loans typically involved issuing seed-grain, with re-payment from the harvest. These basic social agreements were documented in clay tablets, with an agreement on interest accrual. The habit of depositing and storing of wealth in temples continued at least until 209 B.C., as evidenced by Antioch having ransacked or pillaged the temple of Aine in Ecbatana (Media) of gold and silver.

Cuneiform records of the house of Egibi of Babylonia describe the family's financial activities dated as having occurred sometime after 1000 BC and ending sometime during the reign of Darius I, show according to one source a "lending house" (Silver 2002),a family engaging in "professional banking..." (Dandamaev *et al* 2004) and economic activities similar to a degree to modern deposit banking, although another states the family's activities better described as entrepreneurship rather than banking (Wunsch 2007). The provision of credit is apparently also something the Murashu family participated in (Moshenskyi 2008).

Greece

Trapezitica is the first source documenting banking *(de Soto* – p. 41). The speeches of Demosthenes contain numerous references to the issuing of credit (Millett p. 5). Xenophon is credited to have made the first suggestion of the creation of an organisation known in the modern definition as a joint-stock bank in *On Revenues* written *circa* 353 B.C.

The city-states of Greece after the Persian Wars produced a government and culture sufficiently organized for the birth of a private citizenship and therefore an embryonic capitalist society, allowing for the separation of wealth from exclusive state ownership to the possibility of ownership by the individual.

According to one source (Dandamaev *et al*), trapezites were the first to trade using money, during the 5th century B.C, as opposed to earlier trade which occurred using forms of pre-money.

Specific Locus of Funds

The earliest forms of storage utilized were the rudimentary money-boxes which were made similar in form to the construction of a bee-hive, and were found for example in the Mycenae tombs of 1550–1500 BC.

Private and civic entities within ancient Grecian society, especially Greek temples, performed financial transactions. (Gilbart p. 3) The temples were the places where treasure was deposited for safe-keeping. The three temples thought the most important were the temple to Artemis in Ephesus, and temple of Hera within Samos, and within Delphi, the temple to Apollo. These consisted of deposits, currency exchange, validation of coinage, and loans.

The first treasury to the Apollonian temple was built before the end of the 7th century BC, a treasury of the temple was constructed by the city of Siphnos during the 6th century.

Before the destruction by Persians during the 480 invasion, the Athenian Acropolis temple dedicated to Athena stored money; Pericles rebuilt a depository afterward contained within the Parthenon.

During the reign of the Ptolemies, state depositories replaced temples as the location of security-deposits, records exist to show this having occurred by the end of the reign of Ptolemy I (305–284).

As the need for new buildings to house operations increased, construction of these places within the cities began around the courtyards of the agora (markets).

Geographical Loci of Banking Activities

Athens received the Delian leagues' treasury during 454.

During the late 3rd and 2nd century BC, the Aegean island of Delos, became a prominent banking center. During the 2nd century, there were for certain three banks and one temple depository within the city.

Thirty five Hellenistic cities included private banks during the 2nd century (Roberts – p. 130).

Of the settlements of the Greco-Roman world of the 1st century AD, three were of pronounced wealth and centres of banking, Athens, Corinth and Patras.

Loans

Many loans are recorded in writings from the classical age, although a very small proportion were provided by banks. Provision of these were likely an occurrence of Athens, with loans known to have been provided at some time at an annual interest of 12%. Within the boundaries of Athens, bankers loans are recorded as having been issued on eleven occasions altogether (Bogaert 1968).

Banks sometimes made loans available confidentially, which is, they provided funds without being publicly and openly known to have done so, in addition also, to act as intermediaries for persons to loan their own monies without this being known to others. This intermediation *per se* was known as dia tes trapazēs.

A loan was made by a Temple of Athens to the state during 433–427 BCE.

Egypt

Government and Economy

About the time of the 18th century BC, amounts of gold were deposited within the boundaries of the temple buildings of Egypt for reasons of security.

In Egypt from early times, grain having an intrinsic value as food functioned, in addition to precious metals, as money. The regional granaries were used to store and loan the grain of communities, functions similar to banking services although not the same. Under the dynastic rule of the Ptolemies, the numerous scattered government granaries were transformed into a network of grain banks, centralized in Alexandria where the main accounts from all the state granary banks were recorded. This centralized administration was the first known governmental bank (according to *de Soto*), functioning as a trade credit system that transferred payments between accounts without passing money.

According to Muir (2008) there were two types of banks operating within Egypt, royal and private. During the Ptolemaic period, *basilik trápeza* was the term used when referring to *royal bank.*

More generally during the whole Graeco-Roman period (332 B.C. – 642 A.D.), banks were of three types, either privately run, leased, or owned by government, of which included within this last group were some organisations having dual roles including being additionally treasury departments.

Documents made to show the banking of taxes were known as peptoken-records.

The recording of the gathering of money to buy grain in a pharaoh's kingdom as ordered by the Biblical Joseph, is written within the book Genesis of the Bible, and this money was placed within the house of the pharaoh. Joseph bought with the money of the pharaoh a large amount of *corn*, having this then laid in the public granaries.

Rome

Gold coin produced by the Roman Imperial Mint

Roman banking activities were an economic situation which had a crucial presence within temples, for instance the minting of coins occurred within temples, most importantly the Juno Moneta temple, though during the time of the Empire, public deposits gradually ceased to be held in temples, and instead were held in private depositories. Still, the Roman Empire inherited the *spirit of capitalism* from Greece (Parker).

During 352 B.C. a rudimentary public bank (known as *dēmosía trápeza*) was formed, with the passing of consul directive to form a commission of *mensarii* to deal with debt in the impoverished lower classes. Another source shows banking practices during 325 BC when, on account of being in debt, the Plebeians were required to borrow money, so newly appointed *quinqueviri mensarii* were commissioned to provide services to those who had security to provide, in exchange for money from the public treasury. Another source (J.Andreau) has the shops of banking of Ancient Rome firstly opening in the public forums during the period 318 to 310 BC.

In early Ancient Rome deposit bankers were known as *argentarius* and at a later time (from the 2nd century *anno domini* onward) as *nummularius* (Andreau 1999 p. 2) or *mensarii*. The banking-houses were known as *Taberae Argentarioe* and *Mensoe Numularioe*. Money-lenders would set up their stalls in the middle of enclosed courtyards called *macella* on a long bench called a *bancu*, from which the words *banco* and *bank* are derived. As a moneychanger, the merchant at the *bancu* did not so much invest money as merely convert the foreign currency into the only legal tender in Rome – that of the Imperial Mint.

Operations of banking within Roman society were known as *officium argentarii*. Statutes (AD 125/126) of the Empire described "*letter from Caesar to Quietus*" show rental monies to be collected from persons using land belonging to a temple and given to the temple treasurer, as decreed by Mettius Modestus governor of Lycia and Pamphylia. A law, *receptum argentarii*, obliged a bank to pay its clients debts under guarantee.

Cassius Dio advocated the establishment of a state bank, funded by the sale of all the properties owned at the time by the state.

In the 4th century monopolies existed in Byzantium and in the city of Olbia in Sardinia.

The Roman empire at some time formalized the administrative aspect of banking and instituted greater regulation of financial institutions and financial practices. Charging interest on loans and paying interest on deposits became more highly developed and competitive. The development of Roman banks was limited, however, by the Roman preference for cash transactions. During the reign of the Roman emperor Gallienus (AD 260–268), there was a temporary breakdown of the Roman banking system after the banks rejected the flakes of copper produced by his mints. With the ascent of Christianity, banking became subject to additional restrictions, as the charging of interest was seen as immoral. After the fall of Rome, banking temporarily ended in Europe and was not revived until the time of the crusades.

Asia Minor

From the fourth millennia previously agricultural settlements began administrative activities.

The temple of Artemis at Ephesus was the largest depository of Asia. A pot-hoard dated to 600 B.C. was found in excavations by *the British Museum* during the year after 1904. During the time at the cessation of the first Mithridatic war the entire debt record at the time being held, was annulled by the council. Mark Anthony is recorded to have stolen from the deposits on an occasion. The temple served as a depository for Aristotle, Caesar, Dio Chrysostomus, Plautus, Plutarch, Strabo and Xenophon.

The temple to Apollo in Didyma was constructed sometime in the 6th century. A large sum of gold was deposited within the treasury at the time by king Croesus.

Asia

India

In ancient India there is evidence of loans from the Vedic period (beginning 1750 BC). Later during the Maurya dynasty (321 to 185 BC), an instrument called adesha was in use, which was an order on a banker desiring him to pay the money of the note to a third person, which corresponds to the definition of a bill of exchange as we understand it today. During the Buddhist period, there was considerable use of these instruments. Merchants in large towns gave letters of credit to one another.

China

In ancient China, starting in the Qin Dynasty (221 to 206 BC), Chinese currency developed with the introduction of standardized coins that allowed easier trade across China, and led to development of letters of credit. These letters were issued by merchants who acted in ways that today we would understand as banks.

Religious Restrictions on Interest

Most early religious systems in the ancient Near East, and the secular codes arising from them, did not forbid usury. These societies regarded inanimate matter as alive, like plants, animals and people, and capable of reproducing itself. Hence if you lent 'food money', or monetary tokens of any kind, it was legitimate to charge interest. Food money in the shape of olives, dates, seeds or animals was lent out as early as c. 5000 BCE, if not earlier. Among the Mesopotamians, Hittites, Phoenicians and Egyptians, interest was legal and often fixed by the state.

Judaism

The Torah and later sections of the Hebrew Bible criticize interest-taking, but interpretations of the Biblical prohibition vary. One common understanding is that Jews are forbidden to charge interest upon loans made to other Jews, but obliged to charge interest on transactions with non-Jews, or Gentiles. However, the Hebrew Bible itself gives numerous examples where this provision was evaded.

Deuteronomy 23:19 Thou shalt not lend upon interest to thy brother: interest of money, interest of victuals, interest of any thing that is lent upon interest.

Deuteronomy 23:20 Unto a foreigner thou mayest lend upon interest; but unto thy brother thou shalt not lend upon interest; that the LORD thy God may bless thee in all that thou puttest thy hand unto, in the land whither thou goest in to possess it.

Christ drives the Usurers out of the Temple, a woodcut by Lucas Cranach the Elder in Passionary of Christ and Antichrist.

Israelites were forbidden to charge interest on loans made to other Israelites, but allowed to charge interest on transactions with non-Israelites, as the latter were often amongst the Israelites for the purpose of business anyway, but in general, it was seen as advantageous to avoid debt at all, to avoid being bound to someone else. Debt was to be avoided and not used to finance consumption, but only when in need. However, laws against usury were among many the prophets condemn the people for breaking.

It was the interpretation that interest could be charged to non-Israelites that would be used in the 14th century for Jews living within Christian societies in Europe to justify lending money for profit. As this conveniently side stepped the rules against usury in both Judaism and Christianity as the Jews could lend to the Christians as they are not Israelites and the Christians were not involved in the lending but were still free to take the loans.

Christianity

Originally, the charging of interest, known as usury, was banned by Christian churches.

This included charging a fee for the use of money, such as at a bureau de change. However over time the charging of interest became acceptable due to the changing nature of money, the term came to be used for interest above the rate allowed by law.

The rise of Protestantism in the 16th century weakened Rome's influence, and its dictates against usury became irrelevant in some areas. That would free up the development of banking in Northern Europe.

Islam

In Islam it is strictly prohibited to take interest; the Quran strictly prohibits lending money on Interest. "O you who have believed, do not consume usury, doubled and multiplied, but fear Allah that you may be successful" (3:130) "and Allah has permitted trade and has forbidden interest" (2:275).

Holy Quran states that taking of interest and making money through unethical means is not prohibited for Muslims only but were prohibited for earlier communities as well. Two verses (Al Quran – 4:160–161) clearly states that "Because of the wrongdoing of the Jews We forbade them good things which were (before) made lawful unto them, and because of their much hindering from Allah's way, And of their taking usury when they were forbidden it, and of their devouring people's wealth by false pretences, We have prepared for those of them who disbelieve a painful doom."

Riba is forbidden in Islamic economic jurisprudence (fiqh). Islamic jurists discuss two types of riba: an increase in capital with no services provided, which the Qur'an prohibits—and commodity exchanges in unequal quantities, which the Sunnah prohibits; trade in promissory notes (e.g. fiat money and derivatives) is forbidden.

Despite the prohibition of charging interest, during the 20th century a number of developments took place that would lead to an Islamic banking model where no interest is charged but banks would still operate for profit. This would be done through charging for loans in different ways such as through fees and using method of risk sharing and different ownership models such as leasing.

Medieval Europe

Banking, in the modern sense of the word, is traceable to medieval and early Renaissance Italy, to rich cities in the north such as Florence, Venice, and Genoa.

Emergence of Merchant Banks

The original banks were "merchant banks" that Italian grain merchants invented in the Middle Ages. As Lombardy merchants and bankers grew in stature based on the strength of the Lombard plains cereal crops, many displaced Jews fleeing Spanish persecution were attracted to the trade. They brought with them ancient practices from the

Middle and Far East silk routes. Originally intended to finance long trading journeys, they applied these methods to finance grain production and trading.

Map showing silk routes

Jews could not hold land in Italy, so they entered the great trading piazzas and halls of Lombardy, alongside local traders, and set up their benches to trade in crops. They had one great advantage over the locals. Christians were strictly forbidden the sin of usury, defined as lending at interest (Islam makes similar condemnations of usury). The Jewish newcomers, on the other hand, could lend to farmers against crops in the field, a high-risk loan at what would have been considered usurious rates by the Church; but the Jews were not subject to the Church's dictates. In this way they could secure the grain-sale rights against the eventual harvest. They then began to advance payment against the future delivery of grain shipped to distant ports. In both cases they made their profit from the present discount against the future price. This two-handed trade was time-consuming and soon there arose a class of merchants who were trading grain debt instead of grain.

The Jewish trader performed both financing (credit) and underwriting (insurance) functions. Financing took the form of a crop loan at the beginning of the growing season, which allowed a farmer to cultivate (through seeding, growing, weeding, and harvesting) his annual crop. Underwriting in the form of a crop, or commodity, insurance guaranteed the delivery of the crop to its buyer, typically a merchant wholesaler. In addition, traders performed the merchant function by making arrangements to supply the buyer of the crop through alternative sources—grain stores or alternate markets, for instance—in the event of crop failure. He could also keep the farmer (or other commodity producer) in business during a drought or other crop failure, through the issuance of a crop (or commodity) insurance against the hazard of failure of his crop.

Merchant banking progressed from financing trade on one's own behalf to settling trades for others and then to holding deposits for settlement of "billette" or notes written by the people who were still brokering the actual grain. And so the merchant's "benches" (*bank* is derived from the Italian for bench, *banca*, as in a counter) in the great grain markets became centres for holding money against a bill (*billette*, a note, a letter of formal exchange, later a bill of exchange and later still a cheque).

These deposited funds were intended to be held for the settlement of grain trades, but often were used for the bench's own trades in the meantime. The term bankrupt is a corruption of the Italian *banca rotta*, or broken bench, which is what happened when someone lost his traders' deposits. Being "broke" has the same connotation.

Crusades

Adhemar de Monteil in chain mail carrying the Holy Lance in one of the battles of the First Crusade

In the 12th century, the need to transfer large sums of money to finance the Crusades stimulated the re-emergence of banking in western Europe. In 1162, Henry II of England levied a tax to support the crusades—the first of a series of taxes levied by Henry over the years with the same objective. The Templars and Hospitallers acted as Henry's bankers in the Holy Land. The Templars' wide flung, large land holdings across Europe also emerged in the 1100–1300 time frame as the beginning of Europe-wide banking, as their practice was to take in local currency, for which a demand note would be given that would be good at any of their castles across Europe, allowing movement of money without the usual risk of robbery while traveling.

Discounting of Interest

A sensible manner of discounting interest to the depositors against what could be earned by employing their money in the trade of the bench soon developed; in short, selling an "interest" to them in a specific trade, thus overcoming the usury objection. Once again this merely developed what was an ancient method of financing long-distance transport of goods. Medieval trade fairs, such as the one in Hamburg, contributed to the growth of banking in a curious way: moneychangers issued documents redeemable at other fairs, in exchange for hard currency. These documents could be cashed at another fair in a different country or at a future fair in the same location. If redeemable at a future date, they would often be discounted by an amount comparable to a rate of interest. Eventually, these documents evolved into bills of exchange, which could be redeemed at any office of the issuing banker. These bills made it possible to transfer large sums of money without the complications of hauling large chests of gold and hiring armed guards to protect the gold from thieves.

Foreign Exchange Contracts

In 1156, in Genoa, occurred the earliest known foreign exchange contract. Two brothers borrowed 115 Genoese pounds and agreed to reimburse the bank's agents in Constantinople the sum of 460 bezants one month after their arrival in that city. In the following century the use of such contracts grew rapidly, particularly since profits from time differences were seen as not infringing canon laws against usury.

Italian Bankers

A 14th century manuscript depicting bankers in an Italian counting house.

The first bank to be established was established in Venice with guarantee from the State in 1157. According to Macardy this was due to the commercial agency of the Venetians, acting in the interest of the Crusaders of Pope Urban the Second. The reason is given elsewhere as due to costs of the expansion of the empire under Doge Vitale II Michiel, and to relieve the subsequent financial burden on the republic "a forced loan" was made necessary. To this end the Chamber of Loans, was created to manage the affairs of the forced loan, as to the loans repayment at four percent interest. Changes in the enterprises of the Chamber, firstly by the commencing of use of discounting exchanges and later by the receipt of deposits, there developed the functioning of the organisation into *The Bank of Venice*, with an initial capital of 5,000,000 ducats. In any case, banking practice proper began in the mid-parts of the 12th century, and continued until the bank was caused to cease to operate during the French invasion of 1797. The bank was the first national bank to have been established within the boundaries of Europe.

There were banking failures from 1255 to 1262.

In the middle of the 13th century, groups of Italian Christians, particularly the Cahorsins and Lombards, invented legal fictions to get around the ban on Christian usury; for example, one method of effecting a loan with interest was to offer money without interest, but also require that the loan is insured against possible loss or injury, and/or delays in repayment. The Christians effecting these legal fictions became known as the *pope's usurers*, and reduced thc importance of the Jews to European monarchs; later, in the Middle Ages, a distinction evolved between things that were consumable (such as food and fuel) and those that were not, with usury permitted on loans that involved the latter.

Coat of arms for the Medici family

The most powerful banking families came from Florence, including the Acciaiuoli, Mozzi, Bardi and Peruzzi families, which established branches in many other parts of Europe. Probably the most famous Italian bank was the Medici bank, set up by Giovanni di Bicci de' Medici in 1397 and continuing until 1494. (Banca Monte dei Paschi di Siena S.p.A. (BMPS) Italy, is in fact the oldest banking organisation to have surviving banking-operations, or services).

It was the Italian bankers that would take their place and by 1327, Avignon had 43 branches of Italian banking houses. In 1347, Edward III of England defaulted on loans. Later there was the bankruptcy of the Bardi (1343) and Peruzzi (1346). The accompanying growth of Italian banking in France was the start of the Lombard moneychangers in Europe, who moved from city to city along the busy pilgrim routes important for trade. Key cities in this period were Cahors, the birthplace of Pope John XXII, and Figeac.

Of Usury, from Brant's Stultifera Navis (the Ship of Fools); woodcut attributed to Albrecht Dürer

By the later Middle Ages, Christian Merchants who lent money with interest were without opposition, and the Jews lost their privileged position as money-lenders;

After 1400, political forces did, in fact, somewhat turn against the methods of the Italian free enterprise bankers, In 1401 King Martin I of Aragon had some of these bankers expelled. In 1403, Henry IV of England prohibited them from taking profits in any way in his kingdom. In 1409, Flanders imprisoned and then expelled Genoese bankers. In 1410, all Italian merchants were expelled from Paris. In 1407, the Bank of Saint George, the first state-bank of deposit, was founded in Genoa and was to dominate business in the Mediterranean.

15th–17th Centuries – Expansion

Italy

In the times between 1527 and 1572 the Genoese people produced a number of important banking family groups, the Grimaldi, Spinola and Pallavicino families were especially influential and wealthy, also the Doria, although perhaps less influential, and the Pinelli and the Lomellini.

Spain and the Ottoman Empire

In 1401 the magistrates of Barcelona, then the capital of the Principality of Catalonia, established in the city the first replication of the Venetian model of exchange and deposit, Taula de Canvi – the *Table of Exchange*, considered to be the first public bank of Europe.

Halil Inalcik suggests that, in the 16th century, Marrano Jews (Doña Gracia from House of Mendes) fleeing from Iberia introduced the techniques of European capitalism, banking and even the mercantilist concept of state economy to the Ottoman Empire. In the 16th century, the leading financiers in Istanbul were Greeks and Jews. Many of the Jewish financiers were Marranos who had fled from Iberia during the period leading up to the expulsion of Jews from Spain. Some of these families brought great fortunes with them. The most notable of the Jewish banking families in the 16th-century Ottoman Empire was the Marrano banking house of Mendes, which moved to Istanbul in 1552, under the protection of Sultan Suleyman the Magnificent. When Alvaro Mendes arrived in Istanbul in 1588, he is reported to have brought with him 85,000 gold ducats. The Mendès family soon acquired a dominating position in the state finances of the Ottoman Empire and in commerce with Europe.

They thrived in Baghdad during the 18th and 19th centuries under Ottoman rule, performing critical commercial functions such as moneylending and banking. Like the Armenians, the Jews could engage in necessary commercial activities, such as moneylending and banking, that were proscribed for Muslims under Islamic law.

Court Jew

Cornelius Berenberg of the Berenberg banking dynasty

Court Jews were Jewish bankers or businessmen who lent money and handled the finances of some of the Christian European noble houses, primarily in the 17th and 18th centuries. Court Jews were precursors to the modern financier or Secretary of the Treasury. Their jobs included raising revenues by tax farming, negotiating loans, master of the mint, creating new sources for revenue,floating debentures, devising new taxes. and supplying the military. In addition, the Court Jew acted as personal bankers for nobility: he raised money to cover the noble's personal diplomacy and his extravagances.

Court Jews were skilled administrators and businessmen who received privileges in return for their services. They were most commonly found in Germany, Holland, and Austria, but also in Denmark, England, Hungary, Italy, Poland, Lithuania, Portugal, and Spain. According to Dimont, virtually every duchy, principality, and palatinate in the Holy Roman Empire had a Court Jew.

Germany

In the southern German realm, two great banking families emerged in the 15th century, the Fuggers and the Welsers. They came to control much of the European economy and to dominate international high finance in the 16th century. The Fuggers built the first German social housing area for the poor in Augsburg, the Fuggerei. It still exists, but not the original Fugger Bank which lasted from 1486 to 1647.

Dutch bankers played a central role in establishing banking in the Northern German city states. Berenberg Bank is the oldest bank in Germany and the world's second oldest, established in 1590 by Dutch brothers Hans and Paul Berenberg in Hamburg. The bank is still owned by the Berenberg dynasty.

Holland

Throughout the 17th century, precious metals from the New World, Japan and other locales were being channeled into Europe, with corresponding price increases. Thanks to the free coinage, the Bank of Amsterdam, and the heightened trade and commerce, the Netherlands attracted even more coin and bullion to be deposited in their banks. These concepts of Fractional-reserve banking and payment systems were further developed and spread to England and elsewhere.

England

In the City of London there weren't any banking houses operating in a manner recognized as so today until the 17th century, although the London Royal Exchange was established in 1565.

17th–19th Centuries – The Emergence of Modern Banking

The old town hall in Amsterdam where the Bank of Amsterdam was founded in 1609, painting by Pieter Saenredam.

By the end of the 16th century and during the 17th, the traditional banking functions of accepting deposits, moneylending, money changing, and transferring funds were combined with the issuance of bank debt that served as a substitute for gold and silver coins.

New banking practices promoted commercial and industrial growth by providing a safe and convenient means of payment and a money supply more responsive to commercial needs, as well as by "discounting" business debt. By the end of the 17th century, banking was also becoming important for the funding requirements of the combative European states. This would lead on to government regulations and the first central banks. The success of the new banking techniques and practices in Amsterdam and London helped spread the concepts and ideas elsewhere in Europe.

Goldsmiths of London

Modern banking practice, including fractional reserve banking and the issue of banknotes, emerged in the 17th century. At the time, wealthy merchants began to store their gold with the goldsmiths of London, who possessed private vaults and charged a fee for their service. In exchange for each deposit of precious metal, the goldsmiths issued receipts certifying the quantity and purity of the metal they held as a bailee; these receipts could not be assigned, only the original depositor could collect the stored goods.

Gradually the goldsmiths began to lend the money out on behalf of the depositor, which led to the development of modern banking practices; promissory notes (which evolved into banknotes) were issued for money deposited as a loan to the goldsmith.

These practices created a new kind of "money" that was actually debt, that is, goldsmiths' debt rather than silver or gold coin, a commodity that had been regulated and controlled by the monarchy. This development required the acceptance in trade of the goldsmiths' promissory notes, payable on demand. Acceptance in turn required a general belief that coin would be available; and a fractional reserve normally served this purpose. Acceptance also required that the holders of debt be able legally to enforce an unconditional right to payment; it required that the notes (as well as drafts) be negotiable instruments. The concept of negotiability had emerged in fits and starts in European money markets, but it was well developed by the 17th century. Nevertheless, an act of Parliament was required in the early 18th century (1704) to overrule court decisions holding that the gold smiths notes, despite the "customs of merchants", were not negotiable.

The Modern Bank

The first bank to begin the permanent issue of banknotes was the Bank of England in 1695. Initially hand-written and issued on deposit or as a loan, they promised to pay the bearer the value of the note on demand. By 1745, standardized printed notes ranging from £20 to £1,000 were being printed. Fully printed notes that didn't require the name of the payee and the cashier's signature first appeared in 1855.

The Louisiana Purchase of 1803 was handled by Francis Baring and Company of London.

The rise of Protestantism freed many European Christians from Rome's dictates against usury. In the 18th century, services offered by banks increased. Clearing facilities, security investments, cheques and overdraft protections were introduced. Cheques were invented in the 1600s in England and banks settled payments by direct courier to the issuing bank. Around 1770, they began meeting in a central location, and by the 1800s a dedicated space was established, known as a bankers' clearing house. The London clearing house used a method where each bank paid cash to and then was paid cash by an inspector at the end of each day. The first overdraft facility was set up in 1728 by the Royal Bank of Scotland.

The Industrial Revolution and growing international trade increased the number of banks, especially in London. At the same time, new types of financial activities broadened the scope of banking far beyond its origins. The merchant-banking families dealt in everything from underwriting bonds to originating foreign loans. These new "merchant banks" facilitated trade growth, profiting from England's emerging dominance in seaborne shipping. Two immigrant families, Rothschild and Baring, established merchant banking firms in London in the late 18th century and came to dominate world banking in the next century.

A great impetus to country banking came in 1797 when, with England threatened by war, the Bank of England suspended cash payments. A handful of Frenchmen landed in Pembrokeshire, causing a panic. Shortly after this incident, Parliament authorised the Bank of England and country bankers to issue notes of low denomination.

Japanese Banking

Modern banking began during a period spanning the year 1868 to the period known as World War I.

1868 marked the year of the beginning of the Meiji governments' attempts at formulating a functioning banking system, which continued until some time during 1881. The Imperial mint was begun using imported machines from Britain during the early years of the Meiji period.

Masayoshi Matsukata is thought the formative figure of the formation of a later banking initiative.

Development of Central Banking

The Bank of Amsterdam became a model for the functioning of a bank in the capacity of monetary exchange and started the development of central banks. An early central bank was the Sveriges Riksbank, established in 1668, although this was short-lived.

The Bank of England, established in 1694.

In England in the 1690s, public funds were in short supply and were needed to finance the ongoing conflict with France. The credit of William III's government was so low in London that it was impossible for it to borrow the £1,200,000 (at 8 per cent) that the government wanted. In order to induce subscription to the loan, the subscribers were to be incorporated by the name of the Governor and Company of the Bank of England. The bank was given exclusive possession of the government's balances, and was the only limited-liability corporation allowed to issue banknotes. The lenders would give the government cash (bullion) and also issue notes against the government bonds, which can be lent again. The £1.2M was raised in 12 days; half of this was used to rebuild the Navy. The establishment of the Bank of England, the model on which most modern central banks have been based on, was devised by Charles Montagu, 1st Earl of Halifax, in 1694, to the plan which had been proposed by William Paterson three years before, but had not been acted upon. He proposed a loan of £1.2M to the government; in return the subscribers would be incorporated as *The Governor and Company of the Bank of England* with long-term banking privileges including the issue of notes. The Royal Charter was granted on 27 July through the passage of the Tonnage Act 1694.

Although the Bank was originally a private institution, by the end of the 18th century it was increasingly being regarded as a public authority with civic responsibility toward the upkeep of a healthy financial system. The currency crisis of 1797, caused by panicked depositors withdrawing from the Bank led to the government suspending convertibility of notes into specie payment. The bank was soon accused by the bullionists of causing the exchange rate to fall from over issuing banknotes, a charge which the Bank denied. Nevertheless, it was clear that the Bank was being treated as an organ of the state.

Henry Thornton, a merchant banker and monetary theorist has been described as the father of the modern central bank. An opponent of the real bills doctrine, he was a defender of the bullionist position and a significant figure in monetary theory, his process of monetary expansion anticipating the theories of Knut Wicksell regarding the "cumulative process which restates the Quantity Theory in a theoretically coherent form". As a response 1797 currency crisis, Thornton wrote in 1802 *An Enquiry into the Nature and Effects of the Paper Credit of Great Britain*, in which he argued that the increase in paper credit did not cause the crisis. The book also gives a detailed account of the British monetary system as well as a detailed examination of the ways in which the Bank of England should act to counteract fluctuations in the value of the pound.

Walter Bagehot, an influential theorist on the economic role of the central bank.

Until the mid-nineteenth century, commercial banks were able to issue their own banknotes, and notes issued by provincial banking companies were commonly in circulation. Many consider the origins of the central bank to lie with the passage of the Bank Charter Act of 1844. Under this law, authorisation to issue new banknotes was restricted to the Bank of England. The Act served to restrict the supply of new notes reaching circulation, and gave the Bank of England an effective monopoly on the printing of new notes. The Bank accepted the role of 'lender of last resort' in the 1870s after criticism of its lacklustre response to the Overend-Gurney crisis. The journalist Walter Bagehot wrote an influential work on the subject *Lombard Street: A Description of the Money Market*, in which he advocated for the Bank to officially become a lender of last resort during a credit crunch (sometimes referred to as "Bagehot's dictum").

Central banks were established in many European countries during the 19th century. The War of the Second Coalition led to the creation of the Banque de France in 1800, in an effort to improve the public financing of the war. The US Federal Reserve was created by the U.S. Congress through the passing of The Federal Reserve Act in 1913. Australia established its first central bank in 1920, Colombia in 1923, Mexico and Chile in 1925 and Canada and New Zealand in the aftermath of the Great Depression in 1934. By 1935, the only significant independent nation that did not possess a central bank was Brazil, which subsequently developed a precursor thereto in 1945 and the present central bank twenty years later. Having gained independence, African and Asian countries also established central banks or monetary union.

Rothschilds

The Frankfurt terminus of the Taunus railroad, financed by the Rothschilds.
Opened in 1840, it was one of Germany's first railroads.

The Rothschild family pioneered international finance in the early 19th century. The family provided loans to the Bank of England and purchased government bonds in the stock markets. Their wealth has been estimated to possibly be the most in modern history. In 1804, Nathan Mayer Rothschild began to deal on the London stock exchange in financial instruments such as foreign bills and government securities. From 1809 Rothschild began to deal in gold bullion, and developed this as a cornerstone of his business. From 1811 on, in negotiation with Commissary-General John Charles Herries, he undertook to transfer money to pay Wellington's troops, on campaign in Portugal and Spain against Napoleon, and later to make subsidy payments to British allies when these organized new troops after Napoleon's disastrous Russian campaign. His four brothers helped co-ordinate activities across the continent, and the family developed a network of agents, shippers and couriers to transport gold—and information—across Europe. This private intelligence service enabled Nathan to receive in London the news of Wellington's victory at the Battle of Waterloo a full day ahead of the government's official messengers.

The Rothschild family were instrumental in supporting railway systems across the world and in complex government financing for projects such as the Suez Canal. The family bought up a large proportion of the property in Mayfair, London. Major businesses directly founded by Rothschild family capital include Alliance Assurance (1824) (now Royal & SunAlliance); Chemin de Fer du Nord (1845); Rio Tinto Group (1873); Société Le Nickel (1880) (now Eramet); and Imétal (1962) (now Imerys). The Rothschilds financed the founding of De Beers, as well as Cecil Rhodes on his expeditions in Africa and the creation of the colony of Rhodesia.

The Japanese government approached the London and Paris families for funding during the Russo-Japanese War. The London consortium's issue of Japanese war bonds would total £11.5 million (at 1907 currency rates).

From 1919 to 2004 the Rothschilds' Bank in London played a role as place of the gold fixing.

Napoleonic Wars and Paris

Napoleon III had the goal of overtaking London to make Paris the premier financial center of the world, but the war in 1870 reduced the range of Parisian financial influence. Paris had emerged as an international center of finance in the mid-19th century second only to London. It had a strong national bank and numerous aggressive private banks that financed projects all across Europe and the expanding French Empire.

One key development was setting up one of the main branches of the Rothschild family. In 1812, James Mayer Rothschild arrived in Paris from Frankfurt, and set up the bank "De Rothschild Frères". This bank funded Napoleon's return from Elba and became one of the leading banks in European finance. The Rothschild banking family of France funded France's major wars and colonial expansion. The Banque de France, founded in 1796 helped resolve the financial crisis of 1848 and emerged as a powerful central bank. The Comptoir National d'Escompte de Paris (CNEP) was established during the financial crisis and the republican revolution of 1848. Its innovations included both private and public sources in funding large projects, and the creation of a network of local offices to reach a much larger pool of depositors.

Building Societies

Building societies were established as financial institutions owned by its members as a mutual organization. The origins of the building society as an institution lie in late-18th century Birmingham – a town which was undergoing rapid economic and physical expansion driven by a multiplicity of small metalworking firms, whose many highly skilled and prosperous owners readily invested in property.

Many of the early building societies were based in taverns or coffeehouses, which had become the focus for a network of clubs and societies for co-operation and the exchange of ideas among Birmingham's highly active citizenry as part of the movement known as the Midlands Enlightenment. The first building society to be established was Ketley's Building Society, founded by Richard Ketley, the landlord of the *Golden Cross* inn, in 1775.

Members of Ketley's society paid a monthly subscription to a central pool of funds which was used to finance the building of houses for members, which in turn acted as collateral to attract further funding to the society, enabling further construction. The first outside the English Midlands was established in Leeds in 1785.

Mutual Savings Bank

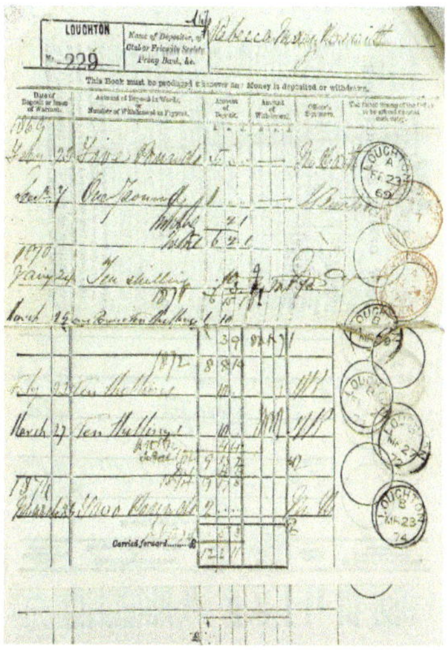

A customer's deposit book, for a Post Office Savings Account.

Mutual savings banks also emerged at that time, as financial institutions chartered by government, without capital stock, and owned by its members who subscribe to a common fund. The institution most frequently identified as the first modern savings bank was the "Savings and Friendly Society" organized by the Reverend Henry Duncan in 1810, in Ruthwell, Scotland. Rev. Duncan established the small bank in order to encourage his working class congregation to develop thrift.

Another precursor to the modern savings bank originated in Germany, with Franz Hermann Schulze-Delitzsch and Friedrich Wilhelm Raiffeisen who developed cooperative banking models that led on to the credit union movement. The traditional banks had viewed poor and rural communities as unbankable because of very small, seasonal flows of cash and very limited human resources. In the history of credit unions the concepts of cooperative banking spread through northern Europe and onto the US at the turn of the 20th century under a wide range of different names.

Postal Savings System

To provide depositors who did not have access to banks a safe, convenient method to save money and to promote saving among the poor, the postal savings system was introduced in Great Britain in 1861. It was vigorously supported by William Ewart Gladstone, then Chancellor of the Exchequer, who saw it as a cheap way to finance the public debt. At the time, banks were mainly in the cities and largely catered to wealthy customers. Rural citizens and the poor had no choice but to keep their funds at home or on their persons. The original Post Office Savings Bank was limited to deposits of £30 a year with a maximum balance of £150. Interest was paid at the rate of two and one-half percent per year on whole pounds in the account.

Similar institutions were created in a number of different countries in Europe and North America. One example was in 1881 the Dutch government created the Rijkspostspaarbank (State post savings bank), a postal savings system to encourage workers to start saving. Four decades later they added the Postcheque and Girodienst services allowing working families to make payments via post offices in the Netherlands.

20th Century

The first decade of the 20th century saw the Panic of 1907 in the US, which led to numerous runs on banks and became known as the bankers panic.

Great Depression

Crowd at New York's American Union Bank during a bank run early in the Great Depression.

During the Crash of 1929 preceding the Great Depression, margin requirements were only 10%. Brokerage firms, in other words, would lend $9 for every $1 an investor had deposited. When the market fell, brokers called in these loans, which could not be paid back. Banks began to fail as debtors defaulted on debt and depositors attempted to withdraw their deposits en masse, triggering multiple bank runs. Government guarantees and Federal Reserve banking regulations to prevent such panics were ineffective or not used. Bank failures led to the loss of billions of dollars in assets. Outstanding debts became heavier, because prices and incomes fell by 20–50% but the debts remained at the same dollar amount. After the panic of 1929, and during the first 10 months of 1930, 744 US banks failed. By April 1933, around $7 billion in deposits had been frozen in failed banks or those left unlicensed after the March Bank Holiday.

Senator Carter Glass and Henry B. Steagall (1933)

Bank failures snowballed as desperate bankers called in loans that borrowers did not have time or money to repay. With future profits looking poor, capital investment and construction slowed or completely ceased. In the face of bad loans and worsening future prospects, the surviving banks became even more conservative in their lending. Banks built up their capital reserves and made fewer loans, which intensified deflationary pressures. A vicious cycle developed and the downward spiral accelerated. In all, over 9,000 banks failed during the 1930s.

In response, many countries significantly increased financial regulation. The U.S. established the Securities and Exchange Commission in 1933, and passed the Glass–Steagall Act, which separated investment banking and commercial banking. This was to avoid more risky investment banking activities from ever again causing commercial bank failures.

World Bank and the Development of Payment Technology

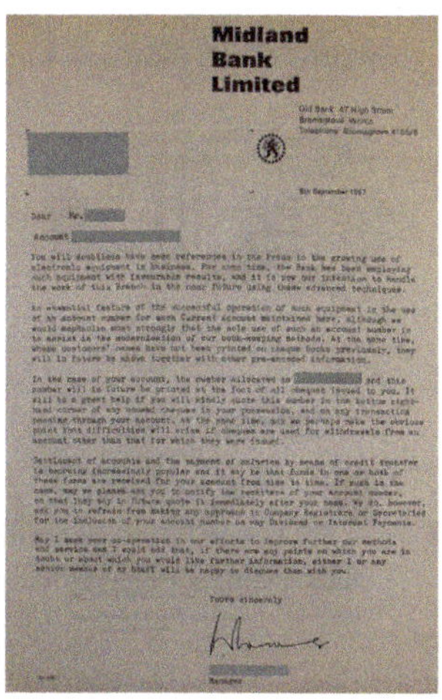

Midland Bank Limited

1967 letter by the Midland Bank to a customer, informing on the introduction of electronic data processing

During the post second world war period and with the introduction of the Bretton Woods system in 1944, two organizations were created: the International Monetary Fund (IMF) and the World Bank. Encouraged by these institutions, commercial banks started to lend to sovereign states in the third world. This was at the same time as inflation started to rise in the west. The Gold standard was eventually abandoned in 1971 and a number of the banks were caught out and became bankrupt due to third world country debt defaults.

This was also a time of increasing use of technology in retail banking. In 1959, banks agreed on a standard for machine readable characters (MICR) that was patented in the United States for use with cheques, which led to the first automated reader-sorter machines. In the 1960s, the first Automated Teller Machines (ATM) or Cash machines were developed and first machines started to appear by the end of the decade. Banks started to become heavy investors in computer technology to automate much of the manual processing, which began a shift by banks from large clerical staffs to new automated systems. By the 1970s the first payment systems started to develop that would lead to electronic payment systems for both international and domestic payments. The international SWIFT payment network was established in 1973 and domestic payment systems were developed around the world by banks working together with governments.

Deregulation and Globalisation

Bishopsgate in the City of London

Global banking and capital market services proliferated during the 1980s after deregulation of financial markets in a number of countries. The 1986 'Big Bang' in London allowing banks to access capital markets in new ways, which led to significant changes to the way banks operated and accessed capital. It also started a trend where retail banks started to acquire investment banks and stock brokers creating universal banks that offered a wide range of banking services. The trend also spread to the US after much of the Glass–Steagall Act was repealed in the 1980s, this saw US retail banks embark on big rounds of mergers and acquisitions and also engage in investment banking activities.

Financial services continued to grow through the 1980s and 1990s as a result of a great increase in demand from companies, governments, and financial institutions, but also because financial market conditions were buoyant and, on the whole, bullish. Interest rates in the United States declined from about 15% for two-year U.S. Treasury notes to about 5% during the 20-year period, and financial assets grew then at a rate approximately twice the rate of the world economy.

This period saw a significant internationalization of financial markets. The increase of U.S. Foreign investments from Japan not only provided the funds to corporations in the U.S., but also helped finance the federal government.

The dominance of U.S. financial markets was disappearing and there was an increasing interest in foreign stocks. The extraordinary growth of foreign financial markets results from both large increases in the pool of savings in foreign countries, such as Japan, and, especially, the deregulation of foreign financial markets, which enabled them to expand their activities. Thus, American corporations and banks started seeking investment opportunities abroad, prompting the development in the U.S. of mutual funds specializing in trading in foreign stock markets.

Such growing internationalization and opportunity in financial services changed the competitive landscape, as now many banks would demonstrate a preference for the "universal banking" model prevalent in Europe. Universal banks are free to engage in all forms of financial services, make investments in client companies, and function as much as possible as a "one-stop" supplier of both retail and wholesale financial services.

21st Century

The early 2000s were marked by consolidation of existing banks and entrance into the market of other financial intermediaries: non-bank financial institution. Large corporate players were beginning to find their way into the financial service community, offering competition to established banks. The main services offered included insurance, pension, mutual, money market and hedge funds, loans and credits and securities. Indeed, by the end of 2001 the market capitalisation of the world's 15 largest financial services providers included four non-banks.

The process of financial innovation advanced enormously in the first decade of the 21st century increasing the importance and profitability of nonbank finance. Such profitability priorly restricted to the non-banking industry, has prompted the Office of the Comptroller of the Currency (OCC) to encourage banks to explore other financial instruments, diversifying banks' business as well as improving banking economic health.

Hence, as the distinct financial instruments are being explored and adopted by both the banking and non-banking industries, the distinction between different financial institutions is gradually vanishing.

The first decade of the 21st century also saw the culmination of the technical innovation in banking over the previous 30 years and saw a major shift away from traditional banking to internet banking.

Financial Crisis

2007 bank run on Northern Rock, a UK bank

The Late-2000s financial crisis caused significant stress on banks around the world. The failure of a large number of major banks resulted in government bail-outs. The collapse and fire sale of Bear Stearns to JPMorgan Chase in March 2008 and the collapse of Lehman Brothers in September that same year led to a credit crunch and global banking crises. In response governments around the world bailed-out, nationalised or arranged fire sales for a large number of major banks. Starting with the Irish government on 29 September 2008, governments around the world provided wholesale guarantees to underwriting banks to avoid panic of systemic failure to the whole banking system. These events spawned the term 'too big to fail' and resulted in a lot of discussion about the moral hazard of these actions.

Major Events in Banking history

- 1100 – Knights Templar run earliest European wide/Mideast banking until the 14th century.
- 1397 – The Medici Bank of Florence is established in Italy and operates until 1494.
- 1542 – The Great Debasement, the English Crown's policy of coin debasement during the reigns of Henry VIII and Edward VI.

- 1553 – The first joint-stock company, the Company of Merchant Adventurers to New Lands, was chartered in London.
- 1602 – The Amsterdam Stock Exchange was established by the Dutch East India Company for dealings in its printed stocks and bonds.
- 1609 – The Amsterdamsche Wisselbank (Amsterdam Exchange Bank) was founded.
- 1656 – The first European bank to use banknotes opened in Sweden for private clients, in 1668 the institution converted to a public bank.
- 1690s – The Massachusetts Bay Colony was the first of the Thirteen Colonies to issue permanently circulating banknotes.
- 1694 – The Bank of England was founded to supply money to the English King.
- 1695 – The Parliament of Scotland created the Bank of Scotland.
- 1716 – John Law opened Banque Générale in France.
- 1717 – Master of the Royal Mint Sir Isaac Newton established a new mint ratio between silver and gold that had the effect of driving silver out of circulation (bimetalism) and putting Britain on a gold standard.
- 1720 – The South Sea Bubble and John Law's Mississippi Scheme failure caused a European financial crisis and forced many bankers out of business.
- 1775 – The first building society, Ketley's Building Society, was established in Birmingham, England.
- 1782 – The Bank of North America opened.
- 1791 – The First Bank of the United States was chartered by the United States Congress for 20 years.
- 1800 – The Rothschild family establishes European wide banking.
- 1800 – Napoleon Bonaparte founds the Bank of France on January 18.
- 1811 – The Senate tied on a vote to renew the charter of the First Bank of the United States charter. Vice President George Clinton broke the tie and voted against renewal, and the bank was dissolved.
- 1816 – The Second Bank of the United States was chartered for five years after the First Bank of the United States lost its charter. This charter was also for 20 years. The bank was created to finance the country in the aftermath of the War of 1812.
- 1817 – The New York Stock Exchange Board was established.

- 1818 – The first savings bank of Paris was established.
- 1862 – To finance the American Civil War, the federal government under U.S. President Abraham Lincoln issued legal tender paper money, called "greenbacks".
- 1874 – The Specie Payment Resumption Act was passed provided for the redemption of United States paper currency, in gold, beginning in 1879.
- 1913 – The Federal Reserve Act created the Federal Reserve System, the central banking system of the United States, and granted it the legal authority to issue legal tender.
- 1930–33 – In the wake of the Wall Street Crash of 1929, 9,000 banks close, wiping out a third of the money supply in the United States.
- 1933 – Executive Order 6102 signed by U.S. President Franklin D. Roosevelt forbade ownership of gold coin, gold bullion, and gold certificates by US citizens beyond a certain amount, effectively ending the convertibility of US dollars into gold.
- 1971 – The Nixon Shock was a series of economic measures taken by U.S. President Richard Nixon which canceled the direct convertibility of the United States dollar to gold by foreign nations. This essentially ended the existing Bretton Woods system of international financial exchange.
- 1986 – The "Big Bang" (deregulation of London financial markets) served as a catalyst to reaffirm London's position as a global centre of world banking.
- 2007 – Start of the Late-2000s financial crisis that saw the a credit crunch that led to the failure and bail-out of a large number of the worlds biggest banks.
- 2008 – Washington Mutual collapses, the largest bank failure in history up to that point.

Investment Banking

An investment bank is typically a private company that provides various financial-related and other services to individuals, corporations, and governments such as raising financial capital by underwriting or acting as the client's agent in the issuance of securities. An investment bank may also assist companies involved in mergers and acquisitions (M&A) and provide ancillary services such as market making, trading of derivatives and equity securities, and FICC services (fixed income instruments, currencies, and commodities).

Unlike commercial banks and retail banks, investment banks do not take deposits. From the passage of Glass–Steagall Act in 1933 until its repeal in 1999 by the Gramm–Leach–Bliley Act, the United States maintained a separation between investment banking and commercial banks. Other industrialized countries, including G7 countries, have historically not maintained such a separation. As part of the Dodd–Frank Wall Street Reform and Consumer Protection Act of 2010 (*Dodd-Frank Act of 2010*), the Volcker Rule asserts some institutional separations of investment banking services from commercial banking.

The two main lines of business in investment banking are called the sell side and the buy side. The "sell side" involves trading securities for cash or for other securities (e.g. facilitating transactions, market-making), or the promotion of securities (e.g. underwriting, research, etc.). The "buy side" involves the provision of advice to institutions that buy investment services. Private equity funds, mutual funds, life insurance companies, unit trusts, and hedge funds are the most common types of buy-side entities.

An investment bank can also be split into private and public functions with a Chinese wall separating the two to prevent information from crossing. The private areas of the bank deal with private insider information that may not be publicly disclosed, while the public areas, such as stock analysis, deal with public information.

An advisor who provides investment banking services in the United States must be a licensed broker-dealer and subject to U.S. Securities and Exchange Commission (SEC) and Financial Industry Regulatory Authority (FINRA) regulation.

History

The Dutch East India Company (VOC) became the first company in history to issue bonds and shares of stock to the general public. In other words, the VOC was officially the first publicly traded company, because it was the first company to be ever actually listed on an official stock exchange. It was also the Dutch who helped lay the foundations for modern practice of investment banking.

Investment banking has changed over the years, beginning as a partnership form focused on underwriting security issuance, i.e. initial public offerings (IPOs) and secondary market offerings, brokerage, and mergers and acquisitions, and evolving into a "full-service" range including securities research, proprietary trading, and investment management. In the modern 21st century, the SEC filings of the major independent investment banks such as Goldman Sachs and Morgan Stanley reflect three product segments: (1) investment banking (fees for M&A advisory services and securities underwriting); (2) asset management (fees for sponsored investment funds), and (3) trading and principal investments (broker-dealer activities including proprietary trading ("dealer" transactions) and brokerage trading ("broker" transactions)).

In the United States, commercial banking and investment banking were separated by the Glass–Steagall Act, which was repealed in 1999. The repeal led to more "universal banks" offering an even greater range of services. Many large commercial banks have therefore developed investment banking divisions through acquisitions and hiring. Notable large banks with significant investment banks include JPMorgan Chase, Bank of America, Credit Suisse, Deutsche Bank, UBS, Barclays, and Wells Fargo. After the financial crisis of 2007–08 and the subsequent passage of the *Dodd-Frank Act of 2010*, regulations have limited certain investment banking operations, notably with the Volcker Rule's restrictions on proprietary trading.

The traditional service of underwriting security issues has declined as a percentage of revenue. As far back as 1960, 70% of Merrill Lynch's revenue was derived from transaction commissions while "traditional investment banking" services accounted for 5%. However, Merrill Lynch was a relatively "retail-focused" firm with a large brokerage network.

Organizational Structure

Core Investment Banking Activities

Investment banking is split into front office, middle office, and back office activities. While large service investment banks offer all lines of business, both "sell side" and "buy side", smaller sell-side investment firms such as boutique investment banks and small broker-dealers focus on investment banking and sales/trading/research, respectively.

Investment banks offer services to both corporations issuing securities and investors buying securities. For corporations, investment bankers offer information on when and how to place their securities on the open market, an activity very important to an investment bank's reputation. Therefore, investment bankers play a very important role in issuing new security offerings.

Front Office

Front office is generally described as a revenue generating role. There are two main areas within front office: investment banking and markets.

- Investment banking involves advising the world's largest organizations on mergers and acquisitions, as well as a wide array of fund raising strategies.
- Markets is divided into "sales and trading" (including "structuring"), and "research".

Corporate Finance

Corporate finance is the traditional aspect of investment banks, which involves helping customers raise funds in capital markets and giving advice on mergers and acquisitions (M&A); this may involve subscribing investors to a security issuance, coordinating with bidders, or negotiating with a merger target. A pitch book of financial information is generated to market the bank to a potential M&A client; if the pitch is successful, the bank arranges the deal for the client. The investment banking division (IBD) is generally divided into industry coverage and product coverage groups. Industry coverage groups focus on a specific industry—such as healthcare, public finance (governments), FIG (financial institutions group), industrials, TMT (technology, media, and telecommunication), P&E (power & energy), consumer/retail, food & beverage, corporate defense and governance—and maintain relationships with corporations within the industry to bring in business for the bank. Product coverage groups focus on financial products—such as mergers and acquisitions, leveraged finance, public finance, asset finance and leasing, structured finance, restructuring, equity, and high-grade debt—and generally work and collaborate with industry groups on the more intricate and specialized needs of a client.

Sales and Trading

On behalf of the bank and its clients, a large investment bank's primary function is buying and selling products. In market making, traders will buy and sell financial products with the goal of making money on each trade. *Sales* is the term for the investment bank's sales force, whose primary job is to call on institutional and high-net-worth investors to suggest trading ideas (on a caveat emptor basis) and take orders. Sales desks then communicate their clients' orders to the appropriate trading rooms, which can price and execute trades, or structure new products that fit a specific need. *Structuring* has been a relatively recent activity as derivatives have come into play, with highly technical and numerate employees working on creating complex structured products which typically offer much greater margins and returns than underlying cash securities. In 2010, investment banks came under pressure as a result of selling complex derivatives contracts to local municipalities in Europe and the US. *Strategists* advise external as well as internal clients on the strategies that can be adopted in various markets. Ranging from derivatives to specific industries, strategists place companies and industries in a quantitative framework with full consideration of the macroeconomic scene. This strategy often affects the way the firm will operate in the market, the direction it would like to take in terms of its proprietary and flow positions, the suggestions salespersons give to clients, as well as the way structurers create new products. Banks also undertake risk through proprietary trading, performed by a special set of traders who do not interface with clients and through "principal risk"—risk undertaken by a trader after he buys or sells a product to a client and does not hedge his total exposure. Banks seek to maximize profitability for a given amount of risk on their balance sheet. The necessity for numerical ability in sales and trading has created jobs for physics, computer science, mathematics and engineering Ph.D.s who act as quantitative analysts.

Research

The securities research division reviews companies and writes reports about their prospects, often with "buy", "hold" or "sell" ratings. Investment banks typically have sell-side analysts which cover various industries. Their sponsored funds or proprietary trading offices will also have buy-side research. While the research division may or may not generate revenue (based on policies at different banks), its resources are used to assist traders in trading, the sales force in suggesting ideas to customers, and investment bankers by covering their clients. Research also serves outside clients with investment advice (such as institutional investors and high-net-worth individuals) in the hopes that these clients will execute suggested trade ideas through the sales and trading division of the bank, and thereby generate revenue for the firm. Research also covers credit research, fixed income research, macroeconomic research, and quantitative analysis, all of which are used internally and externally to advise clients but do not directly affect revenue. All research groups, nonetheless, provide a key service in terms of advisory and strategy. There is a potential conflict of interest between the investment bank and its analysis, in that published analysis can impact the performance of a security (in the secondary markets or an initial public offering) or influence the relationship between the banker and its corporate clients, thereby affecting the bank's profitability .

Front and Middle Office

Risk Management

Risk management involves analyzing the market and credit risk that an investment bank or its clients take onto their balance sheet during transactions or trades. Credit risk focuses around capital markets activities, such as syndicated loans, bond issuance, restructuring, and leveraged finance. Market risk conducts review of sales and trading activities utilizing the VaR model and provide hedge-fund solutions to portfolio managers. Other risk groups include country risk, operational risk, and counterparty risks which may or may not exist on a bank to bank basis. Credit risk solutions are key part of capital market transactions, involving debt structuring, exit financing, loan amendment, project finance, leveraged buy-outs, and sometimes portfolio hedging. Front office market risk activities provide service to investors via derivative solutions, portfolio management, portfolio consulting, and risk advisory. Well-known risk groups in JPMorgan Chase, Morgan Stanley, Goldman Sachs and Barclays engage in revenue-generating activities involving debt structuring, restructuring, syndicated loans, and securitization for clients such as corporates, governments, and hedge funds. J.P. Morgan IB Risk works with investment banking to execute transactions and advise investors, although its Finance & Operation risk groups focus on middle office functions involving internal, non-revenue generating, operational risk controls. Credit default swap, for instance, is a famous credit risk hedging solution for clients invented by J.P. Morgan's Blythe Masters during the 1990s. The Loan Risk Solutions group within Barclays' investment banking division and Risk Management and Financing group housed in Goldman Sach's securities division are client-driven franchises. However, risk management groups such as operational risk, internal risk control, and legal risk are restrained to internal business functions including firm balance-sheet risk analysis and assigning trading cap that are independent of client needs, even though these groups may be responsible for deal approval that directly affects capital market activities. Risk management is a broad area, and like research, its roles can be client-facing or internal.

Middle Office

This area of the bank includes treasury management, internal controls, and internal corporate strategy.

Corporate treasury is responsible for an investment bank's funding, capital structure management, and liquidity risk monitoring.

Internal control tracks and analyzes the capital flows of the firm, the finance division is the principal adviser to senior management on essential areas such as controlling the firm's global risk exposure and the profitability and structure of the firm's various businesses via dedicated trading desk product control teams. In the United States and United Kingdom, a comptroller (or financial controller) is a senior position, often reporting to the chief financial officer.

Internal corporate strategy tackling firm management and profit strategy, unlike corporate strategy groups that advise clients, is non-revenue regenerating yet a key functional role within investment banks.

This list is not a comprehensive summary of all middle-office functions within an investment bank, as specific desks within front and back offices may participate in internal functions.

Back Office

The back office data-checks trades that have been conducted, ensuring that they are not wrong, and transacts the required transfers. Many banks have outsourced operations. It is, however, a critical part of the bank.

Technology

Every major investment bank has considerable amounts of in-house software, created by the technology team, who are also responsible for technical support. Technology has changed considerably in the last few years as more sales and trading desks are using electronic trading. Some trades are initiated by complex algorithms for hedging purposes.

Firms are responsible for compliance with local and foreign government regulations and internal regulations.

Other Businesses

- Global transaction banking is the division which provides cash management, custody services, lending, and securities brokerage services to institutions. Prime brokerage with hedge funds has been an especially profitable business, as well as risky, as seen in the bank run with Bear Stearns in 2008.

- Investment management is the professional management of various securities (stocks, bonds, etc.) and other assets (e.g., real estate), to meet specified investment goals for the benefit of investors. Investors may be institutions (insurance companies, pension funds, corporations etc.) or private investors (both directly via investment contracts and more commonly via investment funds e.g., mutual funds). The investment management division of an investment bank is generally divided into separate groups, often known as private wealth management and private client services.

- Merchant banking can be called "very personal banking"; merchant banks offer capital in exchange for share ownership rather than loans, and offer advice on management and strategy. Merchant banking is also a name used to describe the private equity side of a firm. Current examples include Defoe Fournier & Cie. and JPMorgan Chase's One Equity Partners. The original J.P. Morgan & Co., Rothschilds, Barings and Warburgs were all merchant banks. Originally, "merchant bank" was the British English term for an investment bank.

Industry Profile

There are various trade associations throughout the world which represent the industry in lobbying, facilitate industry standards, and publish statistics. The International Council of Securities Associations (ICSA) is a global group of trade associations.

In the United States, the Securities Industry and Financial Markets Association (SIFMA) is likely the most significant; however, several of the large investment banks are members of the American Bankers Association Securities Association (ABASA), while small investment banks are members of the National Investment Banking Association (NIBA).

In Europe, the European Forum of Securities Associations was formed in 2007 by various European trade associations. Several European trade associations (principally the London Investment Banking Association and the European SIFMA affiliate) combined in November 2009 to form the Association for Financial Markets in Europe (AFME).

In the securities industry in China (particularly mainland China), the Securities Association of China is a self-regulatory organization whose members are largely investment banks.

Global Size and Revenue Mix

Global investment banking revenue increased for the fifth year running in 2007, to a record US$84 billion, which was up 22% on the previous year and more than double the level in 2003. Subsequent to their exposure to United States sub-prime securities investments, many investment banks have experienced losses. As of late 2012, global revenues for investment banks were estimated at $240 billion, down about a third from 2009, as companies pursued less deals and traded less. Differences in total revenue are likely due to different ways of classifying investment banking revenue, such as subtracting proprietary trading revenue.

In terms of total revenue, SEC filings of the major independent investment banks in the United States show that investment banking (defined as M&A advisory services and security underwriting) only made up about 15-20% of total revenue for these banks from 1996 to 2006, with the majority of revenue (60+% in some years) brought in by "trading" which includes brokerage commissions and proprietary trading; the proprietary trading is estimated to provide a significant portion of this revenue.

The United States generated 46% of global revenue in 2009, down from 56% in 1999. Europe (with Middle East and Africa) generated about a third while Asian countries generated the remaining 21%. The industry is heavily concentrated in a small number of major financial centers, including City of London, New York City, Frankfurt, Hong Kong and Tokyo.

According to estimates published by the International Financial Services London, for the decade prior to the financial crisis in 2008, M&A was a primary source of investment banking revenue, often accounting for 40% of such revenue, but dropped during and after the financial crisis. Equity underwriting revenue ranged from 30% to 38% and fixed-income underwriting accounted for the remaining revenue.

Revenues have been affected by the introduction of new products with higher margins; however, these innovations are often copied quickly by competing banks, pushing down trading margins. For example, brokerages commissions for bond and equity trading is a commodity business but structuring and trading derivatives has higher margins because each over-the-counter contract has to be uniquely structured and could involve complex pay-off and risk profiles. One growth area is private investment in public equity (PIPEs, otherwise known as Regulation D or Regulation S). Such transactions are privately negotiated between companies and accredited investors.

Banks also earned revenue by securitizing debt, particularly mortgage debt prior to the financial crisis. Investment banks have become concerned that lenders are securitizing in-house, driving the investment banks to pursue vertical integration by becoming lenders, which is allowed in the United States since the repeal of the Glass-Steagall Act in 1999.

Top 10 Banks

According to the *Financial Times*, in terms of total advisory fees for the whole of 2016, the top ten investment banks were:

Rank	Company	Ticker	Fees ($m)
1.	J.P. Morgan & Co.	JPM	5,727.97
2.	Goldman Sachs	GS	5,040.39
3.	Bank of America Merrill Lynch	BAC	4,498.11
4.	Morgan Stanley	MS	4,453.97
5.	Citigroup	C	3,843.40
6.	Barclays Investment Bank	BARC	3,161.33
7.	Credit Suisse	CS	2,864.58
8.	Deutsche Bank	DBKGn	2,701.96
9.	Wells Fargo Securities	WFC	2,093.97
10.	RBC Capital Markets	Private	1,779.95

The above list is just a ranking of the advisory arm (M&A advisory, syndicated loans, equity capital markets and debt capital markets) of each bank and does not include the generally much larger portion of revenues from sales and trading and asset management.

Mergers and acquisitions and capital markets are also often covered by The Wall Street Journal and Bloomberg.

Financial Crisis of 2007–2008

The 2008 financial credit crisis led to the collapse of several notable investment banks, such as the bankruptcy of Lehman Brothers (one of the largest investment banks in the world) and the hurried sale of Merrill Lynch and the much smaller Bear Stearns to much larger banks, which effectively rescued them from bankruptcy. The entire financial services industry, including numerous investment banks, was rescued by government loans through the Troubled Asset Relief Program (TARP). Surviving U.S. investment banks such as Goldman Sachs and Morgan Stanley converted to traditional bank holding companies to accept TARP relief. Similar situations occurred across the globe with countries rescuing their banking industry. Initially, banks received part of a $700 billion TARP intended to stabilize the economy and thaw the frozen credit markets. Eventually, taxpayer assistance to banks reached nearly $13 trillion, most without much scrutiny, lending did not increase and credit markets remained frozen.

The crisis led to questioning of the business model of the investment bank without the regulation imposed on it by Glass-Steagall. Once Robert Rubin, a former co-chairman of Goldman Sachs, became part of the Clinton administration and deregulated banks, the previous conservatism of underwriting established companies and seeking long-term gains was replaced by lower standards and short-term profit. Formerly, the guidelines said that in order to take a company public, it had to be in business for a minimum of five years and it had to show profitability for three consecutive years. After deregulation, those standards were gone, but small investors did not grasp the full impact of the change.

A number of former Goldman Sachs top executives, such as Henry Paulson and Ed Liddy were in high-level positions in government and oversaw the controversial taxpayer-funded bank bailout. The TARP Oversight Report released by the Congressional Oversight Panel found that the bailout tended to encourage risky behavior and "corrupt[ed] the fundamental tenets of a market economy".

Under threat of a subpoena, Goldman Sachs revealed that it received $12.9 billion in taxpayer aid, $4.3 billion of which was then paid out to 32 entities, including many overseas banks, hedge funds and pensions. The same year it received $10 billion in aid from the government, it also paid out multimillion-dollar bonuses; the total paid in bonuses was $4.82 billion. Similarly, Morgan Stanley received $10 billion in TARP funds and paid out $4.475 billion in bonuses.

Criticisms

The investment banking industry, and many individual investment banks, have come under criticism for a variety of reasons, including perceived conflicts of interest, overly large pay packages, cartel-like or oligopolic behavior, taking both sides in transactions, and more. Investment banking has also been criticised for its opacity.

Conflicts of Interest

Conflicts of interest may arise between different parts of a bank, creating the potential for market manipulation, according to critics. Authorities that regulate investment banking, such as the Financial Conduct Authority (FCA) in the United Kingdom and the SEC in the United States, require that banks impose a "Chinese wall" to prevent communication between investment banking on one side and equity research and trading on the other. However, critics say such a barrier does not always exist in practice. Independent advisory firms that exclusively provide corporate finance advice argue that their advice is not conflicted, unlike bulge bracket banks.

Conflicts of interest often arise in relation to investment banks' equity research units, which have long been part of the industry. A common practice is for equity analysts to initiate coverage of a company in order to develop relationships that lead to highly profitable investment banking business. In the 1990s, many equity researchers allegedly traded positive stock ratings for investment banking business. Alternatively, companies may threaten to divert investment banking business to competitors unless their stock was rated favorably. Laws were passed to criminalize such acts, and increased pressure from regulators and a series of lawsuits, settlements, and prosecutions curbed this business to a large extent following the 2001 stock market tumble after the dot-com bubble.

Philip Augar, author of *The Greed Merchants*, said in an interview that, "You cannot simultaneously serve the interest of issuer clients and investing clients. And it's not just underwriting and sales; investment banks run proprietary trading operations that are also making a profit out of these securities."

Many investment banks also own retail brokerages. During the 1990s, some retail brokerages sold consumers securities which did not meet their stated risk profile. This behavior may have led to investment banking business or even sales of surplus shares during a public offering to keep public perception of the stock favorable.

Since investment banks engage heavily in trading for their own account, there is always the temptation for them to engage in some form of front running – the illegal practice whereby a broker executes orders for their own account before filling orders previously submitted by their customers, thereby benefiting from any changes in prices induced by those orders.

Documents under seal in a decade-long lawsuit concerning eToys.com's IPO but obtained by *New York Times'* Wall Street Business columnist Joe Nocera alleged that IPOs managed by Goldman Sachs and other investment bankers involved asking for kickbacks from their institutional clients who made large profits flipping IPOs which Goldman had intentionally undervalued. Depositions in the lawsuit alleged that clients willingly complied with these demands because they understood it was necessary in order to participate in future hot issues. *Reuters* Wall Street correspondent Felix Salmon retracted his earlier, more conciliatory, statements on the subject and said he believed that the depositions show that companies going public and their initial consumer stockholders are both defrauded by this practice, which may be widespread throughout the IPO finance industry. The case is ongoing, and the allegations remain unproven.

Compensation

Investment banking is often criticized for the enormous pay packages awarded to those who work in the industry. According to Bloomberg Wall Street's five biggest firms paid over $3 billion to their executives from 2003 to 2008, "while they presided over the packaging and sale of loans that helped bring down the investment-banking system."

The highly generous pay packages include $172 million for Merrill Lynch & Co. CEO Stanley O'Neal from 2003 to 2007, before it was bought by Bank of America in 2008, and $161 million for Bear Stearns Co.'s James Cayne before the bank collapsed and was sold to JPMorgan Chase & Co. in June 2008.

Such pay arrangements have attracted the ire of Democrats and Republicans in the United States Congress, who demanded limits on executive pay in 2008 when the U.S. government was bailing out the industry with a $700 billion financial rescue package.

Writing in the Global Association of Risk Professionals, Aaron Brown, a vice president at Morgan Stanley, says “By any standard of human fairness, of course, investment bankers make obscene amounts of money.”

Structure of Banking Industry

The financial system of an economy is expected to support the changes in the economy. Financial system is reflected by the structure of banking industry. Indian economy underwent liberalization programs beginning from 1991-92 and this has influenced the banking industry. The banking industry that was functioning fully under a regulated environment shifted towards a competitive environment. Changes in technology are another factor that has contributed towards the structural change in the banking industry. With the impact of global financial shocks, the Indian financial system also is undergoing the change process to meet the inherent risks in the economy. The structural change in the banking industry that can be highlighted is the increased participation of international financial players in the Indian financial system as well as Indian financial players exhibiting a tendency towards becoming global players.

The Government represented by the Ministry of Finance, the Reserve Bank of India and other regulatory bodies for the banking sector have a coordinated policy measure towards bringing in a cautious change in the structure of the banking industry. Banking industry being the backbone of the nation has to live up to meet the economic needs and provide a protective backdrop for the economic entities by assuming certain inherent risks in the financial system. Besides the change in the overall structure, the structure of each entity within the banking industry has also undergone the necessary changes to meet these economic and risk taking needs. Concerns have also been expressed by international financial community on the need to strengthen the banking industry to support the high growth expectations of the economy.

Most often it has been observed that changing market requirements if not being considered by the financial system in an economy has not reflected in the expected growth rates of the productive economy. A banking structure hence is expected to be strong to support economic growth and contribute towards the long-term progress of the nation. The structure of the banking industry in this context has to be flexible enough to allow for economic expansion and simultaneously provide stability to the financial system of the economy. The consistent trend of economic policies by subsequent Governments hence is considered essential in the formation of the banking structure of an economy.

The banking industry in India exhibits a different structure when compared to other economies and thus caters to our social, economic, political and geographic characteristic. Indian economy is agriculture driven with a large population and wide diversity. Further the high level of financial illiteracy prevalent in India necessitates the need for emphasis of financial inclusion at all strata of the society. This has led to the unique recognition of our social and financial framework that relies more on initiatives from Government and public sector undertakings. The participation of private capital in the banking industry is sought though is still being regulated and monitored to support the socio economic requirements of the country. Public sector participation thus dominates the structure of the banking industry and this has given the Indian financial system benefits in terms of supportive growth, reduced conflict of interest in the administration and ownership structure and the ability to meet risks that are unique to the industry. However, there is also a need to recognize the possible benefits that are foregone by our present structure in terms of cost and quality efficiency required for the ability of the financial system to meet its expectations in the economy.

The structure of banking industry in India can be mapped through the functions performed by banks associated with the economy. The prominent role of the Reserve Bank of India as the central bank governs other banking structures in the economy. Reserve Bank of India monitors and controls the entire banking system of the Indian economic activity. These activities of the Reserve Bank of India do not deal with the government public mechanisms. This helps the Reserve Bank of India to retain its independent status of functions. The Reserve Bank of India acts as a banker to the Government and maintains the deposit and other business activities of other banks that have been allowed to operate in the economy. It is responsible for monitory and credit policies.

Reserve bank of India manages government debt requirements, promotes financial inclusion and encourages development activities in the economy. It monitors and maintains rupee value vs. other global currencies. It exercises credit control and control over money supply in the economy.

Public sector banks dominate commercial banking structure. State Bank of India and its group and nationalized banks account for largest number of branches across the country and also in terms of deposits mobilized and loans sanctioned. Besides they also perform a lead role in the implementation of developmental programs of the government towards rural areas, small borrowers and weaker sections of the society.

In recent times private sector banks also registered significant improvement in their banking activities providing the much needed competition in the banking sector. Foreign banks focus their activities mainly in urban areas.

Offices of commercial banks in India highlight the increasing trend of offices in various bank categories.

TABLE: OFFICES OF COMMERCIAL BANKS IN INDIA - 2006 TO 2010					
Bank Group	As on March 31				
	2006	2007	2008	2009	2010
	(1)	(2)	(3)	(4)	(5)

State Bank of India and its Associates	14310	14673	15846	16878	18114
Nationalised Banks	35858	37431	39234	40854	43187
Public Sector Banks	50168	52104	55080	57732	61301
Old Private Sector Banks	4819	4826	4690	4908	5174
New Private Sector Banks	2016	2598	3632	4328	5213
Private Sector Banks	6835	7424	8322	9236	10387
Foreign Banks	259	272	279	295	310
Regional Rural Banks	14807	14843	15070	15485	15723
Non-Scheduled Commercial Banks	41	46	46	46	47
All Commercial Banks	72110	74689	78797	82794	87768

Besides the primary function of accepting deposits and lending through loans and advances, banks perform a variety of services such as providing safe custody for the valuables of customers, providing foreign exchange, facilitating transfer of money and providing guarantees and letters of credit.

Investment banks are specialized banks providing investment services to individuals and institutions besides arranging loans, lease and mortgage facilities. They help through corporate advisory services, capital market intermediation, consultancy, market research, broking servicesand project finance to their clients.

Development banks are established for the purpose of catering to long term capital needs of business and industry. IFCI, IDBI, IIBI, SFCs provide these facilities. Besides there are national level specialized institutions such as EXIM bank, NHBs, SIDBI, IDFC catering to specific developmental needs of the country.

Co-operative banks are unique that promotes mutual self help among groups. These are formed for a variety of purposes like credit assistance, business promotion and other developmental activities.

These banks operate at three levels. State co-operative banks are apex banks in the state. District cooperative and primary co-operative banks operate at lower levels rendering localized services.

Non banking finance companies offer a variety of services like leasing and hire purchase and investment services. Some NBFCs accept deposits, others render only financial intermediation. Some NBFCs operate as investment companies.

Mutual funds are financial intermediaries that help investors through sale of units under different schemes and offer of returns from investments in these schemes. The schemes may be open ended or close ended. The schemes aim at capital appreciation or regular income or tax savings to the investors.

Another entrant in financial service field is the micro finance institutions. Micro finance institutions provide assistance to low income households through Non Government Organizations (NGOs) or Self Help Groups (SHGs).

Banking operations inevitably involves several types of risks such as credit risk, liquidity risk, market risk, operational risk and systems risk. The effectiveness of risk management by banks depends on technology support, capital adequacy, tools and techniques used, audit and supervision and supportive legal environment. The loan policies followed, interest rates determined, the asset acquisition and management, internal credit rating process and risk tolerance levels fixed for investment purposes are the business strategies adopted by banks. These are some of the banking practices that reveal the approach of a bank to its risk management practices.

Organization of Banking Industry

There are mainly three forms of banks. Unit banks which are popular in US are single unit entities confining there operations to specific localities. As against this in India branch banking is the most applied structure of a banking entity. In this structure a single bank will have number of branches under its control operating at different places. Holding banking companies are large banking entities controlling several subsidiaries. The comparative features of the three types of banks are given in Table.

Table: Comparative features of banking structure

Feature	Unit Bank	Holding Company	Branch Company
Efficiency - Scale	Less	Some	Most
Efficiency - Scope	Most	Most	Some
Flow of Funds	Low	Possible	Easy
Competition	Exists	No	Exists
New Entry	Easy	Little	Easy
Market Access	Tough	Easy	Easy
Liquidity	Low	High	High
Decentralized Power	Most	Little	Moderate
Sensitivity to Society	Most	Little	Moderate
Convenience to Customers	Most	Little	Most

Banks can also be classified on the basis of ownership into nationalized banks, private banks and foreign banks. Another way of classifying banks is on the basis of size. These can be large banks, small banks. The basis of classification can be capital size or deposit size.

Banks can be studied by classifying them on the basis of type of business and level of operations. For example based on area of operation banks may be national banks, regional banks or international banks. On the basis of business specialization they may be classified into community banks, development banks, core banks or service banks.

Commercial banks primarily focus on deposit mobilization and lending operations. It has to operate under the overall regulatory environment created by Central Bank in terms of its operations. Investment banks on the other hand mainly focus on serving investment needs of different types of clients. They perform portfolio management services by marketing different schemes, participating in the initial public issues of corporate firms and performing corporate advisory services.

Branch (Banking)

Former Bank of Montreal branch in Ottawa, now a historical building.

Current Bank of America branch in Porter Ranch, Los Angeles, California

A branch, banking center or financial center is a retail location where a bank, credit union, or other financial institution (and by extension, brokerage firms) offers a wide array of face-to-face and automated services to its customers.

History and Description

During the 3rd century banks in Persia (now Iran) and in other territories started to issue letters of credit known as Sakks, basically checks in today's language, that could be traded in cooperative houses or offices throughout the Persian territories. In the period from 1100-1300 banking started to expand across Europe and banks began opening 'branches' in remote, foreign locations to support international trade. In 1327, Avignon in France had 43 branches of Italian banking houses alone.

The practice of opening satellite branches was popularized in the early 20th century by Amadeo Giannini, then head of the Bank of America. Historically, branches were housed in imposing buildings, often in a neoclassical style of architecture. Today, branches may also take the form of smaller offices within a larger complex, such as a shopping mall.

Traditionally, the branch was the only place of access to a financial institution's services. Services provided by a branch include cash withdrawals and deposits from a demand account with a bank teller, financial advice through a specialist, safe deposit box rentals, bureau de change, insurance sales (where it is allowed by law), etc. In the early 21st century, features such as automated teller machines (ATM), telephone and online banking, allow customers to bank from remote locations and after business hours. This has caused financial institutions to reduce their branch business hours and to merge smaller branches into larger ones. Conversely, they converted some into *mini-branches* with only ATMs for cash withdrawal and depositing; computer terminals for online banking and cheque depositing machines. Some mini-branches may have one or no human staff with only telephone support.

Some financial institutions, in an attempt to show a friendlier image, offer a boutique or coffeehouse-like environment in their branches, with sit-down counters, refreshments, interactive displays, music and playing areas for children. Some branches also have drive-through teller windows or ATMs. Other financial institutions reduce their costs and position their offerings by having no branches and are sometimes known as virtuals or direct banks.

Legal Restrictions in the United States

Historically, branch banking in the United States - especially interstate branch banking - was viewed unfavorably by regulatory authorities, and this was codified with the enactment of the McFadden Act of 1927, which specifically prohibited interstate banking. Over the next few decades, some banks attempted to circumvent McFadden's provisions by establishing bank holding companies that operated so-called independent banks in multiple states. To address this, The Bank Holding Company Act of 1956 prohibited bank holding companies headquartered in one state from having branches in any other state.

Most interstate banking prohibitions were repealed by the Riegle-Neal Interstate Banking and Branching Efficiency Act of 1994. Research has also found that anticompetitive state provisions restricted out-of-state growth when those provisions were more restrictive than the provisions set by the Interstate Banking and Branching Efficiency Act or by neighboring states. Some states have also had restrictive bank branch laws; for example, Illinois outlawed branches (other than the main office) until 1967, and did not allow an unlimited number until 1993.

Types of Branches

Traditional or Brick-and-mortar

These are typically stand alone branches of a financial institution that often are contained in its own building. These branches typically offer full service banking including safe deposit boxes. They may include access to drive-through teller windows.

Instore

These are typically branches located in a retail space such as a grocery, shopping malls or discount store. They may be full service branches or limited service branches. They generally do not include drive-through teller windows or safe deposit boxes. These branches may have limited staff and typically include technology as a means to deliver banking services such as the use of automated teller machines, videoconferencing, and video banking systems.

Foreign Bank Branch

A type of foreign bank that is obligated to follow the regulations of both the home and host countries.operating in the country, regulated by the Office of the Superintendent of Financial Institutions.

Bank Holding Company

A bank holding company is a company that controls one or more banks, but does not necessarily engage in banking itself.

United States

In the United States, a bank holding company, as provided by the Bank Holding Company Act of 1956 (12 U.S.C. 1841(a)(2)(A) *et seq.*), is broadly defined as "any company that has control over a bank". All bank holding companies in the US are required to register with the Board of Governors of the Federal Reserve System.

Regulation

The Federal Reserve Board of Governors, under Regulation Y (12 C.F.R. Pt. 225) has responsibility for regulating and supervising bank holding company activities, such as establishing capital standards, approving mergers and acquisitions and inspecting the operations of such companies. This authority applies even though a bank owned by a holding company may be under the primary supervision of the Office of the Comptroller of the Currency or the Federal Deposit Insurance Corporation.

Bank Holding Company Status

Becoming a bank holding company makes it easier for the firm to raise capital than as a traditional bank. The holding company can assume debt of shareholders on a tax free basis, borrow money, acquire other banks and non-bank entities more easily, and issue stock with greater regulatory ease. It also has a greater legal authority to conduct share repurchases of its own stock.

The downside includes responding to additional regulatory authorities, especially if there are more than 2,000 shareholders (note: prior to the Jobs Act or Jumpstart Our Business Startups Act, the shareholder number was 300), at which point the bank holding company is forced to register with the Securities and Exchange Commission. There are also added expenses of operating with an extra layer of administration.

2008 Credit Crisis

As a result of the global financial crisis of 2008, many traditional investment banks and finance corporations such as Goldman Sachs, Morgan Stanley, American Express, CIT Group and General Motors Acceptance Corporation successfully converted to bank holding companies in order to gain access to liquidity and funding.

Functions of Banks in an Economy

Banks being financial intermediaries provide money in the economy through credit creation and facilitating liquidity. Banks are able to generate credit many times more than the initial deposits they receive from the public subject to regulations relating to cash reserves to be maintained and customers' cash requirements. The resources of banks are generated mainly through a variety of deposits, both short time and long term from the public. The ability of the bank to generate more deposits depends on the interest rate offered and the marketing skills of the bank. Shorter duration and higher interest on deposits will add to the operational risk of the banks.

Bank's role in the economy is necessitated on account of differences in the preference of public in terms of maturity requirements, risk requirements, denomination of currency and access to adequate information. The existence of market imperfection such as transaction and contracting cost also strengthen the need for the functioning of banks. Banking industry differs from other industries in the economy in terms of its asset structure and legal obligations and developmental functions.

Besides offering a variety of loans and advances to different needy clients, banks also provide a lead role in translating the development objectives of the government through lead bank schemes and priority sector lending and financial inclusion. In the process of performing these functions, banks have to manage a variety of risks which are inherent in banking operations. One of the major risks that affect the bank is credit risk which is reflected in the proportion of non-performing assets (NPA) held by the banks. The maturity structure of various assets and liabilities of the bank poses liquidity risk to the bank. The fluctuation in interest rates is another source of risk. Exchange rate risk arises to the bank when they provide foreign currency loans to their customers or when they make investments in foreign securities or accept foreign currency deposits.

Competition in Banking Industry

Competition among commercial and investment banks are influenced by different set of factors. Some of the common factors are size, service quality and regulatory obligations. The ability of the bank to sustain competitive forces depends on their operational efficiency, product innovation, technology support, cost of services, service quality and human resourceskills. For an investment bank the competitive edge depends on their investment performance, innovation in their services, cost of service, number of clients handled by them, confidence in the banks and reputation of the banks.

Given the competitive environment, ability of the bank to foresee changes and their flexibility in adapting to changing conditions will give them an edge. The change factors that have to be initiated by the bank to have an impact on its operations are needs of new customers, their knowledge level, technological changes, regulatory changes, new competitors, new services, quality of human resources and marketing efforts.

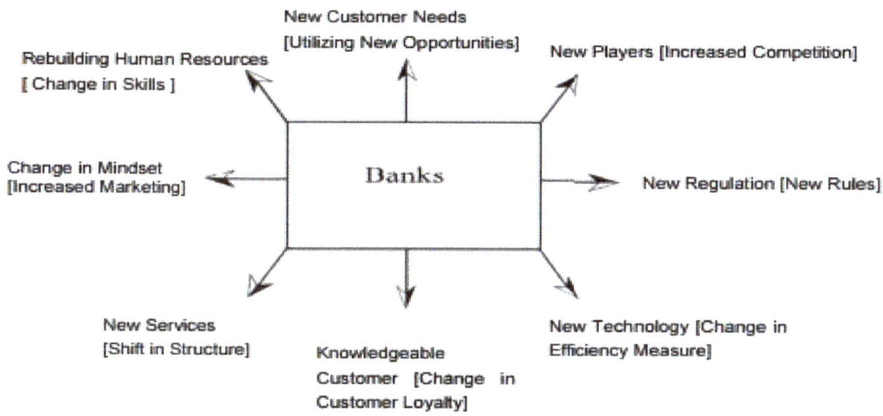

Changes in Bank Operations

To compute the level of competition in a market the Herfindahl-Hirschman index can be applied.

HHI = Sum of squared market share for all banks in a defined locality or economy.

HHI

$$HHI = \sum_{i=1}^{k} A_i^2$$

Where

=Percent of market / deposits / assets of the bank.

= Total number of banks.

Higher the HHI, larger is the competitive dominance of banks in the industry. Smaller score indicates that a few banks have a controlling hold in the banking operations.

References

- O'Sullivan, Arthur; Sheffrin, Steven M. (2003). Economics: Principles in action. Upper Saddle River, New Jersey 07458: Pearson Prentice Hall. p. 421. ISBN 0-13-063085-3
- Rachel Sanderson (October 22, 2010). "UniCredit municipal deal nullified". The Financial Times. Retrieved October 23, 2010
- Rhee RJ. (2010). The Decline of Investment Banking: Preliminary Thoughts on the Evolution of the Industry 1996–2008. Journal of Business and Technology Law
- J Huerta de Soto – 1998 (translated by M.A.Stroup 2012). Money, Bank Credit, and Economic Cycles. Ludwig von Mises Institute. ISBN 1610161890. Retrieved 2012-06-15
- Erin Nothwehrm "Emergency Economic Stabilization Act of 2008" University of Iowa (December 2008). Retrieved June 1, 2012
- G G Aperghis – The Seleukid Royal Economy: The Finances And Financial Administration Of The Seleukid Empire Cambridge University Press, 23 Dec 2004 ISBN 0521837073 Retrieved 2012-06-10
- Edward Niedermeyer, "TARP Oversight Report: Bailout Goals Conflict, Moral Hazard Alive And Well" (January 13, 2011). Retrieved March 7, 2011
- J E Harrison – Themis: A Study of the Social Origins of Greek Religion Cambridge University Press, 24 Jun 2010 ISBN 1108009492 Retrieved 2012-06-16
- G Davies, J H Bank – A history of money: from ancient times to the present day University of Wales Press, 2002 – Retrieved 2012-05-17
- S R Steadman, G McMahon – The Oxford Handbook of Ancient Anatolia: (10,000–323 Bce) Oxford University Press, 5 Sep 2011 ISBN 0195376145 Retrieved 2012-06-25
- R W Bulliet, P K Crossley, D R Headrick, S W Hirsch, L L Johnson – The Earth and Its Peoples: A Global History, Volume 1 Cengage Learning, 1 Jan 2010 Retrieved 2012-06-08
- Journal of the Royal Statistical Society Royal Statistical Society (Great Britain) Statistical Society of London 1874 Retrieved 2012-05-15
- SB MacDonald, AL Gastmann – A History of Credit and Power in the Western World Transaction Publishers, 2004 Retrieved 2012-07-14 ISBN 0765808331
- Thomas Henry Dyer The history of modern Europe: from the fall of Constantinople in 1453 to the war in the Crimea in 1857, Volume 2 John Murray, 1861 Retrieved 2012-05-14

An Overview of Asset Liability Management

2

Asset and liability management is the supervision of the risks that can arise due to discrepancy between assets and liabilities. Wholesale funding, gap analysis, duration analysis, and hedge funds are some of the topics discussed in the section. This chapter elucidates the crucial theories and principles of asset liability management.

Asset Liability Management

Banks hold different categories of assets and liabilities with different maturities carrying different interest rates. The bank's ability in matching this asset and liability structure results in improving its returns. Asset liability management involves managing different risks such as interest rate risk, credit risk, operational risk, exchange rate risk, market risk, liquidity risk, contingency risk and treasury management risk.

Variations in interest rates will impact the value of assets and liabilities that a bank holds. Therefore they need to devise tools and techniques to handle the impact of these changes. Interest rate risk management helps in maximizing bank profits and reduces losses and protects bank assets. The nature of banks having a smaller capital base compared to the larger asset base makes banks vulnerable to capital erosion due to reduction in value of assets.

Bank balance sheet before capital erosion

Liabilities		**Assets**	
Capital	20000	Reserves	85000
Borrowings	10000	Advances	588000
Short term deposits	550000	Investments	100000
Long term deposits	200000	Fixed Assets	7000
Total	780000	Total	780000

Bank balance sheet after capital erosion on account of 2% value reduction in advances shows a 58.8% reduction in capital.

Liabilities		Assets	
Capital	8240	Reserves	85000
Borrowings	10000	Advances	576240
Short term deposits	550000	Investments	100000
Long term deposits	200000	Fixed Assets	7000
Total	768240	Total	768240

There are several models of risk management through asset liability management. They are asset models, liability models, randomness models, multi-dimensional models and computer aided asset liability management (CALM) models. Asset models and liabilities models focus on one aspect of the balance sheet. The randomness model is based on selected criteria that impact the bank performance. Multi-dimensional models look at impact of selected variables on several independent variables. The CALM models are comprehensive and aim at dynamic asset liability management.

In managing risks banks need to focus attention on volume, mix, maturity, rate sensitivity, quality and liquidity and acceptable risk reward ratio. The parameters for ALM are net interest margin, market value of equity and economic equity ratio.

Reserve Bank of India has provided guidelines in terms of asset liability management. The traditional approach focuses on operational limits on credit, loan provisioning, portfolio diversification and collateralization. The innovative methods suggested include loan securitization, capital adequacy and derivative products.

For successful risk management by banks, well developed money market, trading in repo transactions, forward trading, underwriting facilities and derivative markets are essential.

Initially pioneered by financial institutions during the 1970s as interest rates became increasingly volatile, asset and liability management (often abbreviated ALM) is the practice of managing risks that arise due to mismatches between the assets and liabilities.

The process is at the crossroads between risk management and strategic planning. It is not just about offering solutions to mitigate or hedge the risks arising from the interaction of assets and liabilities but is focused on a long-term perspective: success in the process of maximising assets to meet complex liabilities may increase profitability.

Thus modern ALM includes the allocation and management of assets, equity, interest rate and credit risk management including risk overlays, and the calibration of firm-wide tools within these risk frameworks for optimisation and management in the local regulatory and capital environment.

Often an ALM approach passively matches assets against liabilities (fully hedged) and leaves surplus to be actively managed.

ALM Objectives and Scope

The exact roles and perimeter around ALM can vary significantly from one bank (or other financial institutions) to another depending on the business model adopted and can encompass a broad area of risks.

The traditional ALM programs focus on interest rate risk and liquidity risk because they represent the most prominent risks affecting the organization balance-sheet (as they require coordination between assets and liabilities).

But ALM also now seeks to broaden assignments such as foreign exchange risk and capital management. According to the Balance sheet management benchmark survey conducted in 2009 by the audit and consulting company PricewaterhouseCoopers (PwC), 51% of the 43 leading financial institutions participants look at capital management in their ALM unit.

The scope of the ALM function to a larger extent covers the following processes:

1. Liquidity risk: the current and prospective risk arising when the bank is unable to meet its obligations as they come due without adversely affecting the bank's financial conditions. From an ALM perspective, the focus is on the funding liquidity risk of the bank, meaning its ability to meet its current and future cash-flow obligations and collateral needs, both expected and unexpected. This mission thus includes the bank liquidity's benchmark price in the market.
2. Interest rate risk: The risk of losses resulting from movements in interest rates and their impact on future cash-flows. Generally because a bank may have a disproportionate amount of fixed or variable rates instruments on either side of the balance-sheet. One of the primary causes are mismatches in terms of bank deposits and loans.
3. Capital markets risk: The risk from movements in equity and/or credit on the balance sheet. An insurer may wish to harvest either risk or fee premia. Risk is then mitigated by options, futures, derivative overlays which may incorporate tactical or strategic views.
4. Currency risk management: The risk of losses resulting from movements in exchanges rates. To the extent that cash-flow assets and liabilities are denominated in different currencies.
5. Funding and capital management: As all the mechanism to ensure the maintenance of adequate capital on a continuous basis. It is a dynamic and ongoing process considering both short- and longer-term capital needs and is coordinated with a bank's overall strategy and planning cycles (usually a prospective time-horizon of 2 years).
6. Profit planning and growth.

7. In addition, ALM deals with aspects related to credit risk as this function is also to manage the impact of the entire credit portfolio (including cash, investments, and loans) on the balance sheet. The credit risk, specifically in the loan portfolio, is handled by a separate risk management function and represents one of the main data contributors to the ALM team.

The ALM function scope covers both a prudential component (management of all possible risks and rules and regulation) and an optimization role (management of funding costs, generating results on balance sheet position), within the limits of compliance (implementation and monitoring with internal rules and regulatory set of rules). ALM intervenes in these issues of current business activities but is also consulted to organic development and external acquisition to analyse and validate the funding terms options, conditions of the projects and any risks (i.e., funding issues in local currencies).

Today, ALM techniques and processes have been extended and adopted by corporations other than financial institutions; e.g., insurance.

Treasury and ALM

For simplification treasury management can be covered and depicted from a corporate perspective looking at the management of liquidity, funding, and financial risk. On the other hand, ALM is a discipline relevant to banks and financial institutions whose balance sheets present different challenges and who must meet regulatory standards.

For banking institutions, treasury and ALM are strictly interrelated with each other and collaborate in managing both liquidity, interest rate, and currency risk at solo and group level: Where ALM focuses more on risk analysis and medium- and long-term financing needs, treasury manages short-term funding (mainly up to one year) including intra-day liquidity management and cash clearing, crisis liquidity monitoring.

ALM Governance

The responsibility for ALM is often divided between the treasury and Chief Financial Officer (CFO). In smaller organizations, the ALM process can be addressed by one or two key persons (Chief Executive Officer, such as the CFO or treasurer).

The vast majority of banks operate a centralised ALM model which enables oversight of the consolidated balance-sheet with lower-level ALM units focusing on business units or legal entities.

To assist and supervise the ALM unit an Asset Liability Committee (ALCO), whether at the board or management level, is established. It has the central purpose of attaining goals defined by the short- and long-term strategic plans:

- To ensure adequate liquidity while managing the bank's spread between the interest income and interest expense

- To approve a contingency plan
- To review and approve the liquidity and funds management policy at least annually
- To link the funding policy with needs and sources via mix of liabilities or sale of assets (fixed vs. floating rate funds, wholesale vs. retail deposit, money market vs. capital market funding, domestic vs. foreign currency funding...)

Legislative Summary

Relevant ALM legislation deals mainly with the management of interest rate risk and liquidity risk:

- Most global banks have benchmarked their ALM framework to the Basel Committee on Banking Supervision (BCBS) guidance 'Principles for the management and supervision of interest rate risk'. Issued in July 2004, this paper has the objective to support the Pillar 2 approach to interest rate risk in the banking book within the Basel II capital framework.
- In January 2013, the Basel Committee has issued the full text of the revised Liquidity Coverage Ratio (LCR) as one of the key component of the Basel III capital framework. This new coming ratio will ensure that banks will have sufficient adequacy transformation level between their stock of unencumbered high-quality assets (HQLA) and their conversion into cash to meet their liquidity requirements for a 30-calendar-day liquidity stress scenario (and thus hoping to cure shortcoming from Basel II that was not addressing liquidity management).

ALM Concepts

Building an ALM Policy

Policy limits for balance sheet mix on the size of asset/liabilities categories	
Assets	**Policy limits as a % of Total Assets**
Loans and leases	**70%**
Residential mortgage	30%
Commercial loans	20%
Personal loans	15%
Finance leases	5%
Financial investments	15%
Other investments	5%
Inventories	1%
Intangible assets	3%
Cash and cash equivalent	4%
Trade an dother receivables	2%
	100%
Liabilities	
Domestic interest bearing deposits	**75%**
Term deposit	42%
Demand deposit	25%
Brokered deposits	8%
Short-term borrowings	4%
Long-term debt	12%
Non-interest bearing liabilities	5%
Deferred revenue	2%
Trade and other payable	2%
	100%

Illustrative example of a balance sheet mix limits mechanism

As in all operational areas, ALM must be guided by a formal policy and must address:

- Limits on the maximum size of major asset/ liability categories
- Balance sheet mix : in order to follow the old adage 'Don't put all your eggs in one basket'
  - Limits on the mix of balance sheet assets (loans by credit category, financial instruments...) considering levels of risk and return and thus guided by annual planning targets, lending licence constraints and regulatory restrictions on investments.
  - Limits on the mix of balance sheet liabilities such as deposits and other types of funding (all sources of funding are expressed as a % of total assets with the objective to offer comparability and correlate by term and pricing to the mix of assets held) considering the differential costs and volatility of these types of funds
  - Policy limits have to be realistic :based on historical trend analysis and comparable to the peers or the market
- Correlating maturities and terms
- Controlling liquidity position and set limits in terms of ratios and projected net cash-flows, analyse and test alternative sources of liquidity
- Controlling interest rate risk and establishing interest rate risk measurement techniques
- Controlling currency risk
- Controlling the use of derivatives as well as defining management analysis and expert contribution for derivative transactions
- Frequency and content for board reporting
- But also practical decision such as :
  - Who is responsible for monitoring the ALM position of the bank
  - What tools to use to monitor the ALM framework

Note that the ALM policy has not the objective to skip out the institution from elaborating a liquidity policy. In any case, the ALM and liquidity policies need to be correlated as decision on lending, investment, liabilities, equity are all interrelated.

ALM Core Functions

Managing Gaps

The objective is to measure the direction and extent of asset-liability mismatch through the funding or maturity gap. This aspect of ALM stresses the importance of balancing maturities as well as cash-flows or interest rates for a particular set time horizon.

For the management of interest rate risk it may take the form of matching the maturities and interest rates of loans and investments with the maturities and interest rates of deposit, equity and external credit in order to maintain adequate profitability. In other words, it is the management of the spread between interest rate sensitive assets and interest rate sensitive liabilities.

Static/Dynamic Gap Measurement Techniques

Gap analysis suffers from only covering future gap direction of current existing exposures and exercise of options (i.e.: prepayments) at different point in time. Dynamic gap analysis enlarges the perimeter for a specific asset by including 'what if' scenarios on making assumptions on new volumes, (changes in the business activity, future path of interest rate, changes in pricing, shape of yield curve, new prepayments transactions, what its forecast gap positions will look like if entering into a hedge transaction).

Liquidity Risk Management

The role of the bank in the context of the maturity transformation that occurs in the banking book (as traditional activity of the bank is to borrow short and lend long) lets inherently the institution vulnerable to liquidity risk and can even conduct to the so-call risk of 'run of the bank' as depositors, investors or insurance policy holders can withdraw their funds/ seek for cash in their financial claims and thus impacting current and future cash-flow and collateral needs of the bank (risk appeared if the bank is unable to meet in good conditions these obligations as they come due). This aspect of liquidity risk is named funding liquidity risk and arises because of liquidity mismatch of assets and liabilities (unbalance in the maturity term creating liquidity gap). Even if market liquidity risk is not covered into the conventional techniques of ALM (market liquidity risk as the risk to not easily offset or eliminate a position at the prevailing market price because of inadequate market depth or market disruption), these 2 liquidity risk types are closely interconnected. In fact, reasons for banking cash inflows are :

- when counterparties repay their debts (loan repayments): indirect connect due to the borrower's dependence to market liquidity to obtain the funds
- when clients put deposit: indirect connect due to the depositor's dependence to market liquidity to obtain the funds
- when the bank purchases assets hold: direct connect with market liquidity (security's market liquidity as the ease at trading it and thus potential sharp in price)
- when the bank sells debts it has primary bought: direct connect

Liquidity Gap Analysis

Liquidity gap report							
Time interval	1 to 14 days	15 to 28 days	29 days up to 3 months	Over 3 months and up to 6 months	Over 6 months and up to 12 months	Over 1 year	Total
Assets (Inflows)							
Overnight investments	15 456	0	0	0	0	0	15 456
Investments	18 890	16 678	15 034	43 278	27 413	18 996	140 289
Loans	54 234	48 098	42 896	111 567	65 447	50 320	372 562
Other assets	0	0	0	0	0	0	0
Total assets	88 580	64 776	57 930	154 845	92 860	69 316	528 307
Liabilities (Outflows)							
Non maturity deposits	956	4 003	3 045	10 519	9 459	9 774	37 756
Time deposits	39 671	38 004	42 590	90 488	74 933	32 309	317 995
Total deposits	40 627	42 007	45 635	101 007	84 392	42 083	355 751
Overnight borrowings	0	0	0	0	0	0	0
Borrowings	96 551	23 599	1 678	7 990	29 045	5 332	164 195
Other liabilities	0	0	0	0	0	0	0
Total liabilities	137 178	65 606	47 313	108 997	113 437	47 415	519 946
							Cumulative
Periodic net cash-flow	-48 598	-830	10 617	45 848	-20 577	21 901	8 361
Marginal gap		47 768	11 447	35 231	-66 425	42 478	70 499
Internal limits as gap cannot exceed % of cash outflows							
Scenario analysis							
Retained 75% of time deposit	29 753	28 503	31 943	67 866	56 200	24 232	238 496
Projected Net Cash flow	-18 845	27 673	42 560	113 714	35 623	46 133	246 857

Liq gap report2

Measuring liquidity position via liquidity gap analysis is still one of the most common tool used and represents the foundation for scenario analysis and stress-testing.

Maturity liquidity profile		
Accounts		**Time interval classification**
Assets (Inflows)		
Cash		1-14 days time interval
Balances with other banks		
	Current account	Non-withdrawable portion over 1 year period
	Money at call and short notice, term	Effective maturity period
Investments		
	Approved securities	Effective maturity period
	Corporate debentures and bonds	Effective maturity period
	Shares/ units of open ended mutual	Over 5 years
	Investments in subsidiaries/joint	Over 5 years
Advances		
	Bills purchased and discounted	Effective maturity period
	Cash credit/ overdraft	Base on internal model on client's behavior
	Term loans	Interim cash flows may be shown under
	Non performing assets	Over 1 year
Fixed assets		Over 5 years
Other assets		Effective maturity period
Liabilities (Outflows)		
Capital, reserve and surplus		Over 5 years
Current and saving bank deposit		Classified into 2 parts
		-volatile parts: 1-14 days time interval
		-Core balance: over 1 year
Term deposit		Effective maturity period
Certificate of deposit, borrowings		1-14 days time interval
Other liabilities and provisions		
	Bills payable	1-14 days time interval
	Provisions for NPAs	Over 1 year
	Provisions for depreciation in	Over 5 years
	Provisions for NPA in investments	Over 1 year
	Other provisions	Depending on the purpose
	Other liabilities	Effective maturity period

Off-balance sheet position, contingent liabilities/ credit committed/ available - other inflow outflow	
Lines of credit committed to institutions (outflow)	1-14 days time interval
Unavailed portion of cash credit/ overdraft (outflow)	Based on internal models
Letters of credit/ Guarantees (outflow)	Based on internal models and among various
Repos/ bills rediscounted/ swaps, forex, forward (outflow / inflow)	Effective maturity period
Interest payable receivable (inflow/ outflow)	Effective maturity period

Indicative maturity liquidity profile

To do so, ALM team is projecting future funding needs by tracking through maturity and cash-flow mismatches gap risk exposure (or matching schedule). In that situation, the risk depends not only on the maturity of asset-liabilities but also on the maturity of each intermediate cash-flow, including prepayments of loans or unforeseen usage of credit lines.

Actions to Perform

- Determining the number and length of each relevant time interval (time bucket)
- Defining the relevant maturities of the assets and liabilities where a maturing liability will be a cash outflow while a maturing asset will be a cash inflow (based on effective maturities or the 'liquidity duration': estimated time to dispose of the instruments in a crisis situation such as withdrawal from the business). For non maturity assets (such as overdrafts, credit card balances, drawn and undrawn lines of credit or any other off-balance sheet commitments), their movements as well as volume can be predict by making assumptions derived from examining historic data on client's behaviour.

- Slotting every asset, liability and off-balance sheet items into corresponding time bucket based on effective or liquidity duration maturity

In dealing with the liquidity gap, the bank main concern is to deal with a surplus of long-term assets over short-term liabilities and thus continuously to finance the assets with the risk that required funds will not be available or into prohibitive level.

Before any remediation actions, the bank will ensure first to :

1. Spread the liability maturity profile across many time intervals to avoid concentration of most of the funding in overnight to few days time buckets (standard prudent practices admit that no more than 20% of the total funding should be in the overnight to one-week period)
2. Plan any large size funding operation in advance
3. Hold a significant productions of high liquid assets (favorable conversion rate into cash in case distressed liquidity conditions)
4. Put limits for each time bucket and monitor to stay within a comfortable level around these limits (mainly expressed as a ratio where mismatch may not exceed X% of the total cash outflows for a given time interval)

Non-maturing Liabilities Specificity

As these instruments do not have a contractual maturity, the bank needs to dispose of a clear understanding of their duration level within the banking books. This analysis for non-maturing liabilities such as non interest-bearing deposits (savings accounts and deposits) consists of assessing the account holders behavior to determine the turnover level of the accounts or decay rate of deposits (speed at which the accounts 'decay', the retention rate is representing the inverse of a decay rate).

Calculation to define (example):

- Average opening of the accounts : a retail deposit portfolio has been open for an average of 8,3 years
- Retention rate : the given retention rate is 74,3%
- Duration level : translation into a duration of 6,2 years

Various assessment approaches may be used:

1. To place these funds in the longest-dated time bucket as deposits remain historically stable over time due to large numbers of depositors.
2. To divide the total volume into 2 parts: a stable part (core balance) and a floating part.

3. To assign maturities and re-pricing dates to the non-maturing liabilities by creating a portfolio of fixed income instruments that imitates the cash-flows of the liabilities positions.

The 2007 crisis however has evidence fiercely that the withdrawal of client deposits is driven by two major factors (level of sophistication of the counterparty: high-net-worth clients withdraw their funds quicker than retail ones, the absolute deposit size: large corporate clients are leaving faster than SMEs) enhancing simplification in the new deposit run-off models.

Remediation Actions

- A surplus of assets creates a funding requirement, i.e. a negative mismatch that can be financed
  - By long-term borrowings (typically costlier) : long-term debt, preferred stock, equity or demand deposit
  - By short-term borrowings (cheaper but with higher uncertainty level in term of availability and cost) : collateralized borrowings (repo), money market
  - By asset sales : distressed sales (at loss) but sales induce drastic changes in the bank's strategy
- A surplus of liabilities over assets creates the need to find efficient uses for those funds, i.e. a positive mismatch that is not a wrong signal (generally a rare scenario in a bank as the bank always has a target return on capital to achieve and so requires funds to be put to work by acquiring assets) but only means that the bank is sacrificing profits unnecessarily to achieve a liquidity position that is too liquid. This excess of liquidity can be deployed in money market instruments or risk-free assets such as government T-bills or bank certificate of deposit (CDs) if this liability excess belongs to bank's capital (the ALM desk will not take the risk of putting capital in a credit-risk investment).

Measuring Liquidity Risk

The liquidity measurement process consists of evaluating :

- Liquidity consumption (as the bank is consumed by illiquid assets and volatile liabilities)
- Liquidity provision (as the bank is provided by stable funds and by liquid assets)

2 essential factors are to take into account :

- Speed: the speed of market deterioration in 2008 fosters the need to daily measurement of liquidity figures and quick data availability
- Integrity

But daily completeness of data for an internationally operating bank should not represent the forefront of its procupation as the seek for daily consolidation is a lengthy process that may put away the vital concern of quick availability of liquidity figures. So the main focus will be on material entities and business as well as off-balance sheet position (commitments given,movements of collateral posted...)

For the purposes of quantitative analysis, since no single indicator can define adequate liquidity, several financial ratios can assist in assessing the level of liquidity risk. Due to the large number of areas within the bank's business giving rise to liquidity risk, these ratios present the simpler measures covering the major institution concern. In order to cover short-term to long-term liquidity risk they are divided into 3 categories :

1. Indicators of operating cash-flows
2. Ratios of liquidity
3. Financial strength (leverage)

Liquidity risk oriented ratios			
Category	**Ratio name**	**Objective and significance**	**Formula**
Cash-flow ratio	Cash and short term investment to total assets ratio	Indication of how much available cash the bank has to meet share withdrawals or additional loan demand	Cash + short term investment / total assets Short term investment : part of the current assets section of investment that will expire within the year (most part as stocks and bonds that can be liquidated quickly)
Cash-flow ratio	Operating cash flow ratio	Help to gauge the bank's liquidity in the short-term as how well current liabilities are covered by the cash-flow generated by the bank (thus shows its ability to meet near future expenses without to sell assets)	Cash-flow from operations / current liabilities
Ratio of liquidity	Current ratio	Estimation of whether the business can pay debts due within one year out of the current assets: • 1.7 to 2 : the business has enough cash to pay its debts • 1 to 1.5: potential problem to pay debts and raise extra finance	Current assets/ current liabilities • Current assets: cash, accounts receivable, inventory, marketable securities, prepaid expenses • Current liabilities : debt or obligation due within the year, short-term debt, account payable, accrued liabilities and other assets
Ratio of liquidity	Quick ratio (acid test ratio)	Adjustement of the current ratio to eliminate no-cash equivalent assets (inventory) and indicate the size of the buffer of cash	Current assets (-stock) / current liabilities

Ratio of liquidity	Non core funding dependence ratio	Measure of the bank's current position of how much long term earning assets (more than one year) are funded with non core funds (net short term funds: repo,CDs, foreign deposits and other borrowings maturing within one-year) net of short term investments. The lower the ratio the better	Non core liabilities (-Short term investments) / Long term assets
Ratio of liquidity	Core deposits to total assets	Measurement of the extent to which assets are funded through stable deposit base. Correct level : 55%	Core deposit : deposit accounts, withdrawals accounts, savings, money market accounts, retail certificates of deposits
Financial strength	Loans to deposit ratio	Simplified indication on the extent to which a bank is funding liquid assets by stable liabilities. A level of 85 to 95% indicating correct level.	Loans + advances to customer net of allowance for impairment losses (-reverse repo) / customer deposit (-repo)
Financial strength	Loans to asset ratio	Indication that the bank can effectively meet the loan demand as well as other liquidity needs. Correct level : 70 to 80%	

Setting Limits

Setting risk limits still remain a key control tool in managing liquidity as they provide :

- A clear and easily understandable communication tool for risk managers to top management of the adequacy of the level of liquidity to the bank's current exposure but also a good alert system to enhance conditions where the liquidity demands may disrupt the normal course of business
- One of the easiest control framework to implement

Funding Management

As an echo to the deficit of funds resulting from gaps between assets and liabilities the bank has also to address its funding requirement through an effective, robust and stable funding model.

Constraints to Take Into Account

1. Obtaining funds at reasonable costs
2. Fostering funding diversification in the sources and tenor of funding in the short, medium to long-term (funding mix process)
3. Adapting the maturities of liabilities cash-flow in order to match with funds uses

4. Gaining cushion of high liquid assets (refers to the bank's management of its asset funding sources)

Today, banking institutions within industrialized countries are facing structural challenges and remain still vulnerable to new market shocks or setbacks:

- New regulations from Basel III requirements on new capital buffers and liquidity ratios are increasing the pressure on bank's balance sheet
- Prolonged period of low rates has compressed margins and creates incentives to expand the assets hold in order to cover yields and thus growing exposures (rise in credit and liquidity risks)
- Long-term secured funding has fallen half since 2007 with decrease of the average maturity from 10 to 7 years
- Unsecured funding markets are no longer available for many banks (mostly banks located in southern European countries) with cut access to cheap funding
- Client deposits as the reliable source of stable funding is no more under a growth period as depositors shifting away their funds into safer institutions or non-banks institutions as well as following the economic slowdown trends
- The banking system needs to deal with fierce competition of the shadow banking system : entities or activities structured outside the regular banking mechanism that perform bank-like functions such as credit intermediation or funding sources (with bank corporate clients with refinancing rates lower or similar to the banks themselves and of course without financial regulatory restrictions and risk control). Size of the shadow banking system is evaluated to $67 trillion in 2011 according to the Financial Stability Board (FSB), this estimation is based on a proxy measure for non-credit intermediation in Australia, Canada, Japan, Korea, UK, US and the Euro area.

Principal Sources of Funding

After 2007, financial groups have further improved the diversification of funding sources as the crisis has proven that limited mix of funds may turn out to be risky if these sources run dry all of a sudden.

2 forms to obtain funding for banks:

Asset-based Funding Sources

The asset contribution to funding requirement depends on the bank ability to convert easily its assets to cash without loss.

- Cash-flows : as the primary source of asset side funding, occur when investments mature or through amortization of loans (periodic principal and interest cash-flows) and mortgage-backed securities
- Pledging of assets: in order to secure borrowings or line commitments. This practice induces a close management of these assets hold as collateral
- Liquidation of assets or sale of subsidiaries or lines of business (other form of shortening of assets can be also to reduce new loans origination)
- Securitization of assets as the bank originates loans with the intent to transform into pools of loans and selling them to investors

Liability and Equity Funding Sources

Retail Funding

From customers and small businesses and seen as stable sources with poor sensitivity level to market interest rates and bank's financial conditions.

- Deposit account
- Transaction accounts
- Savings accounts
- Public deposit
- Current account

Wholesale Funding

- Borrowing funds under secured and unsecured debt obligations (volatile and subordinated liabilities that are purchased by rate sensitive investors)
    - Short-term :
        - High-grade securities (otherwise the counterparty or broker/ dealer will not accept the collateral or charge high haicut on collateral) sold under repurchase agreement : repo transaction that helps create leverage and short-term liabilities collateralised with longer maturity assets
        - Debt instruments such as commercial paper (promissory note such as Asset-backed commercial paper program or ABCP)
    - Longer terms : collateralized loans and issuance of debt securities such as straight or covered bonds
- Other form of deposit

- Certificate of deposit
- Money market deposit
- Brokered deposit (in the US banking industry)
- Parent company deposit
- Deposit from banks

- Support from legacy governments and central bank facilities.Such as Long Term Refinancing Operations (LTRO) in the Eurozone where the ECB provides financing to Eurozone banks (on 29 February 2012, the last LTRO has contained €529,5 billion 36-months maturity low-interest loans with 800 banks participants).

Equity Funds or Raising Capital

- Common stock
- Preferred stock
- Retained earnings

Putting an Operative Plan for the normal Daily Operations and Ongoing Business Activities

This plan needs to embrace all available funding sources and requires an integrated approach with the strategic business planning process. The objective is to provide realistic projection of funding future under various set of assumptions. This strategy includes :

Assessment of Possible Funding Sources

Liability sensitivity

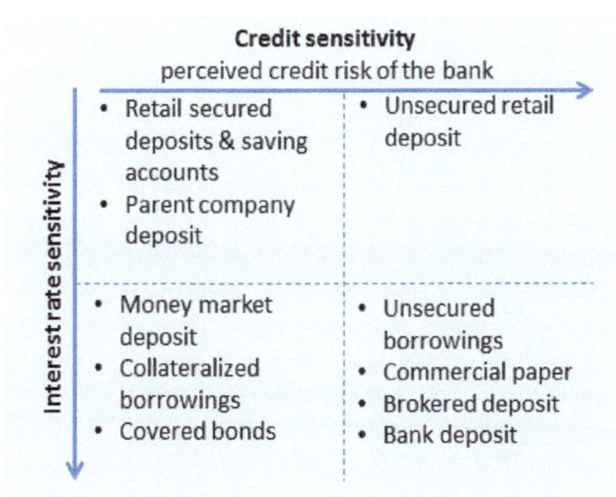

Funding requirement-liability sensitivity table

Main characteristics :

- Concentrations level between funding sources
- Sensitivity to interest-rate and credit risk volatility
- Ability and speed to renew or replace the funding source at favorable terms (evaluation of the possibility to lengthening its maturity for liability source)
- For borrowed funds, documentation of a plan defining repayment of the funds and terms including call features, prepayment penalties, debt covenants
- Possible early redemption option of the source
- Diversification of sources, tenors, investors base and types, currencies and to collateralization requirements (with limits by counterparty, secured versus unsecured level of the market funding, instrument types, securitization vehicles, geographic market and investor types)
- Costs : a bank can privilegiate interest bearing deposit products for retail clients as it is still considered as a cheap form of stable funding but the fierce competition between banks to attract a big market share has increased the acquisition and operational costs generated to manage large volume treatment (personnel, advertising...)

Dependencies to endogenous (bank specific events such as formulas, asset allocation, funding methods...) / exogenous (investment returns, market volatility, inflation, bank ratings...) factors that will influence the bank ability to access one particular source.

Setting for Each Source an Action Plan and Assessment of the bank's Exposure to Changes

Once the bank has established a list of potential sources based on their characteristics and risk/ reward analysis, it should monitor the link between its funding strategy and market conditions or systemic events.

For simplification, the diversify available sources are divided into 3 main time categories:

- Short-term
- Medium-term
- Long-term period

Key aspects to take into account :

1. Assessment of the likehood of funding deficiencies or cost increase across time

periods. In case for example, position on the wholesale funding, providers often require liquid assets as collateral. If that collaterals become less liquid or difficult to evaluate, wholesale funds providers may arbitrate no more funding extension maturity

2. Explanation of the objective, purpose and strategy behind each funding source chosen : a bank may borrow on a long-term basis to fund real estate loans

3. Monitoring of the bank capacity to raise each funds quickly and without bad cost effects as well as the monitoring of the dependence factors affecting its capacity to raise them

4. Maintenance of a constant relation with funding market as market access is critical and affects the ability to both raise new funds and liquid assets. This access to market is expressed first by identification and building of strong relationships with current and potential key providers of funding (even if the bank is solliciting also brokers or third parties to raise funds)

5. As a prudent measure, the choice of any source has to be demonstrated with the effective ability to access the source for the bank. If the bank has never experienced to sold loans in the past or securitization program, it should not anticipate using such funding strategies as a primary source of liquidity

Liquidity Reserve or Highly Liquid Assets Stock

This reserve can also referred to liquidity buffer and represents as the first line of defense in a liquidity crisis before intervention of any measures of the contingency funding plan. It consists of a stock of highly liquid assets without legal, regulatory constraints (the assets need to be readily available and not pledged to payments or clearing houses, we call them cashlike assets). They can include :

- High grade collateral received under repo
- Collateral pledged to the central bank for emergency situation
- Trading assets if they are freely disposable (not used as collateral)

Key actions to undertake :

1. To maintain a central data repository of these unemcombered liquid assets

2. To invest in liquid assets for purely precautionary motives during normal time of business and not during first signs of market turbulence

3. To apply, if possible (smaller banks may suffer from a lack of internal model intelligence), both an economic and regulatory liquidity assets holding position. The LCR (Liquidity Coverage Ratio), one of the new Basel III ratios in that con-

text can represent an excellent 'warning indicator' for monitoring the dedicated level and evolution of the dedicated stock of liquid assets. Indeed, the LCR addresses the sufficiency of a stock of high quality liquid assets to meet short-term liquidity needs under a specified acute stress scenario. It identifies the amount of unencumbered, high quality liquid assets an institution holds that can be used to offset the net cash outflows it would encounter under an acute 30-days stress scenario specified by supervisors. In light of the stricter LCR eligible assets definition, the economic approach could include a larger bulk of other liquid assets (in particular in the trading book)

4. To adapt (scalability approach) the stock of the cushion of liquid assets according to stress scenarios (scenarios including estimation on loss or impairment of unsecured/ secured funding sources, contractual or non contractual cashflows as well as among others withdrawal stickiness measures). As an example, a bank may decide to use high liquid sovereign debt instruments in entering into repurchase transaction in response to one severe stress scenario

5. To evaluate the cost of maintening dedicated stock of liquid assets portfolio as the negative carry between the yield of this portfolio and its penalty rate (cost of funding or rate at which the bank may obtain funding on the financial markets or the interbank market). This negative carry of this high liquid portfolio assets will be then allocated to the respective business lines that are creating the need for such liquidity reserve

Contingency Funding Plan

As the bank should not assume that business will always continue as it is the current business process, the institution needs to explore emergency sources of funds and formalise a contingency plan. The purpose is to find alternative backup sources of funding to those that occur within the normal course of operations.

Dealing with Contingency Funding Plan (CFP) is to find adequate actions as regard to low-probability and high-impact events as opposed to high-probability and low-impact into the day-to-day management of funding sources and their usage within the bank.

To do so, the bank needs to perform the hereafter tasks :

Identification of Plausible Stress Events

Bank specific events : generally linked to bank's business activities and arising from credit, market, operational, reputation or strategic risk. These aspects can be expressed as the inability :

- To fund asset growth
- To renew or replace maturing liabilities

- To use off-balance sheet commitments given
- To hold back unexpected large deposit withdrawals

External events :

- Changes in economic conditions
    - Changes in price volatility of securities
    - Negative press coverage
    - Disruption in the markets from which the bank obtains funds

Estimation of the Severity Levels, Occurrence and Duration of those Stress Events on the Bank Funding Structure

Contingency Funding plan- Monitoring report		
Stress event	Warning indicators	Monitoring tasks
External credit rating downgrade (or significant changes in short to long-term debt ratings)	Rating agency credit watch for potential downgrades Widening credit spreads on senior subordinated debts Fast decline in Credit Default Swap and bank stock price	Maket watch or rating agency reports Debt and credit spreads stock performance
Deterioration of the bank's asset quality	Deteriorating trend in loan performance, default and recovery level, non-performing portfolio trends	Loan provision level and trends Volumes and trends in loan sales (quality level of the credit portfolios, attrition rate...)
High and consistent operating losses	Decline in earning performance	Margin and profitability reports and trends
Inability to access funds into normal conditions Restriction by traditional providers to funding extension requests Difficulty in accessing long-term debt markets	Rising funding costs in a stable market Difficulties to set repo agreement into normal access (in term of haircut or collateral acceptance) Counterpary reluctance to off-balance sheet products Increase margin requirements Concentration trends in high-cost funding	Wire transfer activity reportsr Collateral management report Benchmark analysis of the traditional bank's funding market Funding capacity reports by funding typology Funding source concentration report
Large withdrawal of clients deposit Rapid redemption of Certficate of Deposits	Significant declines in clients deposits Highest stickiness level of the deposit trend (volatile level) Increased early redemption of CDs	Vault cash management reports Cash-flow projection and run-off reports CD early redemption report
Inability to sell assets	Increasing spreads on assets Deterioration in asset market values	Asset impairment reports Pricing trend analysis

Examples of Contingent Funding Plan stress events

This assessment is realised in accordance with the bank current funding structure to establish a clear view on their impacts on the 'normal' funding plan and therefore evaluate the need for extra funding.

This quantitative estimation of additional funding ressources under stress events is declined for:

- Each relevant level of the bank (consolidated level to solo and business lines ones)
- Within the 3 main time categories horizon : short-term (focus on intraday, daily, weekly operations), medium to long-term

In addition, analysis are conducted to evaluate the threat of those stress events on the bank earnings, capital level, business activities as well as the balance sheet composition.

The bank need, in accordance, to develop a monitoring process to :

- Detect early sign of events that could degenerate into crisis situation through set of warning indicators or triggers
- Build an escalation scheme via reporting and action plan in order to provide precautionary measure before any material risk materialized

Overview of Potential and Viable Contingent Funding Sources and Build up of a Central Inventory

Such inventory includes :

- The dedicated liquidity reserve (stock of highly liquid assets that can follow the Basel III new liquidity ratios LCR/ NSFR strict liquid asset definition)
- Other unencombered liquid assets (i.e.,those contained in the trading book) and in relation to economic liquidity reserve view. They can represent :
  - Additional unsecured or secured funding (possible use of securities lending and borrowing)
  - Access to central bank reserves
  - Reduction plan of assets
  - Additional sale plan of unemcombered assets

Determination of the Contingent Funding Sources Value According to Stressed Scenario Events

- Stressed haircut applied
- Variation around cash-flow projection
- Erosion level of the funding ressources
- Confidence level to gain access to the funding markets (tested market access)
- Monetization possibility of less liquid assets such as real-estate or mortgage loans with linked operational procedures and legal structure to put in place if any (as well as investor base, prices applied, transfer of servicing rights, re-course debt or not)

Setting of an Administrative Structure and Crisis-management Team

The last key aspect of an effective Contingency Funding Plan relates to the management of potential crisis with a dedicated team in charge to provide :

- Action plan to take during a given level of stress
- Communication scheme with counterparties, large investors, Central Bank and regulators involved
- Reports and escalation process
- Link with other contingent activities such as the Business Continuity Planning of the bank

Managing the ALM Profile Generated by the Funding Requirements

Gap management report -By business line									
Time Buckets	Overnight	Overnight to one week	One week to one month	One month to three months	Three months to six months	Six months to 12 months	Over 12 months	Non rate sensitive	Total
Assets									
Investments									
MBS	0	0	120	180	145	130	5		580
Other securities	0	0	1627						1627
Swap	0	0	0	0	0	0	0		0
Commercial loans									
Fixed	45	650	1000	3000	3450	3000	7675		18820
Variables	500	230	670	1456	1690	3500	3904		11950
Consumer loans									0
Fixed	0	230	570	720	850	760	456		3586
Variables	0	345	560	722	899	700	433		3659
Real estate loans									0
Fixed	0	0	1240	2400	3600	3900	14500		25640
Variables	0	0	170	2400	6790	8000	15890		33250
Overdrafts & advances to custumers	300	400	171	0	0	0	0		871
Reverse repurchase agreements	2800	670	95	0	0	0	0		3565
Available for sale financial assets	400	700	250	506					1856
Non earning assets								6900	6900
Total assets	**4045**	**3225**	**6473**	**11384**	**17424**	**19990**	**42863**	**6900**	**112304**
%	3,6	2,9	5,8	10,1	15,5	17,8	38,2	6,1	100,0

ALM funding report requirement

Liabilities									
Demand deposit								15600	15600
Interest-bearing Deposits	1200	3403	4405	4789	4985	5009	8900		32691
Wholesale funding									0
Long-short term borrowings	2100	2344	2990	2523	1381		4670		16008
Debt securitities in issue	0	2000	2355	4370	2200	2080			13005
Non funding liabilities								5000	5000
Capital								30000	30000
Total liabilities	**3300**	**7747**	**9750**	**11682**	**8566**	**7089**	**13570**	**50600**	**112304**
	2,9	6,9	8,7	10,4	7,6	6,3	12,1	45,1	100,0
Periodic Gap / Mismatch (Liabilities-Assets)	-745	4522	3277	298	-8858	-12901	-29293	43700	109267
Gap as % of total funding	0,7	4,0	2,9	-0,3	7,9	11,5	26,1	38,9	
Gap as % of total gap	0,7	4,1	3,0	-0,3	8,1	11,8	26,8	40,0	100
Gap limit as % of total funding	20	20	20	20	20	20	20		
Limit breach	No	No	No	No	No	No	Yes		
Cumulative gap	-745	3777	7054	7352	-1506	-14407	-43700	0	
Cumulative gap as % of total funding	-0,7%	3,4%	6,3%	6,5%	-1,3%	-12,8%	-38,9%	0,0%	
Marginal gap	-745	5267	-1245	-2979	-9156	-4043	-16392		
Periodic assets / total assets	3,6%	2,9%	5,8%	10,1%	15,5%	17,8%	38,2%	6,1%	100%
Periodic liabilities / total liabilities	2,9%	6,9%	8,7%	10,4%	7,6%	6,3%	12,1%	45,1%	100%

ALM funding report requirement - Liabilities and gap profile

The objective is to settle an approach of the asset-liabilitiy profile of the bank in accordance with its funding requirement. In fact, how effectively balancing the funding sources and uses with regard to liquidity, interest rate management, funding diversification and the type of business-model the bank is conducting (for example business based on a majority of short-term movements with high frequency changement of the asset profile) or the type of activities of the respective business lines (market making business is requiring more flexible liquidity profile than traditional bank activities).

ALM Report

Funding report summarises the total funding needs and sources with the objective to dispose of a global view where the forward funding requirement lies at the time of the snapshot. The report breakdown is at business line level to a consolidatedone on the firm-wide level. As a widespread standard, a 20% gap tolerance level is applied in each time bucket meaning that gap within each time period defined can support no more than 20% of total funding.

- Marginal gap : difference between change in assets and change in liabilities for a given time period to the next (known also as incremental gap)
- Gap as % of total gap : to prevent an excessive forward gap developing in one time period

Funding Cost Allocation Or Fund Transfer Pricing Concept

The effect of terming out funding is to produce a cost of funds, the objective is to :

- Set an internal price estimation of the cost of financing needed for the coming periods
- Assign it to users of funds

This is the concept of Fund Transfer Pricing (FTP) a process within ALM context to ensure that business lines are funded with adequate tenors and that are charged and accountable in adequation to their current or future estimated situation.

Wholesale Funding

Wholesale funding is a method that banks use in addition to core demand deposits to finance operations and manage risk. Wholesale funding sources include, but are not limited to, Federal funds, public funds (such as state and local municipalities), U.S. Federal Home Loan Bank advances, the U.S. Federal Reserve's primary credit program, foreign deposits, brokered deposits, and deposits obtained through the Internet or CD listing services.

Rationale

Although core deposits continue to be a key liability funding source, many insured depository institutions have experienced difficulty attracting core deposits and are increasingly looking to wholesale funding sources to satisfy funding and liability management needs.

Liquidity Risk

Wholesale funding providers are generally sensitive to changes in the credit risk profile of the institutions to which they provide these funds and to the interest rate environment. For instance, such providers closely track the institution's financial condition and may be likely to curtail such funding if other investment opportunities offer more attractive interest rates. As a result, an institution may experience liquidity problems due to lack of wholesale funding availability when needed. Academic research suggests that the use of wholesale funding was one of the major determinants of bank vulnerability during the 2007-2010 financial crisis.

Gap Analysis

The technique used by banks to analyze the impact of interest rate changes on the assets, liabilities and net worth. Gap is the difference between rate sensitive asset and rate sensitive liabilities. A negative gap is associated with increase in interest rates and a positive gap is associated with decline in interest rates. Estimated loss is computed with reference to value change within each time bucket and aggregate difference between assets and liabilities.

Liabilities	**Assets**
Rate Sensitive Liabilities	Rate Sensitive Assets
Fixed Rate Liabilities	Fixed Rate Assets
Total	Total

A positive funds gap shows financing of rate sensitive assets by fixed rate liabilities. A negative funds gap on the other hand shows fixed rate assets financed by rate sensitive liabilities.

Example

Liabilities		**Assets**	
Rate Sensitive Liabilities		Rate Sensitive Assets	
Short term deposits	550000	Advances	145000
Fixed Rate Liabilities		Investments	100000
Borrowings	10000	Reserves	85000
Long term deposits	200000	Fixed Rate Assets	
		Advances	443000
Capital	20000	Fixed Assets	7000
Total	780000	Total	780000

Liabilities		**Assets**	
Rate Sensitive Liabilities		Rate Sensitive Assets	
Short term deposits	550000	Advances	145000
		Investments	100000
		Reserves	85000
		Fixed Rate Assets	

		Advances	220000
Fixed Rate Liabilities		Fixed Rate Assets	
Borrowings	10000	Advances	223000
Long term deposits	200000		
Capital	20000	Fixed Assets	7000
Total	780000	Total	780000

Total Rate Sensitive Assets (RSA) = 330000

Total Rate Sensitive Liabilities (RSL) = 550000

Funds Gap = 220000 (Negative Gap)

A conservative bank maintains a positive gap and gains from increase in interest rate. An aggressive bank maintains a negative gap and gains from decrease in interest rate. The net interest income likely to affect the bank due to changing interest rate scenarios can be computed by multiplying change in rate with the gap.

Other ways of representing gap include relative gap and gap ratio. When a bank has a positive gap a possible management action at times of rising interest rates would be to increase rate sensitive assets or reduce rate sensitive liabilities. Another possible action is to extend liability maturity or shorten asset maturities. If on the other hand interest rates are falling, a reverse action will be initiated.

In management literature, gap analysis involves the comparison of actual performance with potential or desired performance. If an organization does not make the best use of current resources, or forgoes investment in capital or technology, it may produce or perform below its potential. This concept is similar to an economy's being below the production possibilities frontier.

Gap analysis identifies gaps between the optimized allocation and integration of the inputs (resources), and the current allocation-level. This may reveal areas that can be improved. Gap analysis involves determining, documenting, and approving the difference between business requirements and current capabilities. Gap analysis naturally flows from benchmarking and from other assessments. Once the general expectation of performance in an industry is understood, it is possible to compare that expectation with the company's current level of performance. This comparison becomes the gap analysis. Such analysis can be performed at the strategic or at the operational level of an organization.

Gap analysis is a formal study of what a business is doing currently and where it wants to go in the future. It can be conducted, in different perspectives, as follows:

1. Organization (e.g., Human Resources)
2. Business direction

3. Business processes
4. Information technology

Gap analysis provides a foundation for measuring investment of time, money and human resources required to achieve a particular outcome (e.g. to turn the salary payment process from paper-based to paperless with the use of a system). Note that "GAP analysis" has also been used as a means of classifying how well a product or solution meets a targeted need or set of requirements. In this case, "GAP" can be used as a ranking of "Good", "Average" or "Poor". (This terminology appears in the PRINCE2 project management publication from the OGC (Office of Government Commerce)).

The need for new products or additions to existing lines may emerge from portfolio analysis, in particular from the use of the Boston Consulting Group Growth-share matrix—or the need may emerge from the regular process of following trends in the requirements of consumers. At some point, a gap emerges between what existing products offer and what the consumer demands. The organization must fill that gap to survive and grow.

Gap analysis can identify gaps in the market. Thus, comparing forecast profits to desired profits reveals the *planning gap*. This represents a goal for new activities in general, and new products in particular. The planning gap can be divided into three main elements:

Usage Gap

The usage gap is the gap between the total potential for the market and actual current usage by all consumers in the market. Data for this calculation includes:

- Market usage
- Existing usage

Existing Usage

Existing consumer usage makes up the total current market, from which market shares, for example, are calculated. It usually derives from marketing research, most accurately from panel research, but also from adhoc work. Sometimes it may be available from figures that governments or industries have collected. However, these are often based on categories that make bureaucratic sense but are less helpful in marketing terms. The 'usage gap' is thus:

usage gap = market potential – existing usage

This is an important calculation. Many, if not most, marketers accept existing market size—suitably projected their forecast timescales—as the boundary for expansion plans.

Though this is often the most realistic assumption, it may impose an unnecessary limit on horizons. For example: the original market for video-recorders was limited to professional users who could afford high prices. Only after some time did the technology extend to the mass market.

In the public sector, where service providers usually enjoy a monopoly, the usage gap is probably the most important factor in activity development. However, persuading more consumers to take up family benefits, for example, is probably more important to the relevant government department than opening more local offices.

Usage gap is most important for brand leaders. If a company has a significant share of the whole market, they may find it worthwhile to invest in making the market bigger. This option is not generally open to minor players, though they may still profit by targeting specific offerings as market extensions.

All other gaps relate to the difference between existing sales (market share) and total sales of the market as a whole. The difference is the competitor share. These gaps therefore, relate to competitive activity.

Product Gap

The *product gap*—also called the *segment* or *positioning gap*—is that part of the market a particular organization is excluded from because of product or service characteristics. This may be because the market is segmented and the organization does not have offerings in some segments, or because the organization positions its offerings in a way that effectively excludes certain potential consumers—because competitive offerings are much better placed for these consumers.

This segmentation may result from deliberate policy. Segmentation and positioning are powerful marketing techniques, but the trade-off—against better focus—is that market segments may effectively be put beyond reach. On the other hand, product gap can occur by default; the organization has thought out its positioning, its offerings drifted to a particular market segment.

The product gap may be the main element of the planning gap where an organization can have productive input; hence the emphasis on the importance of correct positioning.

Use to Develop a Better Process

A gap analysis can also be used to analyze gaps in processes and the gulf between the existing outcome and the desired outcome. This step process can be illustrated by the example below:

- Identify the existing process: fishing by using fishing rods
- Identify the existing outcome: we can manage to catch 20 fish per day

- Identify the desired outcome: we want to catch 100 fish per day
- Identify and document the gap: it is a difference of 80 fish
- Identify the process to achieve the desired outcome: we can use an alternative method such as using a fishing net
- Develop the means to fill the gap: acquire and use a fishing net
- Develop and prioritize Requirements to bridge the gap

A gap analysis can also be used to compare one process to others performed elsewhere, which are often identified through benchmarking. In this usage, one compares each process side-by-side and step-by-step and then notes the differences. One then analyzes each deviation to determine if there is any benefit to changing to the alternate process. The results of this analysis (in the context of the benefits and detriments of changing processes) may support the maintenance of the current process, the wholesale adoption of an alternate process, or a fusion of different aspects of each process.

Duration Analysis

Duration analysis aims at maximizing market value of equity. Duration is computed taking weighted average of cash flows of an instrument discounted to present time. Duration gap is computed subtracting weighted liabilities duration from asset duration. The weights are computed by dividing total liabilities by total assets.

Duration analysis assumes precise knowledge of duration of assets and liabilities, market value of assets, a flat interest rate structure, no impact of convexity on valuation and a parallel shift in the change of interest rates.

Computation of duration gap

Assets	**Liabilities**
T Bill Investment	Certificate of Deposit
1 year 7% 30	1 year 6% 50
Loan 2 year 10% 70	3 Year Time Deposit 8% 40
	Capital 10
100	100

When rates increase by 2%

Assets	**Discounted Cash Flows**
T Bill : $\frac{32.70}{(1 + 0.09)}$	30.00

Loan: $\frac{7.00}{(1+0.12)} = 6.25$ $\frac{77.00}{(1+0.12)^2} = 61.38$	67.63
Asset Value	97.63

Liabilities	Discounted Cash Flows
1 Year CD $= \frac{54.00}{(1+0.08)}$	50.00
3 Year TD $= \frac{3.60}{(1+0.11)} = 3.24$ $= \frac{3.60}{(1+0.11)2} = 2.92$ $= \frac{43.60}{(1+0.11)^3} = 31.88$	38.04
Total Liabilities	88.04
Market Value of Bank Capital (97.63 – 88.04)	9.59
Additional Income - (-20 x 0.02)	0.40
Decline in Capital Value of Bank (10 – 9.59 – 0.40)	0.01
Book Value of Bank Capital	10.00

Assets	Duration
T Bill : $D_{A1} = \frac{\frac{32.70}{(1+0.09)}}{30}$	1.000
Loan : $D_{A2} = \frac{\frac{7.00\times(1)}{(1+0.12)} + \frac{77.00\times(2)}{(1+0.12)^2}}{67.63}$	1.908
Weighted Average duration 0.30 x 1.000 0.70 x 1.908	1.635

Impact on equity

Equity	Value
$\Delta V_E = (D_A - W_L D_L) \times A \times \left(\frac{\Delta R}{1+R}\right)$	
$W_L = \left(\frac{L}{A}\right) = \left(\frac{90}{100}\right)$ ΔR	0.9 0.02
$\Delta V_E = [0.034] \times 100 \times \left(\frac{0.02}{1.10}\right)$	-0.063
Macauley's Duration $= -\frac{[0.034]}{(1+0.10)} \times 100 \times \left(\frac{0.02}{1.10}\right)$	-0.057
Decline in Equity Value (Duration Gap)	-0.010

Summary of impact of duration gap on changing interest rate scenarios can be stated as follows.

Duration Gap	Interest rate Change	Assets		Liabilities	Equity
Positive	Increase	Decrease	>	Decrease	Decrease
Positive	Decrease	Increase	>	Increase	Increase
Negative	Increase	Decrease	<	Decrease	Increase
Negative	Decrease	Increase	<	Increase	Decrease
Zero	Increase	Decrease	=	Decrease	No change
Zero	Decrease	Increase	=	Increase	No change

Immunization is the process of achieving a zero duration gap. Immunization of bank portfolio is optimum when the gain from the higher reinvestment rate is offset by capital loss and the change in capital is insensitive to changes in interest rate fluctuations.

Interest Rate Risk Management

The strategies adopted by banks to manage interest rate risks may be broadly classified into two categories. The first is the rearrangement of balance sheet that includes duration gap management. The second is the off-balance sheet adjustment through instruments such as interest rate swap, hedging with financial futures, insurance and risk transfer.

Some of the causes for risk from off balance sheet activities include contingent liabilities, guarantees, standby letters of credit, loan commitments and note issue facilities given by banks. Securitization of loan wherein a debt instrument is issued by a bank based on expected revenues from a defined pool of loans is a strategy used by banks to transfer loan risks to market.

Hedge Fund

A hedge fund is an investment fund that pools capital from accredited individuals or institutional investors and invests in a variety of assets, often with complex portfolio-construction and risk-management techniques. It is administered by a professional investment management firm, and often structured as a limited partnership, limited liability company, or similar vehicle. Hedge funds are generally distinct from mutual funds, as their use of leverage is not capped by regulators, and distinct from private equity funds, as the majority of hedge funds invest in relatively liquid assets.

The term "hedge fund" originated from the paired long and short positions that the first of these funds used to hedge market risk. Over time, the types and nature of the hedging concepts expanded, as did the different types of investment vehicles. Today, hedge funds engage in a diverse range of markets and strategies and employ a wide variety of financial instruments and risk management techniques.

Hedge funds are made available only to certain sophisticated or accredited investors and cannot be offered or sold to the general public. As such, they generally avoid direct regulatory oversight, bypass licensing requirements applicable to investment companies, and operate with greater flexibility than mutual funds and other investment funds. However, following the financial crisis of 2007–2008, regulations were passed in the United States and Europe with intentions to increase government oversight of hedge funds and eliminate certain regulatory gaps.

Hedge funds have existed for many decades and have become increasingly popular. They have now grown to be a substantial fraction of asset management, with assets now totaling around $3 trillion.

Hedge funds are almost always open-ended and allow additions or withdrawals by their investors (generally on a monthly or quarterly basis). The value of an investor's holding is directly related to the fund net asset value.

Many hedge fund investment strategies aim to achieve a positive return on investment regardless of whether markets are rising or falling ("absolute return"). Hedge fund managers often invest money of their own in the fund they manage. A hedge fund typically pays its investment manager an annual management fee (for example 2% of the assets of the fund), and a performance fee (for example 20% of the increase in the fund's net asset value during the year). Both co-investment and performance fees serve to align the interests of managers with those of the investors in the fund. Some hedge funds have several billion dollars of assets under management (AUM).

The word "hedge", meaning a line of bushes around a field, has long been used as a metaphor for the placing of limits on risk. Early hedge funds sought to hedge specific investments against general market fluctuations by shorting the market, hence the name. Nowadays, however, many different investment strategies are used, many of which do not "hedge risk".

History

During the US bull market of the 1920s, there were numerous private investment vehicles available to wealthy investors. Of that period the best known today is the Graham-Newman Partnership, founded by Benjamin Graham and Jerry Newman. This was cited by Warren Buffett in a 2006 letter to the Museum of American Finance as an early hedge fund.

The sociologist Alfred W. Jones is credited with coining the phrase "*hedged* fund" and is credited with creating the first hedge fund structure in 1949 (although this has been disputed.) Jones referred to his fund as being "hedged", a term then commonly used on Wall Street to describe the management of investment risk due to changes in the financial markets.

In the 1970s, hedge funds specialized in a single strategy with most fund managers following the long/short equity model. Many hedge funds closed during the recession of 1969–70 and the 1973–1974 stock market crash due to heavy losses. They received renewed attention in the late 1980s.

During the 1990s, the number of hedge funds increased significantly, with the 1990s stock market rise, the aligned-interest compensation structure (i.e. common financial interests) and the promise of above high returns as likely causes. Over the next decade, hedge fund strategies expanded to include: credit arbitrage, distressed debt, fixed income, quantitative, and multi-strategy. US institutional investors such as pension and endowment funds began allocating greater portions of their portfolios to hedge funds.

During the first decade of the 21st century hedge funds gained popularity worldwide, and by 2008 the worldwide hedge fund industry held US$1.93 trillion in assets under management (AUM). However, the 2008 financial crisis caused many hedge funds to restrict investor withdrawals and their popularity and AUM totals declined. AUM totals rebounded and in April 2011 were estimated at almost $2 trillion. As of February 2011, 61% of worldwide investment in hedge funds came from institutional sources. In June 2011, the hedge fund management firms with the greatest AUM were Bridgewater Associates (US$58.9 billion), Man Group (US$39.2 billion), Paulson & Co. (US$35.1 billion), Brevan Howard (US$31 billion), and Och-Ziff (US$29.4 billion). Bridgewater Associates had $70 billion under management as of 1 March 2012. At the end of that year, the 241 largest hedge fund firms in the United States collectively held $1.335 trillion. In April 2012, the hedge fund industry reached a record high of US$2.13 trillion total assets under management.

Notable Hedge Fund Managers

George Soros, fund manager of Quantum Group of Funds

In June 2015, Forbes listed:

- George Soros of Quantum Group of Funds
- Ray Dalio of Bridgewater Associates, the world's largest hedge fund firm in 2015 with US$155 billion assets under management
- Steven A. Cohen of Point72 Asset Management - formerly known as S.A.C. Capital Advisors
- John Paulson of Paulson & Co. whose hedge funds as of December 2015 had $19 billion assets under management, compared to $18 billion in September 2013 and $36 billion in early 2011
- David Tepper of Appaloosa Management,
- Paul Tudor Jones II of Tudor Investment Corporation
- Daniel Och of Och-Ziff Capital Management Group with more than $40 billion in assets under management in 2013
- Israel Englander of Millennium Management

- Leon G. Cooperman of Omega Advisors
- Michael Platt of BlueCrest Capital Management (UK) Europe's third-biggest hedge-fund firm
- James Dinan of York Capital Management
- Stephen Mandel Jr. of Lone Pine Capital with $26.7 billion under management at end June 2015
- Larry Robbins of Glenview Capital Management with approximately $9.2 billion of assets under management as of July 2014
- Glenn Dubin of Highbridge Capital Management
- Paul Singer of Elliott Management Corporation, an activist hedge fund with more than US$23 billion in assets under management in 2013, and a portfolio worth $8,124,567,000 as of the first quarter of 2015
- Michael Hintze of CQS with $14.4 billion of assets under management as of June 2015
- David Einhorn of Greenlight Capital, as the top twenty billionaire hedge fund managers.
- Bill Ackman of Pershing Square Capital Management LP

Strategies

Hedge fund strategies are generally classified among four major categories: global macro, directional, event-driven, and relative value (arbitrage). Strategies within these categories each entail characteristic risk and return profiles. A fund may employ a single strategy or multiple strategies for flexibility, risk management or diversification. The hedge fund's prospectus, also known as an offering memorandum, offers potential investors information about key aspects of the fund, including the fund's investment strategy, investment type, and leverage limit.

The elements contributing to a hedge fund strategy include: the hedge fund's approach to the market; the particular instrument used; the market sector the fund specializes in (e.g. healthcare); the method used to select investments; and the amount of diversification within the fund. There are a variety of market approaches to different asset classes, including equity, fixed income, commodity, and currency. Instruments used include: equities, fixed income, futures, options and swaps. Strategies can be divided into those in which investments can be selected by managers, known as "discretionary/qualitative", or those in which investments are selected using a computerized system, known as "systematic/quantitative". The amount of diversification within the fund can vary; funds may be multi-strategy, multi-fund, multi-market, multi-manager or a combination.

Sometimes hedge fund strategies are described as "absolute return" and are classified as either "market neutral" or "directional". Market neutral funds have less correlation to overall market performance by "neutralizing" the effect of market swings, whereas directional funds utilize trends and inconsistencies in the market and have greater exposure to the market's fluctuations.

Global Macro

Hedge funds using a global macro investing strategy take sizable positions in share, bond or currency markets in anticipation of global macroeconomic events in order to generate a risk-adjusted return. Global macro fund managers use macroeconomic ("big picture") analysis based on global market events and trends to identify opportunities for investment that would profit from anticipated price movements. While global macro strategies have a large amount of flexibility (due to their ability to use leverage to take large positions in diverse investments in multiple markets), the timing of the implementation of the strategies is important in order to generate attractive, risk-adjusted returns. Global macro is often categorized as a directional investment strategy.

Global macro strategies can be divided into discretionary and systematic approaches. Discretionary trading is carried out by investment managers who identify and select investments whereas systematic trading is based on mathematical models and executed by software with limited human involvement beyond the programming and updating of the software. These strategies can also be divided into trend or counter-trend approaches depending on whether the fund attempts to profit from following trends (long or short-term) or attempts to anticipate and profit from reversals in trends.

Within global macro strategies, there are further sub-strategies including "systematic diversified", in which the fund trades in diversified markets, or "systematic currency", in which the fund trades in currency markets. Other sub-strategies include those employed by commodity trading advisors (CTAs), where the fund trades in futures (or options) in commodity markets or in swaps. This is also known as a "managed future fund". CTAs trade in commodities (such as gold) and financial instruments, including stock indices. They also take both long and short positions, allowing them to make profit in both market upswings and downswings.

Directional

Directional investment strategies use market movements, trends, or inconsistencies when picking stocks across a variety of markets. Computer models can be used, or fund managers will identify and select investments. These types of strategies have a greater exposure to the fluctuations of the overall market than do market neutral strategies. Directional hedge fund strategies include US and international long/short equity hedge funds, where long equity positions are hedged with short sales of equities or equity index options.

Within directional strategies, there are a number of sub-strategies. "Emerging markets" funds focus on emerging markets such as China and India, whereas "sector funds" specialize in specific areas including technology, healthcare, biotechnology, pharmaceuticals, energy and basic materials. Funds using a "fundamental growth" strategy invest in companies with more earnings growth than the overall stock market or relevant sector, while funds using a "fundamental value" strategy invest in undervalued companies. Funds that use quantitative and Financial signal processing techniques for equity trading are described as using a "quantitative directional" strategy. Funds using a "short bias" strategy take advantage of declining equity prices using short positions.

Event-driven

Event-driven strategies concern situations in which the underlying investment opportunity and risk are associated with an event. An event-driven investment strategy finds investment opportunities in corporate transactional events such as consolidations, acquisitions, recapitalizations, bankruptcies, and liquidations. Managers employing such a strategy capitalize on valuation inconsistencies in the market before or after such events, and take a position based on the predicted movement of the security or securities in question. Large institutional investors such as hedge funds are more likely to pursue event-driven investing strategies than traditional equity investors because they have the expertise and resources to analyze corporate transactional events for investment opportunities.

Corporate transactional events generally fit into three categories: distressed securities, risk arbitrage, and special situations. Distressed securities include such events as restructurings, recapitalizations, and bankruptcies. A distressed securities investment strategy involves investing in the bonds or loans of companies facing bankruptcy or severe financial distress, when these bonds or loans are being traded at a discount to their value. Hedge fund managers pursuing the distressed debt investment strategy aim to capitalize on depressed bond prices. Hedge funds purchasing distressed debt may prevent those companies from going bankrupt, as such an acquisition deters foreclosure by banks. While event-driven investing in general tends to thrive during a bull market, distressed investing works best during a bear market.

Risk arbitrage or merger arbitrage includes such events as mergers, acquisitions, liquidations, and hostile takeovers. Risk arbitrage typically involves buying and selling the stocks of two or more merging companies to take advantage of market discrepancies between acquisition price and stock price. The risk element arises from the possibility that the merger or acquisition will not go ahead as planned; hedge fund managers will use research and analysis to determine if the event will take place.

Special situations are events that impact the value of a company's stock, including the restructuring of a company or corporate transactions including spin-offs, share-buy-backs, security issuance/repurchase, asset sales, or other catalyst-oriented situations. To take advantage of special situations the hedge fund manager must identify an upcoming event that will increase or decrease the value of the company's equity and equity-related instruments.

Other event-driven strategies include: credit arbitrage strategies, which focus on corporate fixed income securities; an activist strategy, where the fund takes large positions in companies and uses the ownership to participate in the management; a strategy based on predicting the final approval of new pharmaceutical drugs; and legal catalyst strategy, which specializes in companies involved in major lawsuits.

Relative Value

Relative value arbitrage strategies take advantage of relative discrepancies in price between securities. The price discrepancy can occur due to mispricing of securities compared to related securities, the underlying security or the market overall. Hedge fund managers can use various types of analysis to identify price discrepancies in securities, including mathematical, technical or fundamental techniques. Relative value is often used as a synonym for market neutral, as strategies in this category typically have very little or no directional market exposure to the market as a whole. Other relative value sub-strategies include:

- Fixed income arbitrage: exploit pricing inefficiencies between related fixed income securities.
- Equity market neutral: exploits differences in stock prices by being long and short in stocks within the same sector, industry, market capitalization, country, which also creates a hedge against broader market factors.
- Convertible arbitrage: exploit pricing inefficiencies between convertible securities and the corresponding stocks.
- Asset-backed securities (Fixed-Income asset-backed): fixed income arbitrage strategy using asset-backed securities.
- Credit long / short: the same as long / short equity but in credit markets instead of equity markets.
- Statistical arbitrage: identifying pricing inefficiencies between securities through mathematical modeling techniques
- Volatility arbitrage: exploit the change in implied volatility instead of the change in price.
- Yield alternatives: non-fixed income arbitrage strategies based on the yield instead of the price.

Remuneration of Portfolio Managers

Hedge fund management firms are usually owned by their portfolio managers, who are therefore entitled to any profits that the business makes. As management fees are intended to cover the firm's operating costs, performance fees (and any excess management fees) are generally distributed to the firm's owners as profits. Funds do not tend to report compensation and so published lists of the amounts earned by top managers tend to be estimates based on factors such as the fees charged by their funds and the capital they are thought to have invested in them. Many managers have accumulated large stakes in their own funds and so top hedge fund managers can earn extraordinary amounts of money, perhaps up to $4 billion in a good year.

Earnings at the very top are higher than in any other sector of the financial industry and collectively the top 25 hedge fund managers regularly earn more than all 500 of the chief executives in the S&P 500. Most hedge fund managers are remunerated much less, however, and if performance fees are not earned then small managers at least are unlikely to be paid significant amounts.

In 2011, the top manager earned $3,000m, the tenth earned $210m and the 30th earned $80m. In 2011, the average earnings for the 25 highest compensated hedge fund managers in the United States was $576 million. while the mean total compensation for all hedge fund investment professionals was $690,786 and the median was $312,329. The same figures for hedge fund CEOs were $1,037,151 and $600,000, and for chief investment officers were $1,039,974 and $300,000 respectively.

Of the 1,226 people on the *Forbes* World's Billionaires list for 2012, 36 of the financiers listed "derived significant chunks" of their wealth from hedge fund management. Among the richest 1,000 people in the United Kingdom, 54 were hedge fund managers, according to the *Sunday Times* Rich List for 2012.

Structure

A hedge fund is an investment vehicle that is most often structured as an offshore corporation, limited partnership or limited liability company. The fund is managed by an investment manager in the form of an organization or company that is legally and financially distinct from the hedge fund and its portfolio of assets. Many investment managers utilize service providers for operational support. Service providers include prime brokers, banks, administrators, distributors and accounting firms.

Prime brokers clear trades, and provide leverage and short-term financing. They are usually divisions of large investment banks. The prime broker acts as a counterparty to derivative contracts, and lends securities for particular investment strategies, such as long/short equities and convertible bond arbitrage. It can provide custodial services for the fund's assets, and execution and clearing services for the hedge fund manager.

Hedge fund administrators are responsible for operations, accounting, and valuation services. This back office support allows fund managers to concentrate on trades. Administrators also process subscriptions and redemptions, and perform various shareholder services. Hedge funds in the United States are not required to appoint an administrator, and all of these functions can be performed by an investment manager. A number of conflict of interest situations may arise in this arrangement, particularly in the calculation of a fund's net asset value (NAV). Some funds voluntarily employ external auditors, thereby offering a greater degree of transparency.

A distributor is an underwriter, broker, dealer, or other person who participates in the distribution of securities. The distributor is also responsible for marketing the fund to potential investors. Many hedge funds do not have distributors, and in such cases the investment manager will be responsible for distribution of securities and marketing, though many funds also use placement agents and broker-dealers for distribution.

Most funds use an independent accounting firm to audit the assets of the fund, provide tax services and perform a complete audit of the fund's financial statements. The year-end audit is often performed in accordance with the standard accounting practices enforced within the country the fund it established or the International Financial Reporting Standards (IFRS). The auditor may verify the fund's NAV and assets under management (AUM). Some auditors only provide "NAV lite" services, meaning that the valuation is based on prices received from the manager rather than independent assessment.

Domicile and Taxation

The legal structure of a specific hedge fund, in particular its domicile and the type of legal entity in use, is usually determined by the tax expectations of the fund's investors. Regulatory considerations will also play a role. Many hedge funds are established in offshore financial centers to avoid adverse tax consequences for its foreign and tax-exempt investors. Offshore funds that invest in the US typically pay withholding taxes on certain types of investment income but not US capital gains tax. However, the fund's investors are subject to tax in their own jurisdictions on any increase in the value of their investments. This tax treatment promotes cross-border investments by limiting the potential for multiple jurisdictions to layer taxes on investors.

US tax-exempt investors (such as pension plans and endowments) invest primarily in offshore hedge funds to preserve their tax exempt status and avoid unrelated business taxable income. The investment manager, usually based in a major financial center, pays tax on its management fees per the tax laws of the state and country where it is located. In 2011, half of the existing hedge funds were registered offshore and half onshore. The Cayman Islands was the leading location for offshore funds, accounting for 34% of the total number of global hedge funds. The US had 24%, Luxembourg 10%, Ireland 7%, the British Virgin Islands 6% and Bermuda had 3%.

Basket Options

Deutsche Bank and Barclays created special options accounts for hedge fund clients in the banks' names and claimed to own the assets, when in fact the hedge fund clients had full control of the assets and reaped the profits. The hedge funds would then execute trades — many of them a few seconds in duration — but wait until just after a year had passed to exercise the options, allowing them to report the profits at a lower long-term capital gains tax rate.

—Alexandra Stevenson. July 8, 2015. New York Times

The Senate Permanent Subcommittee on Investigations chaired by Carl Levin resulted in a 2014 report that found that from 1998 and 2013, hedge funds avoided billions of dollars in taxes by using basket options. The Internal Revenue Service began investigating Renaissance Technologies in 2009 and Levin criticized the IRS for taking six years to investigate the company. Using basket options Renaissance avoided "more than $6 billion in taxes over more than a decade".

These banks and hedge funds involved in this case used dubious structured financial products in a giant game of 'let's pretend,' costing the Treasury billions and bypassing safeguards that protect the economy from excessive bank lending for stock speculation.

—Carl Levin. 2015. Senate Permanent Subcommittee on Investigations

A dozen other hedge funds along with Renaissance Technologies used Deutsche Bank's and Barclays' basket options. Renaissance argued that basket options were "extremely important because they gave the hedge fund the ability to increase its returns by borrowing more and to protect against model and programming failures". In July 2015 the United States Internal Revenue claimed hedge funds used basket options "to bypass taxes on short-term trades". These basket options will now be labeled as listed transactions that must be declared on tax returns and a failure to do would result in a penalty.

Investment Manager Locations

In contrast to the funds themselves, investment managers are primarily located onshore. The United States remains the largest center of investment, with US-based funds managing around 70% of global assets at the end of 2011. As of April 2012, there were approximately 3,990 investment advisers managing one or more private hedge funds registered with the Securities and Exchange Commission. New York City and the Gold Coast area of Connecticut are the leading locations for US hedge fund managers.

London is Europe's leading center for hedge fund managers. According to EuroHedge data, around 800 funds located in the UK managed some 85% of European-based hedge fund assets in 2011. Interest in hedge funds in Asia has increased significantly since 2003, especially in Japan, Hong Kong, and Singapore. However, the UK and the US remain the leading locations for management of Asian hedge fund assets.

The Legal Entity

Hedge fund legal structures vary depending on location and the investor(s). US hedge funds aimed at US-based, taxable investors are generally structured as limited partnerships or limited liability companies. Limited partnerships and other flow-through taxation structures assure that investors in hedge funds are not subject to both entity-level and personal-level taxation. A hedge fund structured as a limited partnership must have a general partner. The general partner may be an individual or a corporation. The general partner serves as the manager of the limited partnership, and has unlimited liability. The limited partners serve as the fund's investors, and have no responsibility for management or investment decisions. Their liability is limited to the amount of money they invest for partnership interests. As an alternative to a limited partnership arrangement, U.S. domestic hedge funds may be structured as limited liability companies, with members acting as corporate shareholders and enjoying protection from individual liability.

By contrast, offshore corporate funds are usually used for non-US investors, and when they are domiciled in an applicable offshore tax haven, no entity-level tax is imposed. Many managers of offshore funds permit the participation of tax-exempt US investors, such as pensions funds, institutional endowments and charitable trusts. As an alternative legal structure, offshore funds may be formed as an open-ended unit trust using an unincorporated mutual fund structure. Japanese investors prefer to invest in unit trusts, such as those available in the Cayman Islands.

The investment manager who organizes the hedge fund may retain an interest in the fund, either as the general partner of a limited partnership or as the holder of "founder shares" in a corporate fund. For offshore funds structured as corporate entities, the fund may appoint a board of directors. The board's primary role is to provide a layer of oversight while representing the interests of the shareholders. However, in practice board members may lack sufficient expertise to be effective in performing those duties. The board may include both affiliated directors who are employees of the fund and independent directors whose relationship to the fund is limited.

Types of Funds

- Open-ended hedge funds continue to issue shares to new investors and allow periodic withdrawals at the net asset value ("NAV") for each share.
- Closed-ended hedge funds issue a limited number of tradeable shares at inception.
- Shares of Listed hedges funds are traded on stock exchanges, such as the Irish Stock Exchange, and may be purchased by non-accredited investors.

Side Pockets

A side pocket is a mechanism whereby a fund compartmentalizes assets that are relatively illiquid or difficult to value reliably. When an investment is side-pocketed, its value is calculated separately from the value of the fund's main portfolio. Because side pockets are used to hold illiquid investments, investors do not have the standard redemption rights with respect to the side pocket investment that they do with respect to the fund's main portfolio. Profits or losses from the investment are allocated on a *pro rata* basis only to those who are investors at the time the investment is placed into the side pocket and are not shared with new investors. Funds typically carry side pocket assets "at cost" for purposes of calculating management fees and reporting net asset values. This allows fund managers to avoid attempting a valuation of the underlying investments, which may not always have a readily available market value.

Side pockets were widely used by hedge funds during the 2008 financial crisis amidst a flood of withdrawal requests. Side pockets allowed fund managers to lay away illiquid securities until market liquidity improved, a move that could reduce losses. However, as the practice restricts investors' ability to redeem their investments it is often unpopular and many have alleged that it has been abused or applied unfairly. The SEC also has expressed concern about aggressive use of side pockets and has sanctioned certain fund managers for inappropriate use of them.

Regulation

Hedge funds must conform to the national, federal and state regulatory laws in their respective locations. The U.S. regulations and restrictions that apply to hedge funds differ from its mutual funds. Mutual funds, unlike hedge funds and other private funds, are subject to the Investment Company Act of 1940, which is a highly detailed and extensive regulatory regime. According to a report by the International Organization of Securities Commissions the most common form of regulation pertains to restrictions on financial advisers and hedge fund managers in an effort to minimize client fraud. On the other hand, U.S. hedge funds are exempt from many of the standard registration and reporting requirements because they only accept accredited investors. In 2010, regulations were enacted in the US and European Union, which introduced additional hedge fund reporting requirements. These included the U.S.'s Dodd-Frank Wall Street Reform Act and European Alternative Investment Fund Managers Directive.

In 2007 in an attempt for self-regulation, 14 leading hedge fund managers developed a voluntary set of international standards in best practice and known as the *Hedge Fund Standards* they were designed to create a "... framework of transparency, integrity and good governance" in the hedge fund industry. The Hedge Fund Standards Board was set up to prompt and maintain these standards going forward and by 2016 it had approximately 200 hedge fund managers and institutional investors with a value of US$ 3tn investment endorsing the standards.

United States

Hedge funds within the US are subject to regulatory, reporting and record keeping requirements. Many hedge funds also fall under the jurisdiction of the Commodity Futures Trading Commission and are subject to rules and provisions of the 1922 Commodity Exchange Act which prohibits fraud and manipulation. The Securities Act of 1933 required companies to file a registration statement with the SEC to comply with its private placement rules before offering their securities to the public. The Securities Exchange Act of 1934 required a fund with more than 499 investors to register with the SEC. The Investment Advisers Act of 1940 contained anti-fraud provisions that regulated hedge fund managers and advisers, created limits for the number and types of investors, and prohibited public offerings. The Act also exempted hedge funds from mandatory registration with the U.S. Securities and Exchange Commission (SEC) when selling to accredited investors with a minimum of US$5 million in investment assets. Companies and institutional investors with at least US$25 million in investment assets also qualified.

In December 2004, the SEC began requiring hedge fund advisers, managing more than US$25 million and with more than 14 investors, to register with the SEC under the Investment Advisers Act. The SEC stated that it was adopting a "risk-based approach" to monitoring hedge funds as part of its evolving regulatory regimen for the burgeoning industry. The new rule was controversial, with two commissioners dissenting, and was later challenged in court by a hedge fund manager. In June 2006, the U.S. Court of Appeals for the District of Columbia overturned the rule and sent it back to the agency to be reviewed. In response to the court decision, in 2007 the SEC adopted Rule 206(4)-8, which unlike the earlier challenged rule, "does not impose additional filing, reporting or disclosure obligations" but does potentially increase "the risk of enforcement action" for negligent or fraudulent activity. Hedge fund managers with at least US$100 million in assets under management are required to file publicly quarterly reports disclosing ownership of registered equity securities and are subject to public disclosure if they own more than 5% of the class of any registered equity security. Registered advisers must report their business practices and disciplinary history to the SEC and to their investors. They are required to have written compliance policies, a chief compliance officer and their records and practices may be examined by the SEC.

The U.S.'s Dodd-Frank Wall Street Reform Act was passed in July 2010 and requires SEC registration of advisers who manage private funds with more than US$150 million in assets. Registered managers must file Form ADV with the SEC, as well as information regarding their assets under management and trading positions. Previously, advisers with fewer than 15 clients were exempt, although many hedge fund advisers voluntarily registered with the SEC to satisfy institutional investors. Under Dodd-Frank, investment advisers with less than US$100 million in assets under management became subject to state regulation. This increased the number of hedge funds under state supervision. Overseas advisers who managed more than US$25 million were also required to register with the SEC. The Act requires hedge funds to provide information about their trades and portfolios to regulators including the newly created Financial

Stability Oversight Council. In this regard, most hedge funds and other private funds, including private equity funds, must file Form PF with the SEC, which is an extensive reporting form with substantial data on the funds' activities and positions. Under the "Volcker Rule," regulators are also required to implement regulations for banks, their affiliates, and holding companies to limit their relationships with hedge funds and to prohibit these organizations from proprietary trading, and to limit their investment in, and sponsorship of, hedge funds.

Europe

Within the European Union (EU), hedge funds are primarily regulated through their managers. In the United Kingdom, where 80% of Europe's hedge funds are based, hedge fund managers are required to be authorised and regulated by the Financial Conduct Authority (FCA). Each country has their own specific restrictions on hedge fund activities, including controls on use of derivatives in Portugal, and limits on leverage in France.

In the EU, managers are subject to the EU's Directive on Alternative Investment Fund Managers (AIFMD). According to the EU, the aim of the directive is to provide greater monitoring and control of alternative investment funds. AIFMD requires all EU hedge fund managers to register with national regulatory authorities and to disclose more information, on a more frequent basis. It also directs hedge fund managers to hold larger amounts of capital. AIFMD also introduced a "passport" for hedge funds authorised in one EU country to operate throughout the EU. The scope of AIFMD is broad and encompasses managers located within the EU as well as non-EU managers that market their funds to European investors. An aspect of AIFMD which challenges established practices in the hedge funds sector is the potential restriction of remuneration through bonus deferrals and clawback provisions.

Other

Some hedge funds are established in Offshore centers such as the Cayman Islands, Dublin, Luxembourg, the British Virgin Islands, and Bermuda which have different regulations concerning non-accredited investors, client confidentiality and fund manager independence.

In South Africa, investment fund managers must be approved by, and register with, the Financial Services Board (FSB).

Performance

Measurement

Performance statistics for individual hedge funds are difficult to obtain, as the funds have historically not been required to report their performance to a central repository and restrictions against public offerings and advertisement have led many managers to refuse to provide performance information publicly. However, summaries of individual hedge fund performance are occasionally available in industry journals and databases. and investment consultancy Hennessee Group.

One estimate is that the average hedge fund returned 11.4% per year, representing a 6.7% return above overall market performance before fees, based on performance data from 8,400 hedge funds. Another is that between January 2000 and December 2009 the hedge funds outperformed other investments were significantly less volatile, with stocks falling 2.62% per year over the decade and hedge funds rising 6.54%. More recent data show that hedge fund performance has declined and underperformed the market.

Hedge funds performance is measured by comparing their returns to an estimate of their risk. Common measures are the Sharpe ratio., Treynor measure and Jensen's alpha. These measures work best when returns follow normal distributions without autocorrelation, and these assumptions are often not met in practice.

New performance measures have been introduced that attempt to address some of theoretical concerns with traditional indicators, including: modified Sharpe ratios; the Omega ratio introduced by Keating and Shadwick in 2002; Alternative Investments Risk Adjusted Performance (AIRAP) published by Sharma in 2004; and Kappa developed by Kaplan and Knowles in 2004.

Sector-size Effect

There is a debate over whether alpha (the manager's skill element in performance) has been diluted by the expansion of the hedge fund industry. Two reasons are given. First, the increase in traded volume may have been reducing the market anomalies that are a source of hedge fund performance. Second, the remuneration model is attracting more managers, which may dilute the talent available in the industry.

Hedge Fund Indices

Indices that track hedge fund returns are, in order of development, called Non-investable, Investable and Clone. They play a central and unambiguous role in traditional asset markets, where they are widely accepted as representative of their underlying portfolios. Equity and debt index fund products provide investable access to most developed markets in these asset classes. Hedge funds, however, are actively managed, so that tracking is impossible. Non-investable hedge fund indices on the other hand may be more or less representative, but returns data on many of the reference group of funds is non-public. This may result in biased estimates of their returns. In an attempt to address this problem, clone indices have been created in an attempt to replicate the statistical properties of hedge funds without being directly based on their returns data.

None of these approaches achieves the accuracy of indices in other asset classes for which there is more complete published data concerning the underlying returns.

Non-investable Indices

Non-investable indices are indicative in nature, and aim to represent the performance of some database of hedge funds using some measure such as mean, median or weighted mean from a hedge fund database. The databases have diverse selection criteria and methods of construction, and no single database captures all funds. This leads to significant differences in reported performance between different indices.

Although they aim to be representative, non-investable indices suffer from a lengthy and largely unavoidable list of biases.

Funds' participation in a database is voluntary, leading to self-selection bias because those funds that choose to report may not be typical of funds as a whole. For example, some do not report because of poor results or because they have already reached their target size and do not wish to raise further money.

The short lifetimes of many hedge funds means that there are many new entrants and many departures each year, which raises the problem of survivorship bias. If we examine only funds that have survived to the present, we will overestimate past returns because many of the worst-performing funds have not survived, and the observed association between fund youth and fund performance suggests that this bias may be substantial.

When a fund is added to a database for the first time, all or part of its historical data is recorded ex-post in the database. It is likely that funds only publish their results when they are favorable, so that the average performances displayed by the funds during their incubation period are inflated. This is known as "instant history bias" or "backfill bias".

Investable Indices

Investable indices are an attempt to reduce these problems by ensuring that the return of the index is available to shareholders. To create an investable index, the index provider selects funds and develops structured products or derivative instruments that deliver the performance of the index. When investors buy these products the index provider makes the investments in the underlying funds, making an investable index similar in some ways to a fund of hedge funds portfolio.

To make the index investable, hedge funds must agree to accept investments on the terms given by the constructor. To make the index liquid, these terms must include provisions for redemptions that some managers may consider too onerous to be acceptable. This means that investable indices do not represent the total universe of hedge funds. Most seriously, they under-represent more successful managers, who typically refuse to accept such investment protocols.

Hedge Fund Replication

The most recent addition to the field approach the problem in a different manner. Instead of reflecting the performance of actual hedge funds they take a statistical approach to the analysis of historic hedge fund returns, and use this to construct a model of how hedge fund returns respond to the movements of various investable financial assets. This model is then used to construct an investable portfolio of those assets. This makes the index investable, and in principle they can be as representative as the hedge fund database from which they were constructed.

However, these clone indices rely on a statistical modelling process. Such indices have too short a history to state whether this approach will be considered successful.

Closures

In March 2017, HFR – a hedge fund research data and service provider – reported that there were more hedge-fund closures in 2016 than during the 2009 recession. According to the report, several large public pension funds pulled their investments in hedge funds, because the funds' subpar performance as a group did not merit the high fees they charged.

Despite the hedge fund industry topping $3 trillion for the first time ever in 2016, the number of new hedge funds launched fell short of crisis-era figures. There were 729 hedge fund launches in 2016, fewer than the 784 opened in 2009 and dramatically less than the 968 launches in 2015.

Debates and Controversies

Systemic Risk

Systemic risk refers to the risk of instability across the entire financial system, as opposed to within a single company. Such risk may arise following a destabilizing event or events affecting a group of financial institutions linked through investment activity. Organizations such as the National Bureau of Economic Research and the European Central Bank have charged that hedge funds pose systemic risks to the financial sector, and following the failure of hedge fund Long-Term Capital Management (LTCM) in 1998 there was widespread concern about the potential for systemic risk if a hedge fund failure led to the failure of its counterparties. (As it happens, no financial assistance was provided to LTCM by the US Federal Reserve, so there was no direct cost to US taxpayers, but a large bailout had to be mounted by a number of financial institutions.)

However, these claims are widely disputed by the financial industry, who typically regard hedge funds as "small enough to fail", since most are relatively small in terms of the assets they manage and operate with low leverage, thereby limiting the potential harm to the economic system should one of them fail. Formal analysis of hedge fund leverage before and during the 2008 financial crisis suggests that hedge fund leverage is both fairly modest and counter-cyclical to the market leverage of investment banks and the larger financial sector. Hedge fund leverage decreased prior to the financial crisis, even while the leverage of other financial intermediaries continued to increase. Hedge funds fail regularly, and numerous hedge funds failed during the financial crisis. In testimony to the House Financial Services Committee in 2009, Ben Bernanke, the Federal Reserve Board Chairman said he "would not think that any hedge fund or private equity fund would become a systemically critical firm individually".

Nevertheless, although hedge funds go to great lengths to reduce the ratio of risk to reward, inevitably a number of risks remain. Systemic risk is increased in a crisis if there is "herd" behaviour, which causes a number of similar hedge funds to make losses in similar trades. In addition, while most hedge funds make only modest use of leverage, hedge funds differ from many other market participants, such as banks and mutual funds, in that there are no regulatory constraints on their use of leverage, and some hedge funds seek large amounts of leverage as part of their market strategy. The extensive use of leverage can lead to forced liquidations in a crisis, particularly for hedge funds that invest at least in part in illiquid investments. The close interconnectedness of the hedge funds with their prime brokers, typically investment banks, can lead to domino effects in a crisis, and indeed failing counterparty banks can freeze hedge funds. These systemic risk concerns are exacerbated by the prominent role of hedge funds in the financial markets. The global hedge fund industry has over $2 trillion in assets, and this does not take into account the full effect of leverage, which by definition is market exposure in excess of the amount invested.

An August 2012 survey by the Financial Services Authority concluded that risks were limited and had reduced as a result, *inter alia*, of larger margins being required by counterparty banks, but might change rapidly according to market conditions. In stressed market conditions, investors might suddenly withdraw large sums, resulting in forced asset sales. This might cause liquidity and pricing problems if it occurred across a number of funds or in one large highly leveraged fund.

Transparency

Hedge funds are structured to avoid most direct regulation (although their managers may be regulated) and are not required to publicly disclose their investment activities, except to the extent that investors generally are subject to disclosure requirements. This is in contrast to a regulated mutual fund or exchange-traded fund, which will typically have to meet regulatory requirements for disclosure. An investor in a hedge fund usually has direct access to the investment adviser of the fund, and may enjoy more personalized reporting than investors in retail investment funds. This may include detailed discussions of risks assumed and significant positions. However, this high level of disclosure is not available to non-investors, contributing to hedge funds' reputation for secrecy, while some hedge funds have very limited transparency even to investors.

Funds may choose to report some information in the interest of recruiting additional investors. Much of the data available in consolidated databases is self-reported and unverified. A study was done on two major databases containing hedge fund data. The study noted that 465 common funds had significant differences in reported information (e.g. returns, inception date, net assets value, incentive fee, management fee, investment styles, etc.) and that 5% of return numbers and 5% of NAV numbers were dramatically different. With these limitations, investors have to do their own research, which may cost on the scale of US$50,000 for a fund that is not well-established.

A lack of verification of financial documents by investors or by independent auditors has, in some cases, assisted in fraud. In the mid-2000s, Kirk Wright of International Management Associates was accused of mail fraud and other securities violations which allegedly defrauded clients of close to US$180 million. In December 2008, Bernard Madoff was arrested for running a US$50 billion Ponzi scheme that closely resembled a hedge fund and was incorrectly described as one. Several feeder hedge funds, of which the largest was Fairfield Sentry, channeled money to it. Following the Madoff case, the SEC adopted reforms in December 2009 that required hedge funds managed by registered investment advisers to have their assets in the custody of a qualified custodian and subjected them to an audit requirement.

The process of matching hedge funds to investors has traditionally been fairly opaque, with investments often driven by personal connections or recommendations of portfolio managers. Many funds disclose their holdings, strategy, and historic performance relative to market indices, giving investors some idea of how their money is being allocated, although individual holdings are often not disclosed. Investors are often drawn to hedge funds by the possibility of realizing significant returns, or hedging against volatility in the market. The complexity and fees associated with hedge funds are causing some to exit the market – Calpers, the largest pension fund in the US, announced plans to completely divest from hedge funds in 2014. Some services are attempting to improve matching between hedge funds and investors: HedgeZ is designed to allow investors to easily search and sort through funds; iMatchative aims to match investors to funds through algorithms that factor in an investor's goals and behavioral profile, in hopes of helping funds and investors understand the how their perceptions and motivations drive investment decisions.

Links with Analysts

In June 2006, prompted by a letter from Gary J. Aguirre, the Senate Judiciary Committee began an investigation into the links between hedge funds and independent analysts. Aguirre was fired from his job with the SEC when, as lead investigator of insider trading allegations against Pequot Capital Management, he tried to interview John Mack, then being considered for chief executive officer at Morgan Stanley. The Judiciary Committee and the US Senate Finance Committee issued a scathing report in 2007, which found that Aguirre had been illegally fired in reprisal for his pursuit of Mack and in 2009, the SEC was forced to re-open its case against Pequot. Pequot settled with the SEC for US$28 million and Arthur J. Samberg, chief investment officer of Pequot, was barred from working as an investment advisor. Pequot closed its doors under the pressure of investigations.

The systemic practice of hedge funds submitting periodic electronic questionnaires to stock analysts as a part of market research was reported in by *The New York Times* in July 2012. According to the report, one motivation for the questionnaires was to obtain subjective information not available to the public and possible early notice of trading recommendations that could produce short term market movements.

Value in Mean/variance Efficient Portfolios

According to modern portfolio theory, rational investors will seek to hold portfolios that are mean/variance efficient (that is, portfolios that offer the highest level of return per unit of risk). One of the attractive features of hedge funds (in particular market neutral and similar funds) is that they sometimes have a modest correlation with traditional assets such as equities. This means that hedge funds have a potentially quite valuable role in investment portfolios as diversifiers, reducing overall portfolio risk.

However, there are three reasons why one might not wish to allocate a high proportion of assets into hedge funds. These reasons are:

- Hedge funds are highly individual and it is hard to estimate the likely returns or risks.
- Hedge funds' low correlation with other assets tends to dissipate during stressful market events, making them much less useful for diversification than they may appear.
- Hedge fund returns are reduced considerably by the high fee structures that are typically charged.

Several studies have suggested that hedge funds are sufficiently diversifying to merit inclusion in investor portfolios, but this is disputed for example by Mark Kritzman who performed a mean-variance optimization calculation on an opportunity set that consisted of a stock index fund, a bond index fund, and ten hypothetical hedge funds. The optimizer found that a mean-variance efficient portfolio did not contain any allocation to hedge funds, largely because of the impact of performance fees. To demonstrate this, Kritzman repeated the optimization using an assumption that the hedge funds incurred no performance fees. The result from this second optimization was an allocation of 74% to hedge funds.

The other factor reducing the attractiveness of hedge funds in a diversified portfolio is that they tend to perform poorly during equity bear markets, just when an investor needs part of their portfolio to add value. For example, in January–September 2008, the Credit Suisse/Tremont Hedge Fund Index was down 9.87%. According to the same index series, even "dedicated short bias" funds had a return of –6.08% during September 2008. In other words, even though low average correlations may appear to make hedge funds attractive this may not work in turbulent period, for example around the collapse of Lehman Brothers in September 2008.

- Example - Interest-rate forward contract
- Purchase of T-Bills with a maturity of one year.

Advantages

- Risk of increased interest rate is reduced
- Flexibility can be incorporated in the contract if they are traded in the Over-The- Counter (OTC) market.

Disadvantages

- OTC contracts have less liquidity
- Default risk to the bank

3

Credit Risk: Analysis and Management

Credit risk is the failure of the borrower to not be able to make the required payments. The different types of credit risks are credit default risk, country risk and concentration risk. This chapter has been carefully written to provide an easy understanding of the varied facets of credit risk.

Credit Risk

Bank operations involve sanctioning of loans and advances to customers for variety of purposes. These loans may be business loans for short or long term commitments and consumer finance for purchase of durables, property and vehicles. Other types of loans provided by banks are micro credit for small borrowers and contingent obligations that are off balance sheet transactions.

The loan sanctioning process commences when the bank receives a loan proposal from the customer. The loan requirement may be for equipment purchase or for working capital finance requirements. If it is for equipment purchase the amount will be paid directly to the supplier. If it is a working capital requirement, an operational bank account in the name of the customer will be opened and permission will be granted to draw the amount as and when required.

The loan proposal will be evaluated using an internal rating system or the credit rating offered by external rating agencies. After the loan sanction the bank needs to follow up and monitor the loan accounts. The loan sanctioned may become a default or a bad loan if the outstanding payments (either interest or installment of the principle amount) are overdue by 90 days. Thus credit life cycle involves four stages, credit opportunity, credit assessment, credit management and credit implication.

Credit worthiness of the borrowers will influence loan commitment by the bank. The pre requisites for the loan sanctioned depends on the credit worthiness of the borrower. The requirement of credit worthiness varies depending on type of credit and quantum of loan offered to borrowers.

Besides personal credit worthiness the bankability of the proposal is to be evaluated in terms of projected cash flows, projected investment and past performance of the borrower.

Risk exposure for banks is computed considering three factors. The criteria are the default percentage, exposure value for the bank and the estimated recovery rate.

Loss on default = D x E x (1-R)

Where D is default percentage, E is exposure value and R is recovery rate.

Example of a credit evaluation process is given below.

Credit Risk Evaluation Information Requirement by Banks

Details of Applicants

- Name of the entity
- Registered office address
- Name of the contact person
- Address of factory / establishment
- Address for correspondence
- Office contract details
- Date of incorporation
- Date business commenced
- Date of formation

Details of Applicants

- Account number
- Date of account opening
- Branch of applicant account
- Whether existing borrowing customer
- Line of business
- Nature of product / service offered
- Type of constitution of the business
- Existing activity of the business entity
- Proposed activity of the business entity
- Name of parent company if any

Purpose of Loan

- Expected source of funds
- Business owner
- Expected account turnover
- Return on investment
- Sale proceeds
- Details of Director
- Details of the Board
- Principal shareholders of the company
- and their address

Purpose of Loan

- Exposure of the borrowing entity with other bank groups
- Credit facility availed
- Credit facility applied

  – Type of facility

  – Amount

  – Purpose

  – Tenor

  – Primary security

  – Collateral security

  – Currency of security

Details of Assets

- Land
- Tools
- Electrical
- Machinery
- Other assets

Information on each type of Assets

- Purpose of asset
- Imported / Indigenous
- Supplier
- Total cost
- Promoters contribution
- Loan required

Business Information

- Details of collateral
- Details of customers of business
- Currencies in which business is conducted
- Number of employees

Existing Credit Facility Details

- Types of facility
- Limits (value)
- Outstanding as on the previous accounting date
- Names of banks presently working with
- Security lodged
- Rate of interest
- Repayment terms

Past Performance (Two years)

- Net Sales
- Net profit
- Capital (net worth)
- Total debt
- Imports
- Exports

Future Estimate (Current year and next year)

- Net Sales
- Net profit
- Capital (net worth)
- Total debt
- Imports
- Exports

A credit risk is the risk of default on a debt that may arise from a borrower failing to make required payments. In the first resort, the risk is that of the lender and includes lost principal and interest, disruption to cash flows, and increased collection costs. The loss may be complete or partial. In an efficient market, higher levels of credit risk will be associated with higher borrowing costs. Because of this, measures of borrowing costs such as yield spreads can be used to infer credit risk levels based on assessments by market participants.

Losses can arise in a number of circumstances, for example:

- A consumer may fail to make a payment due on a mortgage loan, credit card, line of credit, or other loan.

The probability of rescheduling is an increasing function of debt service ratio, import ratio, variance of export revenue and domestic money supply growth. The likelihood of rescheduling is a decreasing function of investment ratio due to future economic productivity gains. Debt rescheduling likelihood can increase if the investment ratio rises as the foreign country could become less dependent on its external creditors and so be less concerned about receiving credit from these countries/investors.

Counterparty Risk

A counterparty risk, also known as a default risk, is a risk that a counterparty will not pay as obligated on a bond, derivative, insurance policy, or other contract. Financial institutions or other transaction counterparties may hedge or take out credit insurance or, particularly in the context of derivatives, require the posting of collateral. Offsetting counterparty risk is not always possible, e.g. because of temporary liquidity issues or longer term systemic reasons.

Counterparty risk increases due to positively correlated risk factors. Accounting for correlation between portfolio risk factors and counterparty default in risk management methodology is not trivial.

Mitigation

Lenders mitigate credit risk in a number of ways, including:

- Risk-based pricing – Lenders may charge a higher interest rate to borrowers who are more likely to default, a practice called risk-based pricing. Lenders consider factors relating to the loan such as loan purpose, credit rating, and loan-to-value ratio and estimates the effect on yield (credit spread).
- Covenants – Lenders may write stipulations on the borrower, called covenants, into loan agreements, such as:
    - Periodically report its financial condition,
    - Refrain from paying dividends, repurchasing shares, borrowing further, or other specific, voluntary actions that negatively affect the company's financial position, and
    - Repay the loan in full, at the lender's request, in certain events such as changes in the borrower's debt-to-equity ratio or interest coverage ratio.
- Credit insurance and credit derivatives – Lenders and bond holders may hedge their credit risk by purchasing credit insurance or credit derivatives. These contracts transfer the risk from the lender to the seller (insurer) in exchange for payment. The most common credit derivative is the credit default swap.

- Tightening – Lenders can reduce credit risk by reducing the amount of credit extended, either in total or to certain borrowers. For example, a distributor selling its products to a troubled retailer may attempt to lessen credit risk by reducing payment terms from net 30 to net 15.
- Diversification – Lenders to a small number of borrowers (or kinds of borrower) face a high degree of unsystematic credit risk, called concentration risk. Lenders reduce this risk by diversifying the borrower pool.
- Deposit insurance – Governments may establish deposit insurance to guarantee bank deposits in the event of insolvency and to encourage consumers to hold their savings in the banking system instead of in cash.

Related Acronyms

- ACPM Active credit portfolio management
- CCR Counterparty Credit Risk
- CE Credit Exposure
- CVA Credit valuation adjustment
- EAD Exposure at default
- EL Expected loss
- LGD Loss given default
- PD Probability of default
- KMV quantitative credit analysis
- VAR Value at risk
- PFE Potential future exposure
- EE Expected Exposure

Consumer Credit Risk

Consumer credit risk (also retail credit risk) is the risk of loss due to a customer's non re-payment (default) on a consumer credit product, such as a mortgage, unsecured personal loan, credit card, overdraft etc. (the latter two options being forms of unsecured banking credit).

Consumer Credit Risk Management

Most companies involved in lending to consumers have departments dedicated to the measurement, prediction and control of losses due to credit risk. This field is loosely referred to consumer/retail credit risk management, however the word *management* is commonly dropped.

Scorecards

A common method for predicting credit risk is through the credit scorecard. The scorecard is a statistically based model for attributing a number (*score*) to a customer (or an account) which indicates the predicted probability that the customer will exhibit a certain behaviour. In calculating the score, a range of data sources may be used, including data from an application form, from credit reference agencies or from products the customer already holds with the lender.

The most widespread type of scorecard in use is the application scorecard, which lenders employ when a customer applies for a new credit product. The scorecard tries to predict the probability that the customer, if given the product, would become "bad" within a given timeframe, incurring losses for the lender. The exact definition of what constitutes "bad" varies across different lenders, product types and target markets, however examples may be *"missing three payments within the next 18 months"* or *"default within the next 12 months"*. The score given to a customer is usually a three or four digit integer, and in most cases is proportional to the natural logarithm of the odds (or logit) of the customer becoming "bad". In general a low score indicates a low quality (a high chance of going "bad") and a high score indicates the opposite.

Other scorecard types may include behavioural scorecards - which try to predict the probability of an existing account turning "bad"; propensity scorecards - which try to predict the probability that a customer would accept another product if offered one; and collections scorecards - which try to predict a customer's response to different strategies for collecting owed money.

Credit Strategy

Credit strategy is concerned with turning predictions of customer behaviour (as provided by scorecards) into a decision whether to accept their custom.

To turn an application score into a Yes/No decision, "cut-offs" are generally used. A cut-off is a score at and above which customers have their application accepted and below which applications are declined. The placement of the cut-off is closely linked to the price (APR) that the lender is charging for the product. The higher the price charged, the greater the losses the lender can endure and still remain profitable. So, with a higher price the lender can accept customers with a higher probability of going "bad" and can move the cut-off down. The opposite is true of a lower price. Most lenders go further and charge low scoring customers a higher APR than high scoring customers. This compensates for the added risk of taking on poorer quality business without effecting the lender's place in the market with better quality borrowers. In the UK, lenders must advertise a *typical* rate, which at least 51% of customers must receive.

Application score is also used as a factor in deciding such things as an overdraft or credit card limit. Lenders are generally happier to extend a larger limit to higher scoring customers than to lower scoring customers, because they are more likely to pay borrowings back. Alongside scorecards lie *policy rules* which apply regulatory requirements (such as making sure there is no lending to under 18s) and other lending policy (such as many lenders will not lend to customers who have a CCJ registered against them). Credit Strategy is also concerned with the ongoing management of a customer's account, especially with *revolving* credit products such as credit cards, overdrafts and flexible loans, where the customer's balance can go up as well as down. Behavioural scorecards are used (usually monthly) to provide an updated picture of the credit-quality of the customer/account. As the customer's profile changes, the lender may choose to extend or contract the customer's limits.

Underwriting

Not all decisions can be made automatically through the methods mentioned above. This may be for a number of reasons; insufficient data, regulatory requirements, or a borderline decision. In such cases highly trained professionals called underwriters manually review the case and make a decision. Sometimes this is done in conjunction with the "cut-offs" mentioned above and the data provided by scoring. This is more common in highly regulated products such as mortgages, especially when large sums are involved.

Loan

In finance, a loan is the lending of money from one individual, organization or entity to another individual, organization or entity. A loan is a debt provided by an entity (organization or individual) to another entity at an interest rate, and evidenced by a promissory note which specifies, among other things, the principal amount of money borrowed, the interest rate the lender is charging, and date of repayment. A loan entails the reallocation of the subject asset(s) for a period of time, between the lender and the borrower.

In a loan, the borrower initially receives or *borrows* an amount of money, called the *principal*, from the lender, and is obligated to *pay back* or *repay* an equal amount of money to the lender at a later time.

The loan is generally provided at a cost, referred to as interest on the debt, which provides an incentive for the lender to engage in the loan. In a legal loan, each of these obligations and restrictions is enforced by contract, which can also place the borrower under additional restrictions known as loan covenants. Although this section focuses on monetary loans, in practice any material object might be lent.

Acting as a provider of loans is one of the principal tasks for financial institutions such as banks and credit card companies. For other institutions, issuing of debt contracts such as bonds is a typical source of funding.

Types

Secured

A secured loan is a loan in which the borrower pledges some asset (e.g. a car or property) as collateral.

A mortgage loan is a very common type of loan, used by many individuals to purchase things. In this arrangement, the money is used to purchase the property. The financial institution, however, is given security – a lien on the title to the house – until the mortgage is paid off in full. If the borrower defaults on the loan, the bank would have the legal right to repossess the house and sell it, to recover sums owing to it.

In some instances, a loan taken out to purchase a new or used car may be secured by the car, in much the same way as a mortgage is secured by housing. The duration of the loan period is considerably shorter – often corresponding to the useful life of the car. There are two types of auto loans, direct and indirect. A direct auto loan is where a bank gives the loan directly to a consumer. An indirect auto loan is where a car dealership acts as an intermediary between the bank or financial institution and the consumer.

Unsecured

Unsecured loans are monetary loans that are not secured against the borrower's assets. These may be available from financial institutions under many different guises or marketing packages:

- credit card debt
- personal loans
- bank overdrafts
- credit facilities or lines of credit
- corporate bonds (may be secured or unsecured)
- peer-to-peer lending

The interest rates applicable to these different forms may vary depending on the lender and the borrower. These may or may not be regulated by law. In the United Kingdom, when applied to individuals, these may come under the Consumer Credit Act 1974.

Interest rates on unsecured loans are nearly always higher than for secured loans, because an unsecured lender's options for recourse against the borrower in the event of default are severely limited. An unsecured lender must sue the borrower, obtain a money judgment for breach of contract, and then pursue execution of the judgment against the borrower's unencumbered assets (that is, the ones not already pledged to secured lenders). In insolvency proceedings, secured lenders traditionally have priority over unsecured lenders when a court divides up the borrower's assets. Thus, a higher interest rate reflects the additional risk that in the event of insolvency, the debt may be uncollectible.

Demand

Demand loans are short term loans that are typically in that they do not have fixed dates for repayment and carry a floating interest rate which varies according to the prime lending rate. They can be "called" for repayment by the lending institution at any time. Demand loans may be unsecured or secured.

Subsidized

A subsidized loan is a loan on which the interest is reduced by an explicit or hidden subsidy. In the context of college loans in the United States, it refers to a loan on which no interest is accrued while a student remains enrolled in education.

Concessional

A concessional loan, sometimes called a "soft loan", is granted on terms substantially more generous than market loans either through below-market interest rates, by grace periods or a combination of both. Such loans may be made by foreign governments to developing countries or may be offered to employees of lending institutions as an employee benefit.

Target markets

Personal

Loans can also be subcategorized according to whether the debtor is an individual person (consumer) or a business. Common personal loans include mortgage loans, car loans, home equity lines of credit, credit cards, installment loans and payday loans. The credit score of the borrower is a major component in and underwriting and interest rates (APR) of these loans. The monthly payments of personal loans can be decreased by selecting longer payment terms, but overall interest paid increases as well. For car loans in the U.S., the average term was about 60 months in 2009.

Commercial

Loans to businesses are similar to the above, but also include commercial mortgages and corporate bonds. Underwriting is not based upon credit score but rather credit rating.

Loan Payment

The most typical loan payment type is the fully amortizing payment in which each monthly rate has the same value over time.

The fixed monthly payment P for a loan of L for n months and a monthly interest rate c is:

$$P = L \cdot \frac{c(1+c)^n}{(1+c)^n - 1}$$

Abuses in Lending

Predatory lending is one form of abuse in the granting of loans. It usually involves granting a loan in order to put the borrower in a position that one can gain advantage over him or her. Where the moneylender is not authorized, they could be considered a loan shark.

Usury is a different form of abuse, where the lender charges excessive interest. In different time periods and cultures the acceptable interest rate has varied, from no interest at all to unlimited interest rates. Credit card companies in some countries have been accused by consumer organizations of lending at usurious interest rates and making money out of frivolous “extra charges”.

Abuses can also take place in the form of the customer abusing the lender by not repaying the loan or with an intent to defraud the lender.

United States Taxes

Most of the basic rules governing how loans are handled for tax purposes in the United States are codified by both Congress (the Internal Revenue Code) and the Treasury Department (Treasury Regulations – another set of rules that interpret the Internal Revenue Code).

1. A loan is not gross income to the borrower. Since the borrower has the obligation to repay the loan, the borrower has no accession to wealth.

2. The lender may not deduct (from own gross income) the amount of the loan. The rationale here is that one asset (the cash) has been converted into a different asset (a

promise of repayment). Deductions are not typically available when an outlay serves to create a new or different asset.

3. The amount paid to satisfy the loan obligation is not deductible (from own gross income) by the borrower.

4. Repayment of the loan is not gross income to the lender. In effect, the promise of repayment is converted back to cash, with no accession to wealth by the lender.

5. Interest paid to the lender is included in the lender's gross income. Interest paid represents compensation for the use of the lender's money or property and thus represents profit or an accession to wealth to the lender. Interest income can be attributed to lenders even if the lender doesn't charge a minimum amount of interest.

6. Interest paid to the lender may be deductible by the borrower. In general, interest paid in connection with the borrower's business activity is deductible, while interest paid on personal loans are not deductible. The major exception here is interest paid on a home mortgage.

Income from Discharge of Indebtedness

Although a loan does not start out as income to the borrower, it becomes income to the borrower if the borrower is discharged of indebtedness. Thus, if a debt is discharged, then the borrower essentially has received income equal to the amount of the indebtedness. The Internal Revenue Code lists "Income from Discharge of Indebtedness" in Section 61(a)(12) as a source of gross income.

Example: X owes Y $50,000. If Y discharges the indebtedness, then X no longer owes Y $50,000. For purposes of calculating income, this is treated the same way as if Y gave X $50,000.

For a more detailed description of the "discharge of indebtedness", look at Section 108 (Cancellation of Debt (COD) Income) of the Internal Revenue Code.

Loan Guarantee

A loan guarantee, in finance, is a promise by one party (the guarantor) to assume the debt obligation of a borrower if that borrower defaults. A guarantee can be limited or unlimited, making the guarantor liable for only a portion or all of the debt.

Private Loan Guarantees

There are two main types:

1. Guarantor mortgages
2. Unsecured guarantor loan

Guarantor Mortgages

Popular with young borrowers who do not have a large deposit saved and need to borrow up to 100% of the property value to purchase a property. Generally, their parents will provide a guarantee to the lender to cover any shortfall in the event of default.

There are three main types

1. Guarantor Mortgage – generally, a parent or close family member will guarantee the mortgage debt and will cover the repayment obligations should the borrower default.
2. Family offset mortgage – typically, a parent or grandparent will put their savings into an account linked to the borrower's mortgage. They do not get any interest on these savings whilst offsetting the mortgage but will be able to get their money back in full once the mortgage has been paid down to between 70% and 80% of the property's market value.
3. Family deposit mortgage – a family member will place a deposit in a dedicated savings account and is held as security against the properties mortgage. Interest is paid on this deposit, but if the borrower defaults on their repayments then money will be taken from this savings account.

Unsecured Guarantor Loan

An unsecured personal loan that is popular with borrowers who have a poor credit rating. They also require the guarantor to meet the borrower's obligations if they default on their loan repayments.

Government Loan Guarantees

The term can be used to refer to a government to assume a private debt obligation if the borrower defaults. Most loan guarantee programs are established to correct perceived market failures by which small borrowers, regardless of creditworthiness, lack access to the credit resources available to large borrowers.

Loan guarantees can also be extended to large borrowers for political reasons. For example, Chrysler Corporation, one of the "big three" US automobile manufacturers, obtained a loan guarantee in 1979 amid its near-collapse, and lobbying by labor interests. Somewhat differently, despite intensive lobbying by the Israel lobby, President George H. W. Bush refused $10 billion in loan guarantees to the Israeli government of Yitzhak Shamir because of his pro-settlement policy and because Palestinians and many Arab governments viewed the prior acceptance of loan guarantees as an indicator of America's lack of credibility as a mediator.

Bush requested and received a Congressional delay in discussion of the guarantees, and the Madrid Conference of 1991 was later convened. These loan guarantees were issued later, following the election of Itzhak Rabin and his pledge to end Shamir's settlement policy and reformulate national priorities.

Business and Agricultural Loans

The loans sanctioned by banks for business may be broadly classified into two categories namely working capital advances and project loans. Loan sanction by banks can be based on several methods. Turnover method focuses on projected sales, trade terms, cash flows and business cycle of the proposal. Based on the assessment a credit limit will be sanctioned.

Cash flow method will consider industry capacity, sector projections and regional performance of the project in determining the credit limits of the business. Cash budget method uses sales forecast, market forecast, investment forecast, loan commitment expenses, administrative commitments and project expense estimates.

Projected balance sheet method deals with total performance of the business by analyzing asset structure, investment structure, borrowing structure and capital structure. Projects of these balance sheet criteria in terms of liquidity and cash flows identify the credit limit for the business.

Net owned fund method uses risk estimates, capital commitment of the borrower, security requirements, guarantee requirements and the quality of net owned funds of the borrower. On the basis of these estimates a decision on loan proposal will be taken by the banks.

While sanctioning business loans, a bank follows a standard set of procedures which includes application of analytical tools, choice of appraisal methods, manner of delivery of credit, monitoring of account and scheduling of payments. Similarly for export and import loans a separate set of standard procedures are followed.

Additional loan exposures and loan restructuring proposals are considered by banks on a case to case basis considering specific justification for the proposal.

Agricultural loans are sanctioned by banks during Kharif and Rabi seasons. These loans may be for the purchase of equipment, for irrigation facilities, for the purchase of fertilizers or seeds and other purposes such as land development.

Business Loan

A business loan is a loan specifically intended for business purposes. As with all loans, it involves the creation of a debt, which will be repaid with added interest. There are a number of different types of business loans, including bank loans, mezzanine financing, asset-based financing, invoice financing, microloans, business cash advances and cash flow loans.

Types

Bank Loan

A bank loan may be obtained from a bank and may be either secured or unsecured. For secured loans, banks will require collateral, which may be lost if repayments are not made. The bank will probably wish to see the business's accounts, balance sheet and business plan, as well as studying the principals' credit histories. Many smaller businesses are now however turning towards Alternative Finance Providers, especially in the case of smaller firms.

Loans from credit unions may be referred to as bank loans as well. Business loans from credit unions received the second highest level of satisfaction from borrowers after loans from small banks.

SBA Loans

The US Small Business Administration (SBA) does not make loans; instead it guarantees loans made by individual lenders. The main SBA loan programs are SBA 7(a) which includes both a standard and express option; Microloans (up to $50,000); 504 Loans which provide financing for fixed assets such as real estate or equipment; and Disaster loans. In FY 2016, total 7(a) volume was $11,967,861,900 and total 504 loan volume was $2,517,433,000.

Mezzanine Finance

Mezzanine finance effectively secures a company's debt on its equity, allowing the lender to claim part-ownership of the business if the loan is not paid back on time and in full. This allows the business to borrow without putting up other collateral, but risks diluting the principals' equity share in case of default.

Asset-based Finance

Once considered the finance option of last resort, asset-based lending has become a popular choice for small businesses lacking the credit rating or track record to qualify for other forms of finance. In simple terms, it involves borrowing against one of the company's assets, with the lender focusing on the quality of the collateral rather than the credit rating and prospects of the company. A business may borrow against several different types of asset, including premises, plant, stock or receivables.

Invoice Finance

In recent years, it has become increasingly difficult for SMEs to obtain traditional finance from banks. Alternative options are invoice discounting or factoring, whereby the company borrows against its outstanding invoices, with the ability to obtain funds as soon as new invoices are created. It is often questioned which option is best for your business – factoring or discounting – and the answer depends on how the business wants to be perceived by customers. With factoring, the finance company charges interest on the loan until the invoice is paid, as well as fees, and the finance company takes ownership of the debtor ledger and uses its own credit control team to secure payment. With invoice discounting, the business maintains control of its own ledger and chases debts itself.

Microloans

Smaller loans, usually for loan amounts of $100,000 USD or less, are referred to as "microloans." Banks are less likely to make these loans than alternative lenders. When they do, the decision is usually based on the personal credit score of the business and/or the business credit score.

Online Lenders

There has been a rise in the number of online lenders offering small business loans. Online alternative lenders originated an estimated $12 billion in small business loans in 2014, with unsecured consumer loans representing $7 billion and small business loans accounting for approximately $5 billion. Nonbank lenders that make small business loans have doubled their outstanding portfolio balance every year since 2000. Some online originate loans from their own capital. Others may use a "marketplace" model, in which they match borrowers to loan products from a variety of lenders. Others use crowdfunding platforms that allow businesses to raise capital from a wide variety of sources.

Secured and Unsecured Business Loans

Business loans may be either secured or unsecured. With a secured loan, the borrower pledges an asset (such as plant, equipment, stock or vehicles) against the debt. If the debt is not repaid, the lender may claim the secured asset. Unsecured loans do not have collateral, though the lender will have a general claim on the borrower's assets if repayment is not made. Should the borrower become bankrupt, unsecured creditors will usually realise a smaller proportion of their claims than secured creditors. As a consequence, secured loans will generally attract a lower rate of interest.

Lenders that make business loans often use a UCC filing to alert other creditors of their security interest in the property of the business. UCC filings may be placed against specific assets, or a blanket UCC filing secures interest in all property. UCC filings may affect the business credit score and may make it more difficult to obtain subsequent financing.

Personal Guarantees

Many lenders require principals with 20% or greater ownership in the business to provide a personal guarantee. The personal guarantee allows the lender to attempt to collect the debt from the personal assets of the guarantors. Small business lenders may waive the personal guarantee requirement if the business has strong business credit scores and revenue. In May 2016, changes to the Member Business Lending rule by the National Credit Union Administration board further improved these loans, by allowing credit unions discretion in obtaining a personal guarantee from a borrower.

Microfinance

Micro finance is a source of financial services for entrepreneurs and small businesses lacking access to banking and related services. The two main mechanisms for the delivery of financial services to such clients are: (1) relationship-based banking for individual entrepreneurs and small businesses; and (2) group-based models, where several entrepreneurs come together to apply for loans and other services as a group. In some regions, for example Southern Africa, microfinance is used to describe the supply of financial services to low-income employees, which is closer to the retail finance model prevalent in mainstream banking.

For some, microfinance is a movement whose object is "a world in which as many poor and near-poor households as possible have permanent access to an appropriate range of high quality financial services, including not just credit but also savings, insurance, and fund transfers." Many of those who promote microfinance generally believe that such access will help poor people out of poverty, including participants in the Microcredit Summit Campaign. For others, microfinance is a way to promote economic development, employment and growth through the support of micro-entrepreneurs and small businesses.

Microfinance is a broad category of services, which includes microcredit. Microcredit is provision of credit services to poor clients. Microcredit is one of the aspects of microfinance and the two are often confused. Critics may attack microcredit while referring to it indiscriminately as either 'microcredit' or 'microfinance'. Due to the broad range of microfinance services, it is difficult to assess impact, and very few studies have tried to assess its full impact. Proponents often claim that microfinance lifts people out of poverty, but the evidence is mixed. What it does do, however, is to enhance financial inclusion.

Background

Microfinance and Poverty

In developing economies and particularly in rural areas, many activities that would be classified in the developed world as financial are not monetized: that is, money is not used to carry them out. This is often the case when people need the services money can provide but do not have dispensable funds required for those services, forcing them to revert to other means of acquiring them. In their book *The Poor and Their Money*, Stuart Rutherford and Sukhwinder Arora cite several types of needs:

- *Lifecycle Needs*: such as weddings, funerals, childbirth, education, home building, widowhood and old age.
- *Personal Emergencies*: such as sickness, injury, unemployment, theft, harassment or death.
- *Disasters*: such as fires, floods, cyclones and man-made events like war or bulldozing of dwellings.
- *Investment Opportunities*: expanding a business, buying land or equipment, improving housing, securing a job, etc.

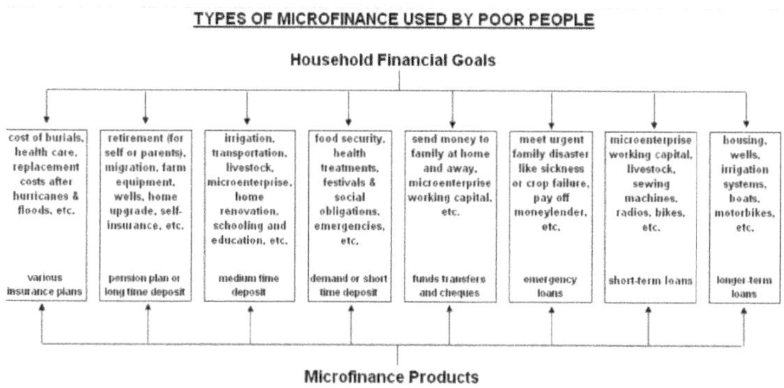

Financial needs and financial services.

People find creative and often collaborative ways to meet these needs, primarily through creating and exchanging different forms of non-cash value. Common substitutes for cash vary from country to country but typically include livestock, grains, jewelry and precious metals. As Marguerite Robinson describes in The Micro finance Revolution, the 1980s demonstrated that "micro finance could provide large-scale outreach profitably," and in the 1990s, "micro finance began to develop as an industry" (2001, p. 54). In the 2000s, the micro finance industry's objective is to satisfy the unmet demand on a much larger scale, and to play a role in reducing poverty. While much progress has been made in developing a viable, commercial micro finance sector in the last few decades, several issues remain that need to be addressed before the industry will be able to satisfy massive worldwide demand. The obstacles or challenges to building a sound commercial micro finance industry include:

- Inappropriate donor subsidies
- Poor regulation and supervision of deposit-taking micro finance institutions (MFIs)

- Few MFIs that meet the needs for savings, remittances or insurance
- Limited management capacity in MFIs
- Institutional inefficiencies
- Need for more dissemination and adoption of rural, agricultural micro finance methodologies

Microfinance is the proper tool to reduce income inequality, allowing citizens from lower socio-economical classes to participate in the economy. Moreover, its involvement has shown to lead to a downward trend in income inequality (Hermes, 2014).

Ways In Which Poor People Manage Their Money

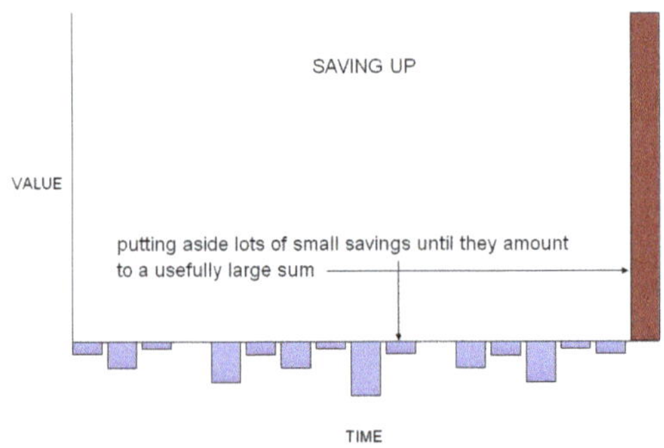

Saving up

Rutherford argues that the basic problem that poor people face as money managers is to gather a 'usefully large' amount of money. Building a new home may involve saving and protecting diverse building materials for years until enough are available to proceed with construction. Children's schooling may be funded by buying chickens and raising them for sale as needed for expenses, uniforms, bribes, etc. Because all the value is accumulated before it is needed, this money management strategy is referred to as 'saving up'.

Often, people don't have enough money when they face a need, so they borrow. A poor family might borrow from relatives to buy land, from a moneylender to buy rice, or from a microfinance institution to buy a sewing machine. Since these loans must be repaid by saving after the cost is incurred, Rutherford calls this 'saving down'. Rutherford's point is that microcredit is addressing only half the problem, and arguably the less important half: poor people borrow to help them save and accumulate assets. Microcredit institutions should fund their loans through savings accounts that help poor people manage their myriad risks.

Most needs are met through a mix of saving and credit. A benchmark impact assessment of Grameen Bank and two other large microfinance institutions in Bangladesh found that for every $1 they were lending to clients to finance rural non-farm micro-enterprise, about $2.50 came from other sources, mostly their clients' savings. This parallels the experience in the West, in which family businesses are funded mostly from savings, especially during start-up.

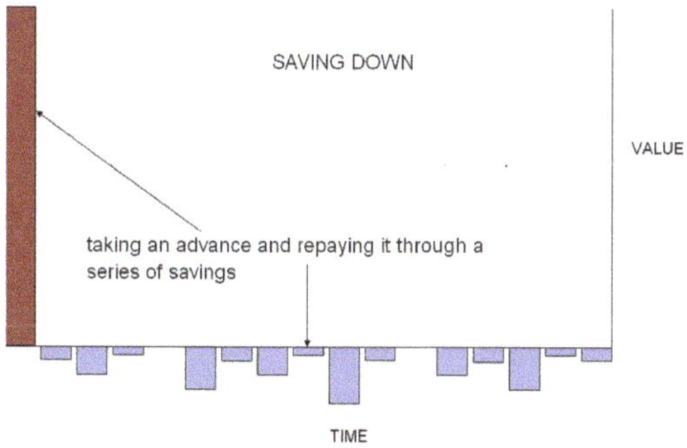

Saving down

Recent studies have also shown that informal methods of saving are unsafe. For example, a study by Wright and Mutesasira in Uganda concluded that "those with no option but to save in the informal sector are almost bound to lose some money—probably around one quarter of what they save there."

The work of Rutherford, Wright and others has caused practitioners to reconsider a key aspect of the microcredit paradigm: that poor people get out of poverty by borrowing, building microenterprises and increasing their income. The new paradigm places more attention on the efforts of poor people to reduce their many vulnerabilities by keeping more of what they earn and building up their assets. While they need loans, they may find it as useful to borrow for consumption as for microenterprise. A safe, flexible place to save money and withdraw it when needed is also essential for managing household and family risk.

Examples

The microfinance project of "saving up" is exemplified in the slums of the south-eastern city of Vijayawada, India. This microfinance project functions as an unofficial banking system where Jyothi, a "deposit collector", collects money from slum dwellers, mostly women, in order for them to accumulate savings. Jyothi does her rounds throughout the city, collecting Rs5 a day from people in the slums for 220 days, however not always 220 days in a row since these women do not always have the funds available to put them into savings. They ultimately end up with Rs1000 at the end of the process. However, there are some issues with this microfinance saving program. One of the issues is that while saving, clients are actually losing part of their savings. Jyothi takes interest from each client—about 20 out of every 220 payments, or Rs100 out of 1,100 or 8%. When these slum dwellers find someone they trust, they are willing to pay up to 30% to someone to safely collect and keep their savings. There is also the risk of entrusting their savings to unlicensed, informal, peripatetic collectors. However, the slum dwellers are willing to accept this risk because they are unable to save at home, and unable to use the remote and unfriendly banks in their country. This microfinance project also has many benefits, such as empowering women and giving parents the ability to save money for their children's education. This specific microfinance project is a great example of the benefits and limitations of the "saving up" project (Rutherford, 2009).

The microfinance project of "saving through" is shown in Nairobi, Kenya which includes a Rotating Savings and Credit Associations or ROSCAs initiative. This is a small scale example, however Rutherford (2009) describes a woman he met in Nairobi and studied her ROSCA. Everyday 15 women would save 100 shillings so there would be a lump sum of 1,500 shillings and everyday 1 of the 15 women would receive that lump sum. This would continue for 15 days and another woman within this group would receive the lump sum. At the end of the 15 days a new cycle would start. This ROSCA initiative is different from the "saving up" example above because there are no interest rates affiliated with the ROSCA, additionally everyone receives back what they put forth. This initiative requires trust and social capital networks in order to work, so often these ROSCAs include people who know each other and have reciprocity. The ROSCA allows for marginalized groups to receive a lump sum at one time in order to pay or save for specific needs they have.

Microfinance Debates and Challenges

There are several key debates at the boundaries of microfinance.

Interest Rates

This shop in South Sudan was opened using money borrowed from the Finance Sudan Limited (FSL) Program. This program was established in 2006 as one of the only microfinance lenders in the country.

One of the principal challenges of microfinance is providing small loans at an affordable cost. The global average interest and fee rate is estimated at 37%, with rates reaching as high as 70% in some markets. The reason for the high interest rates is not primarily cost of capital. Indeed, the local microfinance organizations that receive zero-interest loan capital from the online microlending platform Kiva charge average interest and fee rates of 35.21%. Rather, the main reason for the high cost of microfinance loans is the high transaction cost of traditional microfinance operations relative to loan size.

Microfinance practitioners have long argued that such high interest rates are simply unavoidable, because the cost of making each loan cannot be reduced below a certain level while still allowing the lender to cover costs such as offices and staff salaries. For example, in Sub-Saharan Africa credit risk for microfinance institutes is very high, because customers need years to improve their livelihood and face many challenges during this time. Financial institutes often do not even have a system to check the person's identity. Additionally they are unable to design new products and enlarge their business to reduce the risk. The result is that the traditional approach to microfinance has made only limited progress in resolving the problem it purports to address: that the world's poorest people pay the world's highest cost for small business growth capital. The high costs of traditional microfinance loans limit their effectiveness as a poverty-fighting tool. Offering loans at interest and fee rates of 37% mean that borrowers who do not manage to earn at least a 37% rate of return may actually end up poorer as a result of accepting the loans.

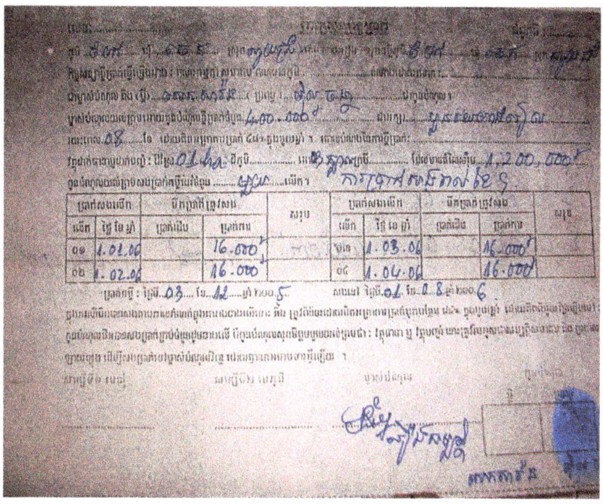

Example of a loan contract, using flat rate calculation, from rural Cambodia. Loan is for 400,000 riels at 4% flat (16,000 riels) interest per month.

According to a recent survey of microfinance borrowers in Ghana published by the Center for Financial Inclusion, more than one-third of borrowers surveyed reported struggling to repay their loans. Some resorted to measures such as reducing their food intake or taking children out of school in order to repay microfinance debts that had not proven sufficiently profitable.

In recent years, the microfinance industry has shifted its focus from the objective of increasing the volume of lending capital available, to address the challenge of providing microfinance loans more affordably. Microfinance analyst David Roodman contends that, in mature markets, the average interest and fee rates charged by microfinance institutions tend to fall over time. However, global average interest rates for microfinance loans are still well above 30%.

The answer to providing microfinance services at an affordable cost may lie in rethinking one of the fundamental assumptions underlying microfinance: that microfinance borrowers need extensive monitoring and interaction with loan officers in order to benefit from and repay their loans. The P2P microlending service Zidisha is based on this premise, facilitating direct interaction between individual lenders and borrowers via an internet community rather than physical offices. Zidisha has managed to bring the cost of microloans to below 10% for borrowers, including interest which is paid out to lenders. However, it remains to be seen whether such radical alternative models can reach the scale necessary to compete with traditional microfinance programs.

Use of Loans

Practitioners and donors from the charitable side of microfinance frequently argue for restricting microcredit to loans for productive purposes—such as to start or expand a microenterprise. Those from the private-sector side respond that, because money is fungible, such a restriction is impossible to enforce, and that in any case it should not be up to rich people to determine how poor people use their money.

Reach Versus Depth of Impact

These goats are being raised by Rwandan women as part of a farm cooperative funded by microfinance.

There has been a long-standing debate over the sharpness of the trade-off between 'outreach' (the ability of a microfinance institution to reach poorer and more remote people) and its 'sustainability' (its ability to cover its operating costs—and possibly also its costs of serving new clients—from its operating revenues). Although it is generally agreed that microfinance practitioners should seek to balance these goals to some extent, there are a wide variety of strategies, ranging from the minimalist profit-orientation of BancoSol in Bolivia to the highly integrated not-for-profit orientation of BRAC in Bangladesh. This is true not only for individual institutions, but also for governments engaged in developing national microfinance systems. BRAC was ranked the number one NGO in the world in 2015 and 2016 by the Geneva-based NGO Advisor.

Gender

Microfinance generally agree that women should be the primary focus of service delivery. Evidence shows that they are less likely to default on their loans than men. Industry data from 2006 for 704 MFIs reaching 52 million borrowers includes MFIs using the solidarity lending methodology (99.3% female clients) and MFIs using individual lending (51% female clients). The delinquency rate for solidarity lending was 0.9% after 30 days (individual lending—3.1%), while 0.3% of loans were written off (individual lending—0.9%). Because operating margins become tighter the smaller the loans delivered, many MFIs consider the risk of lending to men to be too high. This focus on women is questioned sometimes, however a recent study of microenterpreneurs from Sri Lanka published by the World Bank found that the return on capital for male-owned businesses (half of the sample) averaged 11%, whereas the return for women-owned businesses was 0% or slightly negative.

Microfinance's emphasis on female-oriented lending is the subject of controversy, as it is claimed that microfinance improves the status of women through an alleviation of poverty. It is argued that by providing women with initial capital, they will be able to support themselves independent of men, in a manner which would encourage sustainable growth of enterprise and eventual self-sufficiency. This claim has yet to be proven in any substantial form. Moreover, the attraction of women as a potential investment base is precisely because they are constrained by socio-cultural norms regarding such concepts of obedience, familial duty, household maintenance and passivity. The result of these norms is that while micro-lending may enable women to improve their daily subsistence to a more steady pace, they will not be able to engage in market-oriented business practice beyond a limited scope of low-skilled, low-earning, informal work. Part of this is a lack of permissivity in the society; part a reflection of the added burdens of household maintenance that women shoulder alone as a result of microfinancial empowerment; and part a lack of training and education surrounding gendered conceptions of economics. In particular, the shift in norms such that women continue to be responsible for all the domestic private sphere labour as well as undertaking public economic support for their families, independent of male aid increases rather than decreases burdens on already limited persons.

If there were to be an exchange of labour, or if women's income were supplemental rather than essential to household maintenance, there might be some truth to claims of establishing long-term businesses; however when so constrained it is impossible for women to do more than pay off a current loan only to take on another in a cyclic pattern which is beneficial to the financier but hardly to the borrower. This gender essentializing crosses over from institutionalized lenders such as the Grameen Bank into interpersonal direct lending through charitable crowd-funding operations, such as Kiva. More recently, the popularity of non-profit global online lending has grown, suggesting that a redress of gender norms might be instituted through individual selection fomented by the processes of such programs, but the reality is as yet uncertain. Studies have noted that the likelihood of lending to women, individually or in groups, is 38% higher than rates of lending to men.

This is also due to a general trend for interpersonal microfinance relations to be conducted on grounds of similarity and internal/external recognition: lenders want to see something familiar, something supportable in potential borrowers, so an emphasis on family, goals of education and health, and a commitment to community all achieve positive results from prospective financiers. Unfortunately, these labels disproportionately align with women rather than men, particularly in the developing world. The result is that microfinance continues to rely on restrictive gender norms rather than seek to subvert them through economic redress in terms of foundation change: training, business management and financial education are all elements which might be included in parameters of female-aimed loans and until they are the fundamental reality of women as a disadvantaged section of societies in developing states will go untested.

Benefits and Limitations

Microfinancing produces many benefits for poverty stricken, or low- income households. One of the benefits is that it is very accessible. Banks today simply won't extend loans to those with little to no assets, and generally don't engage in small size loans typically associated with microfinancing. Through microfinancing small loans are produced and accessible. Microfinancing is based on the philosophy that even small amounts of credit can help end the cycle of poverty. Another benefit produced from the microfinancing initiative is that it presents opportunities, such as extending education and jobs. Families receiving microfinancing are less likely to pull their children out of school for economic reasons. As well, in relation to employment, people are more likely to open small businesses that will aid the creation of new jobs. Overall, the benefits outline that the microfinancing initiative is set out to improve the standard of living amongst impoverished communities (Rutherford, 2009).

There are also many challenges within microfinance initiatives which may be social or financial. Here, more articulate and better-off community members may cheat poorer or less-educated neighbours. This may occur intentionally or inadvertently through loosely run organizations. As a result, many microfinance initiatives require a large amount of social capital or trust in order to work effectively. The ability of poorer people to save may also fluctuate over time as unexpected costs may take priority which could result in them being able to save little or nothing some weeks. Rates of inflation may cause funds to lose their value, thus financially harming the saver and not benefiting collector (Rutherford, 2009).

History of Microfinance

Over the past centuries, practical visionaries, from the Franciscan monks who founded the community-oriented pawnshops of the 15th century to the founders of the European credit union movement in the 19th century (such as Friedrich Wilhelm Raiffeisen) and the founders of the microcredit movement in the 1970s (such as Muhammad Yunus and Al Whittaker), have tested practices and built institutions designed to bring the kinds of opportunities and risk-management tools that financial services can provide to the doorsteps of poor people. While the success of the Grameen Bank (which now serves over 7 million poor Bangladeshi women) has inspired the world, it has proved difficult to replicate this success. In nations with lower population densities, meeting the operating costs of a retail branch by serving nearby customers has proven considerably more challenging. Hans Dieter Seibel, board member of the European Microfinance Platform, is in favour of the group model. This particular model (used by many Microfinance institutions) makes financial sense, he says, because it reduces transaction costs. Microfinance programmes also need to be based on local funds.

The history of microfinancing can be traced back as far as the middle of the 1800s, when the theorist Lysander Spooner was writing about the benefits of small credits to entrepreneurs and farmers as a way of getting the people out of poverty. Independently of Spooner, Friedrich Wilhelm Raiffeisen founded the first cooperative lending banks to support farmers in rural Germany.

The modern use of the expression "microfinancing" has roots in the 1970s when organizations, such as Grameen Bank of Bangladesh with the microfinance pioneer Muhammad Yunus, were starting and shaping the modern industry of microfinancing. Another pioneer in this sector is Akhtar Hameed Khan.

Microfinance Standards and Principles

A group of Indian women have assembled to make bamboo products that they intend to resell.

Poor people borrow from informal moneylenders and save with informal collectors. They receive loans and grants from charities. They buy insurance from state-owned companies. They receive funds transfers through formal or informal remittance networks. It is not easy to distinguish microfinance from similar activities. It could be claimed that a government that orders state banks to open deposit accounts for poor consumers, or a moneylender that engages in usury, or a charity that runs a heifer pool are engaged in microfinance. Ensuring financial services to poor people is best done by expanding the number of financial institutions available to them, as well as by strengthening the capacity of those institutions. In recent years there has also been increasing emphasis on expanding the diversity of institutions, since different institutions serve different needs.

Some principles that summarize a century and a half of development practice were encapsulated in 2004 by CGAP and endorsed by the Group of Eight leaders at the G8 Summit on June 10, 2004:

1. Poor people need not just loans but also savings, insurance and money transfer services.
2. Microfinance must be useful to poor households: helping them raise income, build up assets and/or cushion themselves against external shocks.
3. "Microfinance can pay for itself." Subsidies from donors and government are scarce and uncertain and so, to reach large numbers of poor people, microfinance must pay for itself.
4. Microfinance means building permanent local institutions.
5. Microfinance also means integrating the financial needs of poor people into a country's mainstream financial system.
6. "The job of government is to enable financial services, not to provide them."
7. "Donor funds should complement private capital, not compete with it."
8. "The key bottleneck is the shortage of strong institutions and managers." Donors should focus on capacity building.
9. Interest rate ceilings hurt poor people by preventing microfinance institutions from covering their costs, which chokes off the supply of credit.
10. Microfinance institutions should measure and disclose their performance—both financially and socially.

Microfinance is considered a tool for socio-economic development, and can be clearly distinguished from charity. Families who are destitute, or so poor they are unlikely to be able to generate the cash flow required to repay a loan, should be recipients of charity. Others are best served by financial institutions.

Scale of Microfinance Operations

No systematic effort to map the distribution of microfinance has yet been undertaken. A benchmark was established by an analysis of 'alternative financial institutions' in the developing world in 2004. The authors counted approximately 665 million client accounts at over 3,000 institutions that are serving people who are poorer than those served by the commercial banks. Of these accounts, 120 million were with institutions normally understood to practice microfinance. Reflecting the diverse historical roots of the movement, however, they also included postal savings banks (318 million accounts), state agricultural and development banks (172 million accounts), financial cooperatives and credit unions (35 million accounts) and specialized rural banks (19 million accounts).

Two women talk about financial matters. The woman on the right is a loan officer for the Small Enterprise Foundation (SEF). The conversation shown is taking place in Tzaneen, South Africa in February 2010.

Regionally, the highest concentration of these accounts was in India (188 million accounts representing 18% of the total national population). The lowest concentrations were in Latin America and the Caribbean (14 million accounts representing 3% of the total population) and Africa (27 million accounts representing 4% of the total population, with the highest rate of penetration in West Africa, and the highest growth rate in Eastern and Southern Africa). Considering that most bank clients in the developed world need several active accounts to keep their affairs in order, these figures indicate that the task the microfinance movement has set for itself is still very far from finished.

By type of service, "savings accounts in alternative finance institutions outnumber loans by about four to one. This is a worldwide pattern that does not vary much by region."

An important source of detailed data on selected microfinance institutions is the *MicroBanking Bulletin*, which is published by Microfinance Information Exchange. At the end of 2009, it was tracking 1,084 MFIs that were serving 74 million borrowers ($38 billion in outstanding loans) and 67 million savers ($23 billion in deposits).

Another source of information regarding the environment of microfinance is the Global Microscope on the Microfinance Business Environment, prepared by the Economist Intelligence Unit (EIU), the Inter-American Development Bank, and others. The 2011 report contains information on the environment of microfinance in 55 countries among two categories, Regulatory Framework and the Supporting Institutional Framework. This publication, also known as the Microscope, was first developed in 2007, focusing only on Latin America and the Caribbean, but by 2009, this report had become a global study.

As yet there are no studies that indicate the scale or distribution of 'informal' microfinance organizations like ROSCA's and informal associations that help people manage costs like weddings, funerals and sickness. Numerous case studies have been published, however, indicating that these organizations, which are generally designed and managed by poor people themselves with little outside help, operate in most countries in the developing world.

Help can come in the form of more and better-qualified staff, thus higher education is needed for microfinance institutions. This has begun in some universities, as Oliver Schmidt describes.

Microfinance in the United States and Canada

In Canada and the US, microfinance organizations target marginalized populations unable to access mainstream bank financing. Close to 8% of Americans are unbanked, meaning around 9 million are without any kind of bank account or formal financial services. Most of these institutions are structured as nonprofit organizations. Microloans in the U.S. context is defined as the extension of credit up to $50,000. In Canada, CRA guidelines restrict microfinance loans to a maximum of $25,000. The average microfinance loan size in the US is US$9,732, ten times the size of an average microfinance loan in developing countries (US$973).

Impact

While all microfinance institutions aim at increasing incomes and employment, in developing countries the empowerment of women, improved nutrition and improved education of the borrower's children are frequently aims of microfinance institutions. In the US and Canada, aims of microfinance include the graduation of recipients from welfare programs and an improvement in their credit rating. In the US, microfinance has created jobs directly and indirectly, as 60% of borrowers were able to hire others. According to reports, every domestic microfinance loan creates 2.4 jobs. These entrepreneurs provide wages that are, on average, 25% higher than minimum wage. Small business loans eventually allow small business owners to make their businesses their primary source of income, with 67% of the borrowers showing a significant increase in their income as a result of their participation in certain micro-loan programs. In addition, these business owners are able to improve their housing situation, 70% indicating their housing has improved. Ultimately, many of the small business owners that use social funding are able to graduate from government funding.

United States

In the late 1980s, microfinance institutions developed in the United States. They served low-income and marginalized minority communities. By 2007, there were 500 microfinance organizations operating in the US with 200 lending capital.

There were three key factors that triggered the growth in domestic microfinance:

1. Change in social welfare policies and focus on economic development and job creation at the macro level.
2. Encouragement of employment, including self-employment, as a strategy for improving the lives of the poor.

3. The increase in the proportion of Latin American and Asian immigrants who came from societies where microenterprises are prevalent.

These factors incentivized the public and private supports to have microlending activity in the United States.

Canada

Microfinance in Canada took shape through the development of credit unions. These credit unions provided financial services to the Canadians who could not get access to traditional financial means. Two separate branches of credit unions developed in Canada to serve the financially marginalized segment of the population. Alphonse Desjardins introduced the establishment of savings and credit services in late 1900 to the Quebecois who did not have financial access. Approximately 30 years later Father Moses Coady introduced credit unions to Nova Scotia. These were the models of the modern institutions still present in Canada today.

Efforts to transfer specific microfinance innovations such as solidarity lending from developing countries to Canada have met with little success.

Selected microfinance institutions in Canada are:

- Rise Asset Development

Founded by Sandra Rotman in 2009, Rise is a Rotman and CAMH initiative that provides small business loans, leases, and lines of credit to entrepreneurs with mental health and/or addiction challenges.

- Alterna Savings

Formed in 2005 through the merging of the Civil Service Savings and Loan Society and the Metro Credit Union, Alterna is a financial alternative to Canadians. Their banking policy is based on cooperative values and expert financial advising.

- Access Community Capital Fund

Based in Toronto, Ontario, ACCESS is a Canadian charity that helps entrepreneurs without collateral or credit history find affordable small loans.

- Montreal Community Loan Fund

Created to help eradicate poverty, Montreal Community Loan Fund provides accessible credit and technical support to entrepreneurs with low income or credit for start-ups or expansion of organizations that cannot access traditional forms of credit.

- Momentum

Using the community economic development approach, Momentum offers opportunities to people living in poverty in Calgary. Momentum provides individuals and families who want to better their financial situation take control of finances, become computer literate, secure employment, borrow and repay loans for business, and purchase homes.

- Vancity

Founded in 1946, Vancity is now the largest English speaking credit union in Canada.

Limitations

Complications specific to Canada include the need for loans of a substantial size in comparison to the ones typically seen in many international microfinance initiatives. Microfinance is also limited by the rules and limitations surrounding money-lending. For example, Canada Revenue Agency limits the loans made in these sort of transactions to a maximum of $25,000. As a result, many people look to banks to provide these loans. Also, microfinance in Canada is driven by profit which, as a result, fails to advance the social development of community members. Within marginalized or impoverished Canadian communities, banks may not be readily accessible to deposit or take out funds. These banks which would have charged little or no interest on small amounts of cash are replaced by lending companies. Here, these companies may charge extremely large interest rates to marginalized community members thus increasing the cycle of poverty and profiting off of another's loss (Rutherford, 2009).

In Canada, microfinancing competes with pay-day loans institutions which take advantage of marginalized and low-income individuals by charging extremely high, predatory interest rates. Communities with low social capital often don't have the networks to implement and support microfinance initiatives, leading to the proliferation of pay day loan institutions. Pay day loan companies are unlike traditional microfinance in that they don't encourage collectivism and social capital building in low income communities, however exist solely for profit.

Micro Finance on the Indian Subcontinent

Loans to poor people by banks have many limitations including lack of security and high operating costs. As a result, microfinance was developed as an alternative to provide loans to poor people with the goal of creating financial inclusion and equality.

Muhammad Yunus, a Nobel Prize winner, introduced the concept of Microfinance in Bangladesh in the form of the "Grameen Bank". The National Bank for Agriculture and Rural Development (NABARD) took this idea and started the concept of microfinance in India. Under this mechanism, there exists a link between SHGs (Self-help groups), NGOs and banks. SHGs are formed and nurtured by NGOs and only after accomplishing a certain level of maturity in terms of their internal thrift and credit operations are they entitled to seek credit from the banks. There is an involvement from the concerned

NGO before and even after the SHG-Bank linkage. The SHG-Bank linkage programme, which has been in place since 1992 in India, has provided about 22.4 lakh for SHG finance by 2006. It involves commercial banks, regional rural banks (RRBs) and cooperative banks in its operations.

In 2013, Grameen Capital India was able to loan $144 million to microfinance groups. In addition to Grameen Bank, Equitas has been another microfinance organization in Tamil Nadu. The South and Western states are the ones attracting the greatest number of microfinance loans.

Microfinance is defined as, financial services such as savings accounts, insurance funds and credit provided to poor and low income clients so as to help them increase their income, thereby improving their standard of living.

In this context the main features of microfinance are:

- Loan given without security
- Loans to those people who live below the poverty line
- Members of SHGs may benefit from micro finance
- Maximum limit of loan under micro finance Rs 25,000/-
- Terms and conditions offered to poor people are decided by NGOs
- Microfinance is different from Microcredit- under the latter, small loans are given to the borrower but under microfinance alongside many other financial services including savings accounts and insurance. Therefore, microfinance has a wider concept than microcredit.

In June 2014, CRISIL released its latest report on the Indian Microfinance Sector titled "India's 25 Leading MFI's". This list is the most comprehensive and up to date overview of the microfinance sector in India and the different microfinance institutions operating in the sub-continent.

Many loan officers in India create emotional connection with borrowers before loan reaches maturity by mentioning details about borrowers' personal life and family and also demonstrating affection in many different ways as a strategy to generate pressure during recovery.

Inclusive Financial Systems

The microcredit era that began in the 1970s has lost its momentum, to be replaced by a 'financial systems' approach. While microcredit achieved a great deal, especially in urban and near-urban areas and with entrepreneurial families, its progress in delivering financial services in less densely populated rural areas has been slow.

The new financial systems approach pragmatically acknowledges the richness of centuries of microfinance history and the immense diversity of institutions serving poor people in developing world today. It is also rooted in an increasing awareness of diversity of the financial service needs of the world's poorest people, and the diverse settings in which they live and work.

Brigit Helms in her book 'Access for All: Building Inclusive Financial Systems', distinguishes between four general categories of microfinance providers, and argues for a pro-active strategy of engagement with all of them to help them achieve the goals of the microfinance movement.

Informal financial service providers

> These include moneylenders, pawnbrokers, savings collectors, money-guards, ROSCAs, ASCAs and input supply shops. Because they know each other well and live in the same community, they understand each other's financial circumstances and can offer very flexible, convenient and fast services. These services can also be costly and the choice of financial products limited and very short-term. Informal services that involve savings are also risky; many people lose their money.

Member-owned organizations

> These include self-help groups, credit unions, and a variety of hybrid organizations like 'financial service associations' and CVECAs. Like their informal cousins, they are generally small and local, which means they have access to good knowledge about each other's financial circumstances and can offer convenience and flexibility. Grameen Bank is a member-owned organization. Since they are managed by poor people, their costs of operation are low. However, these providers may have little financial skill and can run into trouble when the economy turns down or their operations become too complex. Unless they are effectively regulated and supervised, they can be 'captured' by one or two influential leaders, and the members can lose their money.

NGOs

> The Microcredit Summit Campaign counted 3,316 of these MFIs and NGOs lending to about 133 million clients by the end of 2006. Led by Grameen Bank and BRAC in Bangladesh, Prodem in Bolivia, Opportunity International, and FINCA International, headquartered in Washington, DC, these NGOs have spread around the developing world in the past three decades; others, like the Gamelan Council, address larger regions. They have proven very innovative, pioneering banking techniques like solidarity lending, village banking and mobile banking that have overcome barriers to serving poor populations. However, with boards that don't necessarily represent either their capital or their customers, their governance structures can be fragile, and they can become overly dependent on external donors.

Formal financial institutions

> In addition to commercial banks, these include state banks, agricultural development banks, savings banks, rural banks and non-bank financial institutions. They are regulated and supervised, offer a wider range of financial services, and control a branch network that can extend across the country and internationally. However, they have proved reluctant to adopt social missions, and due to their high costs of operation, often can't deliver services to poor or remote populations. The increasing use of alternative data in credit scoring, such as trade credit is increasing commercial banks' interest in microfinance.

With appropriate regulation and supervision, each of these institutional types can bring leverage to solving the microfinance problem. For example, efforts are being made to link self-help groups to commercial banks, to network member-owned organizations together to achieve economies of scale and scope, and to support efforts by commercial banks to 'down-scale' by integrating mobile banking and e-payment technologies into their extensive branch networks.

Microcredit and the Web

Due to the unbalanced emphasis on credit at the expense of microsavings, as well as a desire to link Western investors to the sector, peer-to-peer platforms have developed to expand the availability of microcredit through individual lenders in the developed world. New platforms that connect lenders to micro-entrepreneurs are emerging on the Web, for example MYC4, Kiva, Zidisha, myELEN, Opportunity International and the Microloan Foundation. Another Web-based microlender United Prosperity uses a variation on the usual microlending model; with United Prosperity the micro-lender provides a guarantee to a local bank which then lends back double that amount to the micro-entrepreneur. In 2009, the US-based nonprofit Zidisha became the first peer-to-peer microlending platform to link lenders and borrowers directly across international borders without local intermediaries.

The volume channeled through Kiva's peer-to-peer platform is about $100 million as of November 2009 (Kiva facilitates approximately $5M in loans each month). In comparison, the needs for microcredit are estimated about 250 bn USD as of end 2006. Most experts agree that these funds must be sourced locally in countries that are originating microcredit, to reduce transaction costs and exchange rate risks.

There have been problems with disclosure on peer-to-peer sites, with some reporting interest rates of borrowers using the flat rate methodology instead of the familiar banking Annual Percentage Rate. The use of flat rates, which has been outlawed among regulated financial institutions in developed countries, can confuse individual lenders into believing their borrower is paying a lower interest rate than, in fact, they are.

Microfinance and Social Interventions

There are currently a few social interventions that have been combined with micro financing to increase awareness of HIV/AIDS. Such interventions like the "Intervention with Microfinance for AIDS and Gender Equity" (IMAGE) which incorporates microfinancing with "The Sisters-for-Life" program a participatory program that educates on different gender roles, gender-based violence, and HIV/AIDS infections to strengthen the communication skills and leadership of women "The Sisters-for-Life" program has two phases where phase one consists of ten one-hour training programs with a facilitator with phase two consisting of identifying a leader amongst the group, train them further, and allow them to implement an Action Plan to their respective centres.

Microfinance has also been combined with business education and with other packages of health interventions. A project undertaken in Peru by Innovations for Poverty Action found that those borrowers randomly selected to receive financial training as part of their borrowing group meetings had higher profits, although there was not a reduction in "the proportion who reported having problems in their business". Pro Mujer, a non-governmental organisation (NGO) with operations in five Latin American countries, combines microfinance and healthcare. This approach shows, that microfinance can not only help businesses to prosper; it can also foster human development and social security. Pro Mujer uses a "one-stop shop" approach, which means in one building, the clients find financial services, business training, empowerment advice and healthcare services combined.

According to technology analyst David Garrity, Microfinance and Mobile Financial Services (MFS) have provided marginal populations with access to basic financial services, including savings programs and insurance policies.

Impact and Criticism

Most criticisms of microfinance have actually been criticisms of microcredit. Criticism focuses on the impact on poverty, the level of interest rates, high profits, overindebtedness and suicides. Other criticism include the role of foreign donors and working conditions in companies affiliated to microfinance institutions, particularly in Bangladesh.

Impact

The impact of microcredit is a subject of much controversy. Proponents state that it reduces poverty through higher employment and higher incomes. This is expected to lead to improved nutrition and improved education of the borrowers' children. Some argue that microcredit empowers women. In the US and Canada, it is argued that microcredit helps recipients to graduate from welfare programs.

Critics say that microcredit has not increased incomes, but has driven poor households into a debt trap, in some cases even leading to suicide. They add that the money from loans is often used for durable consumer goods or consumption instead of being used for productive investments, that it fails to empower women, and that it has not improved health or education. Moreover, as the access to micro-loans is widespread, borrowers tend to acquire several loans from different companies, making it nearly impossible to pay the debt back. As a result of such tragic events, microfinance institutions in India have agreed on setting an interest rate ceiling of 15 percent. This is important because microfinance loan recipients have a higher level of security in repaying the loans and a lower level of risk in failing to repay them.

The available evidence indicates that in many cases microcredit has facilitated the creation and the growth of businesses. It has often generated self-employment, but it has not necessarily increased incomes after interest payments. In some cases it has driven borrowers into debt traps. There is no evidence that microcredit has empowered women. In short, microcredit has achieved much less than what its proponents said it would achieve, but its negative impacts have not been as drastic as some critics have argued. Microcredit is just one factor influencing the success of small businesses, whose success is influenced to a much larger extent by how much an economy or a particular market grows. For example, local competition in the area of lack of a domestic markets for certain goods can influence how successful small businesses who receive microcredit are.

Mission Drift in Microfinance

Mission drift refers to the phenomena through which the MFIs or the micro finance institutions increasingly try to cater to customers who are better off than their original customers, primarily the poor families. Roy Mersland and R. Øystein Strøm in their research on Mission Drift suggest that this selection bias can come not only through an increase in the average loan size, which allows for financially stronger individuals to get the loans, but also through MFI's particular lending methodology, main market of operation, or even the gender bias as further mission drift measures. And as it may follow, this selective funding would lead to lower risks and lower costs for the firm.

However, economists Beatriz Armendáriz and Ariane Szafarz suggests that this phenomenon is not driven by cost minimization alone. She suggests that it happens because of the interplay between the company's mission, the cost differential between poor and unbanked wealthier clients and region specific characteristics pertaining the heterogeneity of their clientele. But in either way, this problem of selective funding leads to an ethical tradeoff where on one hand there is an economic reason for the company to restrict its loans to only the individuals who qualify the standards, and on the other hand there is an ethical responsibility to help the poor people get out of poverty through the provision of capital.

Role of Foreign Donors

The role of donors has also been questioned. CGAP recently commented that "a large proportion of the money they spend is not effective, either because it gets hung up in unsuccessful and often complicated funding mechanisms (for example, a government apex facility), or it goes to partners that are not held accountable for performance. In some cases, poorly conceived programs have retarded the development of inclusive financial systems by distorting markets and displacing domestic commercial initiatives with cheap or free money."

Working Conditions in Enterprises Affiliated to MFIs

There has also been criticism of microlenders for not taking more responsibility for the working conditions of poor households, particularly when borrowers become quasi-wage labourers, selling crafts or agricultural produce through an organization controlled by the MFI. The desire of MFIs to help their borrower diversify and increase their incomes has sparked this type of relationship in several countries, most notably Bangladesh, where hundreds of thousands of borrowers effectively work as wage labourers for the marketing subsidiaries of Grameen Bank or BRAC. Critics maintain that there are few if any rules or standards in these cases governing working hours, holidays, working conditions, safety or child labour, and few inspection regimes to correct abuses. Some of these concerns have been taken up by unions and socially responsible investment advocates.

Abuse

In Nigeria cases of fraud have been reported. Dubious banks promised their clients outrageous interest rates. These banks were closed shortly after clients had deposited money and their deposits were lost. The officials of Nigeria Deposit Insurance Corporation (NDIC) have warned customers about so-called "wonder banks". One initiative to prevent people from depositing money to wonder banks is the mini-series "e go better" that warns about the practices of these wonder banks.

Mr. Mohammud Yunus is credited with micro finance movement in Bangladesh. Micro finance aims at developing banking habits among poor sections of the economy and to extend bank credit to sections that are traditionally neglected as un-bankable.

Micro finance schemes provide small loans without collateral. It encourages small savings deposits from the borrowers. Micro credit is often associated with a group of borrowers such as self help groups. Micro finance also aims at empowering women to achieve self reliance.

The special features of micro finance include (1) supply leading finance principle which means it is the supplier of money who takes initiative to identify the borrower for lending purposes. (2) Imperfect information paradigm which implies that the borrowers are neglected weaker sections of the society whose level of education and awareness are low. (3) Informal credit markets wherein sanctioning of loans is not based on traditional prudential norms but on the basis of borrower welfare. (4) Encouraging savings of the poor is another fundamental micro finance initiative.

Micro finance concept has been extended to adapt to changing needs in changing economies. Micro finance has been extended by commercial banks adopting group lending methods. Loans are sanctioned to a group of borrowers who register themselves as a group for borrowing purposes. The borrowers are of similar economic status and they may use the credit both for personal use as well as an economic or business activity. No collaterals are insisted while sanctioning loans.

Microcredit

Microcredit is the extension of very small loans (microloans) to impoverished borrowers who typically lack collateral, steady employment and a verifiable credit history. It is designed not only to support entrepreneurship and alleviate poverty, but also in many cases to empower women and uplift entire communities by extension. In many communities, women lack the highly stable employment histories that traditional lenders tend to require. Many are illiterate, and therefore unable to complete paperwork required to get conventional loans. As of 2009 an estimated 74 million people held microloans that totalled US$38 billion. Grameen Bank reports that repayment success rates are between 95 and 98 percent.

Microcredit is part of microfinance, which provides a wider range of financial services, especially savings accounts, to the poor. Modern microcredit is generally considered to have originated with the Grameen Bank founded in Bangladesh in 1983. Many traditional banks subsequently introduced microcredit despite initial misgivings. The United Nations declared 2005 the International Year of Microcredit. As of 2012, microcredit is widely used in developing countries and is presented as having "enormous potential as a tool for poverty alleviation."

Critics argue, however, that microcredit has not had a positive impact on gender relationships, does not alleviate poverty, has led many borrowers into a debt trap and constitutes a "privatization of welfare". The first randomized evaluation of microcredit, conducted by Esther Duflo and others, showed mixed results: there was no effect on household expenditure, gender equity, education or health, but the number of new businesses increased by one third compared to a control group.

History

Early Beginnings

Ideas relating to microcredit can be found at various times in modern history, such as the Starr-Bowkett Society. Jonathan Swift inspired the Irish Loan Funds of the 18th and 19th centuries. In the mid-19th century, Individualist anarchist Lysander Spooner wrote about the benefits of numerous small loans for entrepreneurial activities to the poor as a way to alleviate poverty. At about the same time, but independently to Spooner, Friedrich Wilhelm Raiffeisen founded the first cooperative lending banks to support farmers in rural Germany. In the 1950s, Akhtar Hameed Khan began distributing group-oriented credit in East Pakistan. Khan used the Comilla Model, in which credit is distributed through community-based initiatives. The project failed due to the over-involvement of the Pakistani government, and the hierarchies created within communities as certain members began to exert more control over loans than others.

Modern Microcredit

Nobel laureate Muhammad Yunus, the founder of Grameen Bank, which is generally considered the first modern microcredit institution.

The origins of microcredit in its current practical incarnation can be linked to several organizations founded in Bangladesh, especially the Grameen Bank. The Grameen Bank, which is generally considered the first modern microcredit institution, was founded in 1983 by Muhammad Yunus. Yunus began the project in a small town called Jobra, using his own money to deliver small loans at low-interest rates to the rural poor. Grameen Bank was followed by organizations such as BRAC in 1972 and ASA in 1978. Microcredit reached Latin America with the establishment of PRODEM in Bolivia in 1986; a bank that later transformed into the for-profit BancoSol. Microcredit quickly became a popular tool for economic development, with hundreds of institutions emerging throughout the third world. Though the Grameen Bank was formed initially as a non-profit organization dependent upon government subsidies, it later became a corporate entity and was renamed Grameen II in 2002. Muhammad Yunus was awarded the Nobel Peace Prize in 2006 for his work providing microcredit services to the poor.

Principles

Economic Principles

Microcredit organizations were initially created as alternatives to the "loan-sharks" known to take advantage of clients. Indeed, many microlenders began as non-profit organizations and operated with government funds or private subsidies. By the 1980s, however the "financial systems approach," influenced by neoliberalism and propagated by the Harvard Institute for International Development, became the dominant ideology among microcredit organizations. The commercialization of microcredit officially began in 1984 with the formation of Unit Desa (BRI-UD) within the Bank Rakyat Indonesia. Unit Desa offered 'kupedes' microloans based on market interest rates.

Many microcredit organizations now function as independent banks. This has led to their charging higher interest rates on loans and placing more emphasis on savings programs. Notably, Unit Desa has charged in excess of 20 per cent on small business loans. The application of neoliberal economics to microcredit has generated much debate among scholars and development practitioners, with some claiming that microcredit bank directors, such as Muhammad Yunus, apply the practices of loan sharks for their personal enrichment. Indeed, the academic debate foreshadowed a Wall-street style scandal involving the Mexican microcredit organization Compartamos.

Even so, the numbers indicate that ethical microlending and investor profit can go hand-in-hand. In the 1990s a rural finance minister in Indonesia showed how Unit Desa could lower its rates by about 8% while still bringing attractive returns to investors.

Group Lending

Though lending to groups has long been a key part of microcredit, microcredit initially began with the principle of lending to individuals. Despite the use of solidarity circles in 1970s Jobra, Grameen Bank and other early microcredit institutions initially focused on individual lending. (A solidarity circle is a group of borrowers that provide mutual encouragement, information, and assistance in times of need, though loans remain the responsibility of individuals.) Indeed, Muhammad Yunus propagated the notion that every person has the potential to become an entrepreneur. The use of group-lending was motivated by economics of scale, as the costs associated with monitoring loans and enforcing repayment are significantly lower when credit is distributed to groups rather than individuals. Many times the loan to one participant in group-lending depends upon the successful repayment from another member, thus transferring repayment responsibility off of microcredit institutions to loan recipients.

Lending to Women

Lending to women has become an important principle in microcredit, with banks and NGOs such as BancoSol, WWB, and Pro Mujer catering to women exclusively. Pro Mujer also implemented a new strategy to combine microcredits with health-care services, since the health of their clients is crucial to the success of microcredits. Though Grameen Bank initially tried to lend to both men and women at equal rates, women presently make up ninety-five percent of the bank's clients. Women continue to make up seventy-five percent of all microcredit recipients worldwide. Exclusive lending to women began in the 1980s when Grameen Bank found that women have higher repayment rates, and tend to accept smaller loans than men.

Examples

Bangladesh

Mumbai Headquarters of the National Bank for Agriculture and Rural Development of India, which on-lends funds to banks providing microcredit.

Grameen Bank in Bangladesh is the oldest and probably best-known microfinance institution in the world. Grameen Bank launched their US operations in New York in April 2008. Bank of America has announced plans to award more than $3.7 million in grants to nonprofits to use in backing microloan programs. The Accion U.S. Network, the US subsidiary of the better-known Accion International, has provided over $450 million in microloans since 1991, with an over 90% repayment rate. One research study of the Grameen model shows that poorer individuals are safer borrowers because they place more value on the relationship with the bank. Even so, efforts to replicate Grameen-style solidarity lending in developed countries have generally not succeeded. For example, the Calmeadow Foundation tested an analogous peer-lending model in three locations in Canada during the 1990s. It concluded that a variety of factors — including difficulties in reaching the target market, the high risk profile of clients, their general distaste for the joint liability requirement, and high overhead costs — made solidarity lending unviable without subsidies. Microcredits have also been introduced in Israel, Russia, Ukraine and other nations where micro-loans help small business entrepreneurs overcome cultural barriers in the mainstream business society. The Israel Free Loan Association (IFLA) has lent more than $100 million in the past two decades to Israeli citizens of all backgrounds.

India

In India, the National Bank for Agriculture and Rural Development (NABARD) finances more than 500 banks that on-lend funds to self-help groups (SHGs). SHGs comprise twenty or fewer members, of whom the majority are women from the poorest castes and tribes. Members save small amounts of money, as little as a few rupees a month in a group fund. Members may borrow from the group fund for a variety of purposes ranging from household emergencies to school fees. As SHGs prove capable of managing their funds well, they may borrow from a local bank to invest in small business or farm activities. Banks typically lend up to four rupees for every rupee in the group fund. In Asia borrowers generally pay interest rates that range from 30% to 70% without commission and fees. Nearly 1.4 million SHGs comprising approximately 20 million women now borrow from banks, which makes the Indian SHG-Bank Linkage model the largest microfinance program in the world. Similar programs are evolving in Africa and Southeast Asia with the assistance of organizations like IFAD, Opportunity International, Catholic Relief Services, Compassion International, CARE, APMAS, Oxfam, Tearfund and World Vision.

Venezuela

In Venezuela, businessman Victor Vargas, owner of Banco Occidental de Descuento (BOD), established a microcredit program tied with entrepreneurship education. Vargas and BOD set up a network of entrepreneur schools throughout Venezuela. Aspiring entrepreneurs attend a three-month program. If they graduate, they are given a line of credit in the form of a micro-loan from Vargas's BOD. In 2015 alone, 20,000 Venezuelans graduated from the program and received microcredit opportunities.

Peer-to-peer Lending over the Web

The principles of microcredit have also been applied in attempting to address several non-poverty-related issues. Among these, multiple Internet-based organizations have developed platforms that facilitate a modified form of peer-to-peer lending where a loan is not made in the form of a single, direct loan, but as the aggregation of a number of smaller loans—often at a negligible interest rate.

Examples of platforms that connect lenders to micro-entrepreneurs via Internet are Kiva, Zidisha, and the Microloan Foundation. Another WWW-based microlender, United Prosperity, uses a variation on the usual microlending model; with United Prosperity the micro-lender provides a guarantee to a local bank which then lends back double that amount to the micro-entrepreneur. United Prosperity claims this provides both greater leverage and allows the micro-entrepreneur to develop a credit history with their local bank for future loans. In 2009, the US-based nonprofit Zidisha became the first peer-to-peer microlending platform to link lenders and borrowers directly across international borders without local intermediaries. Vittana allows peer-to-peer lending for student loans in developing countries.

Impact of Microcredit

The impact of microcredit is a subject of much controversy. Proponents state that it reduces poverty through higher employment and higher incomes. This is expected to lead to improved nutrition and improved education of the borrowers' children. Some argue that microcredit empowers women. In the US, UK and Canada, it is argued that microcredit helps recipients to graduate from welfare programs.

Critics say that microcredit has not increased incomes, but has driven poor households into a debt trap, in some cases even leading to suicide. They add that the money from loans is often used for durable consumer goods or consumption instead of being used for productive investments, that it fails to empower women, and that it has not improved health or education.

The available evidence indicates that in many cases microcredit has facilitated the creation and the growth of businesses. It has often generated self-employment, but it has not necessarily increased incomes after interest payments. In some cases it has driven borrowers into debt traps. There is no evidence that microcredit has empowered women. In short, microcredit has achieved much less than what its proponents said it would achieve, but its negative impacts have not been as drastic as some critics have argued. Microcredit is just one factor influencing the success of a small businesses, whose success is influenced to a much larger extent by how much an economy or a particular market grows.

Improvement

Many microfinance institutions also offer savings facilities, such as Banco Palma in Brazil shown here.

Many scholars and practitioners suggest an integrated package of services ('a credit-plus' approach) rather than just providing credits. When access to credit is combined with savings facilities, non-productive loan facilities, insurance, enterprise development (production-oriented and management training, marketing support) and welfare-related services (literacy and health services, gender and social awareness training), the adverse effects discussed above can be diminished. Some argue that more experienced entrepreneurs who are getting loans should be qualified for bigger loans to ensure the success of the program.

One of the principal challenges of microcredit is providing small loans at an affordable cost. The global average interest and fee rate is estimated at 37%, with rates reaching as high as 70% in some markets. The reason for the high interest rates is not primarily cost of capital. Indeed, the local microfinance organizations that receive zero-interest loan capital from the online microlending platform Kiva charge average interest and fee rates of 35.21%. Rather, the principal reason for the high cost of microcredit loans is the high transaction cost of traditional microfinance operations relative to loan size. Microcredit practitioners have long argued that such high interest rates are simply unavoidable. The result is that the traditional approach to microcredit has made only limited progress in resolving the problem it purports to address: that the world's poorest people pay the world's highest cost for small business growth capital. The high costs of traditional microcredit loans limit their effectiveness as a poverty-fighting tool. Borrowers who do not manage to earn a rate of return at least equal to the interest rate may actually end up poorer as a result of accepting the loans. According to a recent survey of microfinance borrowers in Ghana published by the Center for Financial Inclusion, more than one-third of borrowers surveyed reported struggling to repay their loans. In recent years, microcredit providers have shifted their focus from the objective of increasing the volume of lending capital available, to address the challenge of providing microfinance loans more affordably. Analyst David Roodman contends that in mature markets, the average interest and fee rates charged by microfinance institutions tend to fall over time.

Professor Dean Karlan from Yale University advocates also giving the poor access to savings accounts.

Credit Analysis

Credit analysis is the method by which one calculates the creditworthiness of a business or organization. In other words, It is the evaluation of the ability of a company to honor its financial obligations. The audited financial statements of a large company might be analyzed when it issues or has issued bonds. Or, a bank may analyze the financial statements of a small business before making or renewing a commercial loan. The term refers to either case, whether the business is large or small.

The objective of credit analysis is to look at both the borrower and the lending facility being proposed and to assign a risk rating. The risk rating is derived by estimating the probability of default by the borrower at a given confidence level over the life of the facility, and by estimating the amount of loss that the lender would suffer in the event of default.

Credit analysis involves a wide variety of financial analysis techniques, including ratio and trend analysis as well as the creation of projections and a detailed analysis of cash flows. Credit analysis also includes an examination of collateral and other sources of repayment as well as credit history and management ability. Analysts attempt to predict the probability that a borrower will default on its debts, and also the severity of losses in the event of default. Credit spreads—the difference in interest rates between theoretically "risk-free" investments such as U.S. treasuries or LIBOR and investments that carry some risk of default—reflect credit analysis by financial market participants.

Before approving a commercial loan, a bank will look at all of these factors with the primary emphasis being the cash flow of the borrower. A typical measurement of repayment ability is the debt service coverage ratio. A credit analyst at a bank will measure the cash generated by a business (before interest expense and excluding depreciation and any other non-cash or extraordinary expenses). The debt service coverage ratio divides this cash flow amount by the debt service (both principal and interest payments on all loans) that will be required to be met. Commercial bankers like to see debt service coverage of at least 120 percent. In other words, the debt service coverage ratio should be 1.2 or higher to show that an extra cushion exists and that the business can afford its debt requirements.

Classic Credit Analysis

Traditionally most banks have relied on subjective judgment to assess the credit risk of a corporate borrower. Essentially, bankers used information on various borrower characteristics – such as character (reputation), capital (leverage), capacity (volatility of earnings), conditions (purpose of the loan), and collateral – in deciding whether or not to make a given loan. These characteristics are commonly referred to as the 5 Cs. Developing this type of expert system is time-consuming and expensive. That is why, from time to time, banks have tried to clone their decision-making process. Even so, in the granting of credit to corporate customers, many banks continue to rely primarily on their traditional expert system for evaluating potential borrowers.

Credit Scoring Systems

In recent decades, a number of objective, quantitative systems for scoring credits have been developed. In univariate (one variable) accounting-based credit-scoring systems, the credit analyst compares various key accounting ratios of potential borrowers with industry or group norms and trends in these variables.

Today, Standard & Poor's, Moody's, and Risk Management Association can all provide banks with industry ratios. The univariate approach enables an analyst starting an inquiry to determine whether a particular ratio for a potential borrower differs markedly from the norm for its industry. In reality, however, the unsatisfactory level of one ratio is frequently mitigated by the strength of some other measure. A firm, for example, may have a poor profitability ratio but an above-average liquidity ratio. One limitation of the univariate approach is the difficulty of making trade-offs between such weak and strong ratios. Of course, a good credit analyst can make these adjustments. However, some univariate measures – such as the specific industry group, public versus private company, and region – are categorical rather than ratio-level values. It is more difficult to make judgments about variables of this type.

Although univariate models are still in use today in many banks, most academics and an increasing number of practitioners seem to disapprove of ratio analysis as a means of assessing the performance of a business enterprise. Many respected theorists downgrade the arbitrary rules of thumb (such as company ratio comparisons) that are widely used by practitioners and favor instead the application of more rigorous statistical techniques.

Education and Training

Typical education credentials often require a bachelor's degree in business, statistics, accounting (to include an emphasis in finance or economics). An MBA is not required however is increasingly being held or pursued by analysts, often to become more competitive for advancement opportunities. Commercial bankers also undergo intense credit training provided by their bank or a third-party company.

Credit Evaluation

Credit evaluation begins with submission of loan proposal by the borrower. Banks follow a comprehensive approach for credit evaluation. First the project for which loan is sought will be evaluated in terms of capital adequacy, projected cash flows, current performance, past performance of the borrower in terms of repayments and adherence to banking procedures.

Besides these banks follow an internal credit rating system based on predetermined criteria or they may depend on external credit rating offered by reputed credit rating agencies. After assessing the project, the next issue will be evaluation of securities offered as collateral for the loan.

Next in the assessment will be the history of the borrower, the present management and its competence and other qualitative parameters obtained through reports from various sources such as other banks having business relationship with the borrower, suppliers of the borrower and other credit information agencies.

Once a loan decision has been made, the bank staff will have to monitor and take up necessary follow up action. Banks insist on receiving periodical reports from the borrower and also conduct field visits to the premises of the borrower to ascertain the progress and utilization of loan amount.

Banks usually compute certain key ratios and analyze the cash flow position of the borrower besides proper valuation of securities for accessing the credit worthiness of the proposal.

Reserve Bank of India has provided guidelines for loan appraisal and evaluation and insists on adoption of "Know Your Customer Norms" (KYC) from the borrowers.

Some of the hindrances in proper credit evaluation in banks include the administrative procedures, competence of the staff and non integration of credit sanction and follow up procedures. Non adherence to prudential norms suggested by RBI is another deterrent in the credit evaluation process.

Hindrances in Credit Evaluation

Focus on asset based lending than cash flow based lending
Industry specific evaluation tools not being used.
RBI guidelines on committee approval for credit sanction not being followed fully since the
committee members do not beet frequently as and when required
Additional evaluations required in case of sensitive sectors such as funding of capital market securities or real estate proposals or commodity markets.

Computation of Credit Risk

Credit risk is inherent in the bank lending process. Therefore banks have to meticulously plan, understand and apply risk measures. All personnel and departments involved in credit management must have a thorough understanding of credit risk. Banks follow systematic methods of risk computation and apply them for loan decisions. They develop and organize credit information for this purpose.

The internal rating system followed by banks requires both financial as well as qualitative information on the project and the borrower. Certain key ratios and cash flow projections are the basis for the quantitative measurement of risk. The risk measures computed by banks could be a one-time measure for a borrower or a measure that is monitored throughout the loan servicing period.

These methods are known as point-in-time measure and life-cycle measure. Any method or model adopted by the bank needs to be evaluated as to its reliability. Usually past borrower data will be used to examine the reliability of models developed for credit risk analysis.

By constant review and updating of the error probability of these models that banks will be able to reduce risk substantially and make them desirable for application. Besides internal rating system banks also depend on information provided by rating agencies. Based on credit analysis the loan proposals will be rated and graded. These ratings and grades may undergo change on account of new developments or changes affecting the business of the borrower.

Accordingly the probability of default and the probability of loss will have to be kept flexible and needs review periodically.

Type of factor	Examples
Size of operation	Amount of capital and net assets
Safety	Current ratio, capital adequacy ratio, and current account balance ratio
Profitability	Return on assets, operating profits, years required to pay back interest-bearing liabilities, and interest coverage ratio
Others	Rate of growth in sales and profits

Type of factor	Examples
Industry	Growth potential size of market fluctuations, and entry barriers
Firm	Ownership relations with parent companies or affiliate firms, the management's ability, and existence of an external audit system

Type of Factor	Real Estate Finance	Project Finance
Quantitative	Credit extension period, loan to value (LTV), and debt service coverage ratio (DSCR)	Credit extension period and DSCR
Qualitative	Characteristics of real estate, e.g., locations and other conditions, adequacy of cash flow schedule, and risks attached to sponsors of the project	Risk attached to the project, e.g., risks attached to sponsors and operators of the project, the risk of eing unable to complete the project, and transfer risk

Credit risk measurement involves computation of probability of default, loss given default and exposure at default. The evaluation process identifies expected and unexpected loss from credit risk. While expected loss is easily measurable through the credit risk models, unexpected losses are difficult since the frequency of occurrence of such events is less. Several other measures besides credit modeling such as Monte Carlo simulation have to be applied by the banks to estimate the unexpected loss.

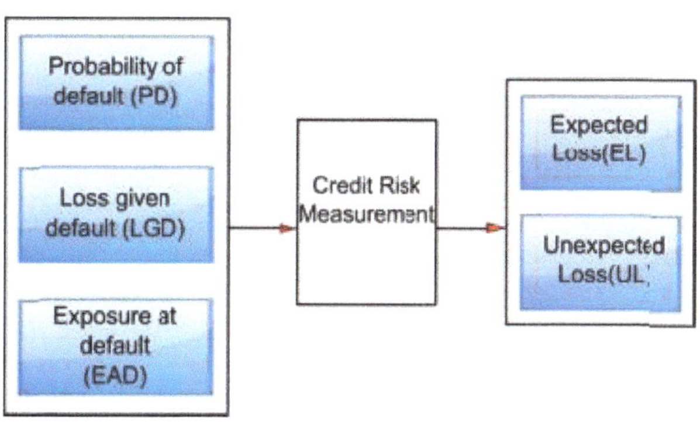

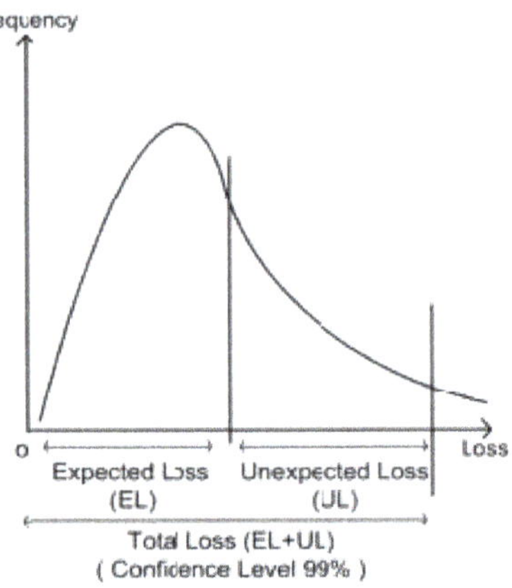

Credit Risk Management

For effective credit risk management, banks have to establish an integrated credit risk management system. In this executives at Board level as well as bank staffs dealing in credit risk at branch level are to be involved. Proper procedures, documentation, methods of appraisal and credit audit are to be incorporated in the system.

Credit risk involves probability of loss of loan sanctioned. This loss comprises non-payment of interest or principle, counter party obligations not met, settlement claims not met, default on account of restrictions imposed, foreign exchange remittances and inability of the borrower to meet contingent expenditures.

Credit risk is affected by bank specific internal factors or external factors such as changes in the economy. Internal risk factors can be managed by adopting a systematic credit risk management policy and procedure. Managing external factors involves diversification of credit among different industry groups and different borrowers.

Prudential norms for credit risk management calls for a comprehensive policy framework laying down strategies, organizational structure, system support, credit risk rating framework, credit risk limits, credit risk modeling, credit risk pricing, risk mitigation, low review mechanism and credit audit.

Banks have several choices regarding the model for credit risk computation. Certain popular models in use are Altman's model, credit metrics model, value at risk model and KMV model. Depending on the suitability and the requirements of banks a model can be chosen and adopted for credit risk measurement.

The main aim of credit risk management is not only quantifying risk but also reducing exposure of credit risk by adopting safety measures through collateral securities, guarantees, credit derivatives and balance sheet netting.

RBI guidelines on credit exposure and management call for adoption of prudential norms. This specifies both quantitative and qualitative restrictions on loan sanctions.

Risk-based Pricing

Risk-based pricing is a methodology adopted by many lenders in the mortgage and financial services industries. It has been in use for many years as lenders try to measure loan risk in terms of interest rates and other fees. The interest rate on a loan is determined not only by the time value of money, but also by the lender's estimate of the probability that the borrower will default on the loan. A borrower who the lender thinks is less likely to default will be offered a better (lower) interest rate. This means that different borrowers will pay different rates. In theory, borrowers who are safer—or who are engaged in safer activities—should be more likely to borrow and resources should therefore be allocated more efficiently.

The lender may consider a variety of factors in assessing the probability of default. These factors might be characteristics of the individual borrower, like the borrower's credit score or employment status. These factors might also be characteristics of the loan; for example, a mortgage lender might offer different rates to the same borrower, depending on whether that borrower wished to buy a single-family house or a condominium.

Concerns have been raised about the extent to which risk-based pricing increases borrowing costs for the poor, who are generally more likely to default, and thereby further increases their likelihood of default. Some supporters of risk-based pricing have argued that, at least in certain contexts, default prediction should be limited by ethical considerations and focus on factors that are under borrowers' control. Supporters also argue that risk-based pricing expands access to credit for high-risk borrowers (who are often lower-income), by allowing lenders to price this increased risk into the loan.

Risk Factors

Credit score and history, property use, property type, loan amount, loan purpose, income, and asset amounts, as well as documentation levels, property location, and others, are common risk based factors currently used. Lenders 'price' loans according to these individual factors and their multiple derivatives. Each derivative either positively or negatively affects the cost of an interest rate. For example, lower credit scores equal higher interest rates and vice versa; typically, those who provide less verifiable income documentation due to self-employment benefits will qualify for a higher interest rate than someone who fully documents all reported income. Mortgage and other financial service industries value credit score and history most when pricing mortgage interest rates.

Property Types

Pertaining to residential mortgages and their risk based pricing methods, the *Property Type* is sub-categorized as follows:

- Single Family Residence (SFR)
- Multi-Family 2-4 Units (MF)
- Townhome/Condominium (TC)

SFRs are considered to have the highest dollar value per square foot and are thus the most favorably priced of the property types in the eyes of the lending institution. The property is stand alone, or 'detached' from other property.

Multi-family and townhome/condominiums are typically 'negatively priced', where the lender will assess a .5% to .75% increase in the actual interest rate or the price of an interest rate, due to their relative lower dollar per square foot values.

Criticism

The main criticism among mainstream consumers has been that risk-based pricing can make 'shopping' for the best interest rates much more difficult. It is almost impossible to tell at first glance if one can be qualified to get an advertised rate or exactly what interest rate they qualify for at all. Consumer-rights advocates also believe that risk-based pricing in the extreme, especially in the form of predatory lending, hurts financially disadvantaged and vulnerable consumers by cutting them off from reasonably affordable capital and exposing them unwittingly to soaring interest rates and unsustainable financing schemes that erode equity and may lead to default. Risk-based pricing can be manipulated to wield deceptive marketing practices, such as the bait and switch. The fairness of similar lending practices within the mortgage industry is being investigated by the United States Congress. Some supporters of risk based pricing have suggested that it should be accompanied by heightened disclosure and transparency requirements and standardization of loan terms to facilitate comparison shopping and ameliorate these problems.

Credit Default Swap

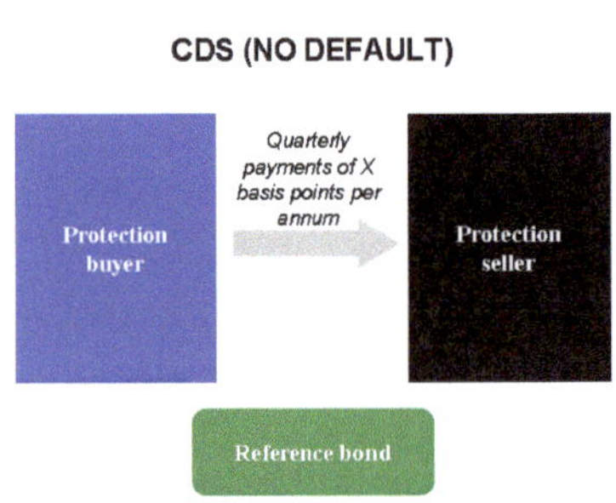

If the reference bond performs without default, the protection buyer pays quarterly payments to the seller until maturity

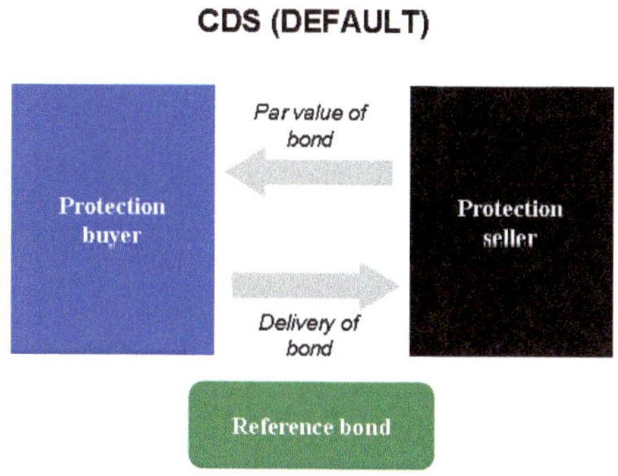

If the reference bond defaults, the protection seller pays par value of the bond to the buyer, and the buyer transfers ownership of the bond to the seller

A credit default swap (CDS) is a financial swap agreement that the seller of the CDS will compensate the buyer (usually the creditor of the reference loan) in the event of a loan default (by the debtor) or other credit event. That is, the seller of the CDS insures the buyer against some reference loan defaulting. The buyer of the CDS makes a series of payments (the CDS "fee" or "spread") to the seller and, in exchange, receives a payoff if the loan defaults. It was invented by Blythe Masters from JP Morgan in 1994.

In the event of default the buyer of the CDS receives compensation (usually the face value of the loan), and the seller of the CDS takes possession of the defaulted loan. However, anyone can purchase a CDS, even buyers who do not hold the loan instrument and who have no direct insurable interest in the loan (these are called "naked" CDSs). If there are more CDS contracts outstanding than bonds in existence, a protocol exists to hold a credit event auction; the payment received is usually substantially less than the face value of the loan.

Credit default swaps have existed since 1994, and increased in use in the early 2000s. By the end of 2007, the outstanding CDS amount was $62.2 trillion, falling to $26.3 trillion by mid-year 2010 and reportedly $25.5 trillion in early 2012. CDSs are not traded on an exchange and there is no required reporting of transactions to a government agency. During the 2007–2010 financial crisis the lack of transparency in this large market became a concern to regulators as it could pose a systemic risk. In March 2010, the Depository Trust & Clearing Corporation announced it would give regulators greater access to its credit default swaps database.

CDS data can be used by financial professionals, regulators, and the media to monitor how the market views credit risk of any entity on which a CDS is available, which can be compared to that provided by the Credit Rating Agencies. U.S. Courts may soon be following suit.

Most CDSs are documented using standard forms drafted by the International Swaps and Derivatives Association (ISDA), although there are many variants. In addition to the basic, single-name swaps, there are basket default swaps (BDSs), index CDSs, funded CDSs (also called credit-linked notes), as well as loan-only credit default swaps (LCDS). In addition to corporations and governments, the reference entity can include a special purpose vehicle issuing asset-backed securities.

Some claim that derivatives such as CDS are potentially dangerous in that they combine priority in bankruptcy with a lack of transparency. A CDS can be unsecured (without collateral) and be at higher risk for a default.

Description

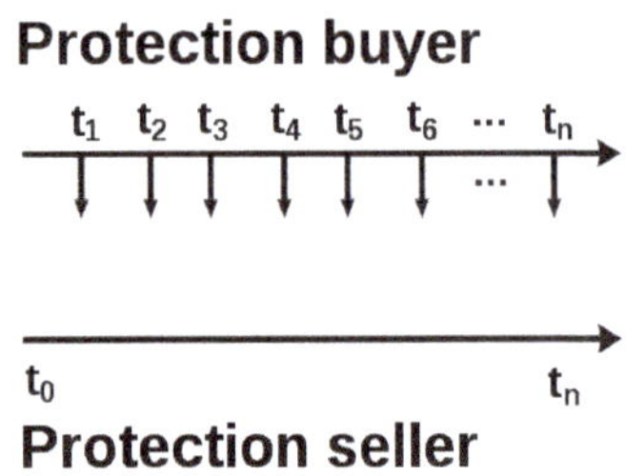

Buyer purchased a CDS at time t_0 and makes regular premium payments at times t_1, t_2, t_3, and t_4. If the associated credit instrument suffers no credit event, then the buyer continues paying premiums at t_5, t_6 and so on until the end of the contract at time t_n.

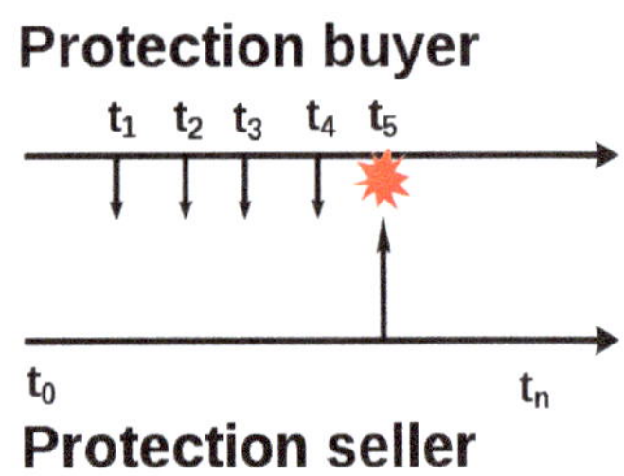

However, if the associated credit instrument suffered a credit event at t_5, then the seller pays the buyer for the loss, and the buyer would cease paying premiums to the seller.

A CDS is linked to a "reference entity" or "reference obligor", usually a corporation or government. The reference entity is not a party to the contract. The buyer makes regular premium payments to the seller, the premium amounts constituting the "spread" charged by the seller to insure against a credit event. If the reference entity defaults, the protection seller pays the buyer the par value of the bond in exchange for physical delivery of the bond, although settlement may also be by cash or auction.

A default is often referred to as a "credit event" and includes such events as failure to pay, restructuring and bankruptcy, or even a drop in the borrower's credit rating. CDS contracts on sovereign obligations also usually include as credit events repudiation, moratorium and acceleration. Most CDSs are in the \$10–\$20 million range with maturities between one and 10 years. Five years is the most typical maturity.

An investor or speculator may "buy protection" to hedge the risk of default on a bond or other debt instrument, regardless of whether such investor or speculator holds an interest in or bears any risk of loss relating to such bond or debt instrument. In this way, a CDS is similar to credit insurance, although CDS are not subject to regulations governing traditional insurance. Also, investors can buy and sell protection without owning debt of the reference entity. These "naked credit default swaps" allow traders to speculate on the creditworthiness of reference entities. CDSs can be used to create synthetic long and short positions in the reference entity. Naked CDS constitute most of the market in CDS. In addition, CDSs can also be used in capital structure arbitrage.

A "credit default swap" (CDS) is a credit derivative contract between two counterparties. The buyer makes periodic payments to the seller, and in return receives a payoff if an underlying financial instrument defaults or experiences a similar credit event. The CDS may refer to a specified loan or bond obligation of a "reference entity", usually a corporation or government.

As an example, imagine that an investor buys a CDS from AAA-Bank, where the reference entity is Risky Corp. The investor—the buyer of protection—will make regular payments to AAA-Bank—the seller of protection. *If* Risky Corp defaults on its debt, the investor receives a one-time payment from AAA-Bank, and the CDS contract is terminated.

If the investor actually owns Risky Corp's debt (i.e., is owed money by Risky Corp), a CDS can act as a hedge. But investors can also buy CDS contracts referencing Risky Corp debt without actually owning any Risky Corp debt. This may be done for speculative purposes, to bet against the solvency of Risky Corp in a gamble to make money, or to hedge investments in other companies whose fortunes are expected to be similar to those of Risky Corp.

If the reference entity (i.e., Risky Corp) defaults, one of two kinds of settlement can occur:

- the investor delivers a defaulted asset to Bank for payment of the par value, which is known as *physical settlement*;
- AAA-Bank pays the investor the difference between the par value and the market price of a specified debt obligation (even if Risky Corp defaults there is usually some *recovery*, i.e., not all the investor's money is lost), which is known as *cash settlement*.

The "spread" of a CDS is the annual amount the protection buyer must pay the protection seller over the length of the contract, expressed as a percentage of the notional amount. For example, if the CDS spread of Risky Corp is 50 basis points, or 0.5% (1 basis point = 0.01%), then an investor buying $10 million worth of protection from AAA-Bank must pay the bank $50,000. Payments are usually made on a quarterly basis, in arrears. These payments continue until either the CDS contract expires or Risky Corp defaults.

All things being equal, at any given time, if the maturity of two credit default swaps is the same, then the CDS associated with a company with a *higher* CDS spread is considered *more likely* to default by the market, since a higher fee is being charged to protect against this happening. However, factors such as liquidity and estimated loss given default can affect the comparison. Credit spread rates and credit ratings of the underlying or reference obligations are considered among money managers to be the best indicators of the likelihood of sellers of CDSs having to perform under these contracts.

Differences From Insurance

CDS contracts have obvious similarities with insurance, because the buyer pays a premium and, in return, receives a sum of money if an adverse event occurs.

However, there are also many differences, the most important being that an insurance contract provides an indemnity against the losses *actually suffered* by the policy holder on an asset in which it holds an insurable interest. By contrast a CDS provides an equal payout to all holders, calculated using an agreed, market-wide method. The holder does not need to own the underlying security and does not even have to suffer a loss from the default event. The CDS can therefore be used to speculate on debt objects.

The other differences include:

- The seller might in principle not be a regulated entity (though in practice most are banks);
- The seller is not required to maintain reserves to cover the protection sold (this was a principal cause of AIG's financial distress in 2008; it had insufficient reserves to meet the "run" of expected payouts caused by the collapse of the housing bubble);
- Insurance requires the buyer to disclose all known risks, while CDSs do not (the CDS seller can in many cases still determine potential risk, as the debt instrument being "insured" is a market commodity available for inspection, but in the case of certain instruments like CDOs made up of "slices" of debt packages, it can be difficult to tell exactly what is being insured);
- Insurers manage risk primarily by setting loss reserves based on the Law of large numbers and actuarial analysis. Dealers in CDSs manage risk primarily by means of hedging with other CDS deals and in the underlying bond markets;
- CDS contracts are generally subject to mark-to-market accounting, introducing income statement and balance sheet volatility while insurance contracts are not;
- Hedge accounting may not be available under US Generally Accepted Accounting Principles (GAAP) unless the requirements of FAS 133 are met. In practice this rarely happens.
- to cancel the insurance contract the buyer can typically stop paying premiums, while for CDS the contract needs to be unwound.

Risk

When entering into a CDS, both the buyer and seller of credit protection take on counterparty risk:

- The buyer takes the risk that the seller may default. If AAA-Bank and Risky Corp. default simultaneously ("double default"), the buyer loses its protection against default by the reference entity. If AAA-Bank defaults but Risky Corp. does not, the buyer might need to replace the defaulted CDS at a higher cost.

- The seller takes the risk that the buyer may default on the contract, depriving the seller of the expected revenue stream. More important, a seller normally limits its risk by buying offsetting protection from another party — that is, it hedges its exposure. If the original buyer drops out, the seller squares its position by either unwinding the hedge transaction or by selling a new CDS to a third party. Depending on market conditions, that may be at a lower price than the original CDS and may therefore involve a loss to the seller.

In the future, in the event that regulatory reforms require that CDS be traded and settled via a central exchange/clearing house, such as ICE TCC, there will no longer be 'counterparty risk', as the risk of the counterparty will be held with the central exchange/clearing house.

As is true with other forms of over-the-counter derivative, CDS might involve liquidity risk. If one or both parties to a CDS contract must post collateral (which is common), there can be margin calls requiring the posting of additional collateral. The required collateral is agreed on by the parties when the CDS is first issued. This margin amount may vary over the life of the CDS contract, if the market price of the CDS contract changes, or the credit rating of one of the parties changes. Many CDS contracts even require payment of an upfront fee (composed of "reset to par" and an "initial coupon.").

Another kind of risk for the seller of credit default swaps is jump risk or jump-to-default risk. A seller of a CDS could be collecting monthly premiums with little expectation that the reference entity may default. A default creates a sudden obligation on the protection sellers to pay millions, if not billions, of dollars to protection buyers. This risk is not present in other over-the-counter derivatives.

Sources of Market Data

Data about the credit default swaps market is available from three main sources. Data on an annual and semiannual basis is available from the International Swaps and Derivatives Association (ISDA) since 2001 and from the Bank for International Settlements (BIS) since 2004. The Depository Trust & Clearing Corporation (DTCC), through its global repository Trade Information Warehouse (TIW), provides weekly data but publicly available information goes back only one year. The numbers provided by each source do not always match because each provider uses different sampling methods. Daily, intraday and real time data is available from S&P Capital IQ through their acquisition of Credit Market Analysis in 2012.

According to DTCC, the Trade Information Warehouse maintains the only "global electronic database for virtually all CDS contracts outstanding in the marketplace."

The Office of the Comptroller of the Currency publishes quarterly credit derivative data about insured U.S commercial banks and trust companies.

Uses

Credit default swaps can be used by investors for speculation, hedging and arbitrage.

Speculation

Credit default swaps allow investors to speculate on changes in CDS spreads of single names or of market indices such as the North American CDX index or the European iTraxx index. An investor might believe that an entity's CDS spreads are too high or too low, relative to the entity's bond yields, and attempt to profit from that view by entering into a trade, known as a basis trade, that combines a CDS with a cash bond and an interest rate swap.

Finally, an investor might speculate on an entity's credit quality, since generally CDS spreads increase as credit-worthiness declines, and decline as credit-worthiness increases. The investor might therefore buy CDS protection on a company to speculate that it is about to default. Alternatively, the investor might sell protection if it thinks that the company's creditworthiness might improve. The investor selling the CDS is viewed as being "long" on the CDS and the credit, as if the investor owned the bond. In contrast, the investor who bought protection is "short" on the CDS and the underlying credit.

Credit default swaps opened up important new avenues to speculators. Investors could go long on a bond without any upfront cost of buying a bond; all the investor need do was promise to pay in the event of default. Shorting a bond faced difficult practical problems, such that shorting was often not feasible; CDS made shorting credit possible and popular. Because the speculator in either case does not own the bond, its position is said to be a synthetic long or short position.

For example, a hedge fund believes that Risky Corp will soon default on its debt. Therefore, it buys $10 million worth of CDS protection for two years from AAA-Bank, with Risky Corp as the reference entity, at a spread of 500 basis points (=5%) per annum.

- If Risky Corp does indeed default after, say, one year, then the hedge fund will have paid $500,000 to AAA-Bank, but then receives $10 million (assuming zero recovery rate, and that AAA-Bank has the liquidity to cover the loss), thereby making a profit. AAA-Bank, and its investors, will incur a $9.5 million loss minus recovery unless the bank has somehow offset the position before the default.

- However, if Risky Corp does not default, then the CDS contract runs for two years, and the hedge fund ends up paying $1 million, without any return, thereby making a loss. AAA-Bank, by selling protection, has made $1 million without any upfront investment.

Note that there is a third possibility in the above scenario; the hedge fund could decide to liquidate its position after a certain period of time in an attempt to realise its gains or losses. For example:

- After 1 year, the market now considers Risky Corp *more likely* to default, so its CDS spread has *widened* from 500 to 1500 basis points. The hedge fund may choose to *sell* $10 million worth of protection for 1 year to AAA-Bank at this higher rate. Therefore, over the two years the hedge fund pays the bank 2 * 5% * $10 million = $1 million, but receives 1 * 15% * $10 million = $1.5 million, giving a total profit of $500,000.

- In another scenario, after one year the market now considers Risky much *less likely* to default, so its CDS spread has *tightened* from 500 to 250 basis points. Again, the hedge fund may choose to *sell* $10 million worth of protection for 1 year to AAA-Bank at this lower spread. Therefore, over the two years the hedge fund pays the bank 2 * 5% * $10 million = $1 million, but receives 1 * 2.5% * $10 million = $250,000, giving a total loss of $750,000. This loss is smaller than the $1 million loss that would have occurred if the second transaction had not been entered into.

Transactions such as these do not even have to be entered into over the long-term. If Risky Corp's CDS spread had widened by just a couple of basis points over the course of one day, the hedge fund could have entered into an offsetting contract immediately and made a small profit over the life of the two CDS contracts.

Credit default swaps are also used to structure synthetic collateralized debt obligations (CDOs). Instead of owning bonds or loans, a synthetic CDO gets credit exposure to a portfolio of fixed income assets without owning those assets through the use of CDS. CDOs are viewed as complex and opaque financial instruments. An example of a synthetic CDO is Abacus 2007-AC1, which is the subject of the civil suit for fraud brought by the SEC against Goldman Sachs in April 2010. Abacus is a synthetic CDO consisting of credit default swaps referencing a variety of mortgage-backed securities.

Naked Credit Default Swaps

In the examples above, the hedge fund did not own any debt of Risky Corp. A CDS in which the buyer does not own the underlying debt is referred to as a *naked credit default swap*, estimated to be up to 80% of the credit default swap market. There is currently a debate in the United States and Europe about whether speculative uses of credit default swaps should be banned. Legislation is under consideration by Congress as part of financial reform.

Critics assert that naked CDSs should be banned, comparing them to buying fire insurance on your neighbor's house, which creates a huge incentive for arson. Analogizing to the concept of insurable interest, critics say you should not be able to buy a CDS—insurance against default—when you do not own the bond. Short selling is also viewed as gambling and the CDS market as a casino. Another concern is the size of the CDS market. Because naked credit default swaps are synthetic, there is no limit to how many can be sold. The gross amount of CDSs far exceeds all "real" corporate bonds and loans outstanding. As a result, the risk of default is magnified leading to concerns about systemic risk.

Financier George Soros called for an outright ban on naked credit default swaps, viewing them as "toxic" and allowing speculators to bet against and "bear raid" companies or countries. His concerns were echoed by several European politicians who, during the Greek Financial Crisis, accused naked CDS buyers of making the crisis worse.

Despite these concerns, Secretary of Treasury Geithner and Commodity Futures Trading Commission Chairman Gensler are not in favor of an outright ban on naked credit default swaps. They prefer greater transparency and better capitalization requirements. These officials think that naked CDSs have a place in the market.

Proponents of naked credit default swaps say that short selling in various forms, whether credit default swaps, options or futures, has the beneficial effect of increasing liquidity in the marketplace. That benefits hedging activities. Without speculators buying and selling naked CDSs, banks wanting to hedge might not find a ready seller of protection. Speculators also create a more competitive marketplace, keeping prices down for hedgers. A robust market in credit default swaps can also serve as a barometer to regulators and investors about the credit health of a company or country.

Despite assertions that speculators are making the Greek crisis worse, Germany's market regulator BaFin found no proof supporting the claim. Some suggest that without credit default swaps, Greece's borrowing costs would be higher. As of November 2011, the Greek bonds have a bond yield of 28%.

A bill in the U.S. Congress proposed giving a public authority the power to limit the use of CDSs other than for hedging purposes, but the bill did not become law.

Hedging

Credit default swaps are often used to manage the risk of default that arises from holding debt. A bank, for example, may hedge its risk that a borrower may default on a loan by entering into a CDS contract as the buyer of protection. If the loan goes into default, the proceeds from the CDS contract cancel out the losses on the underlying debt.

There are other ways to eliminate or reduce the risk of default. The bank could sell (that is, assign) the loan outright or bring in other banks as participants. However, these options may not meet the bank's needs. Consent of the corporate borrower is often required. The bank may not want to incur the time and cost to find loan participants.

If both the borrower and lender are well-known and the market (or even worse, the news media) learns that the bank is selling the loan, then the sale may be viewed as signaling a lack of trust in the borrower, which could severely damage the banker-client relationship. In addition, the bank simply may not want to sell or share the potential profits from the loan. By buying a credit default swap, the bank can lay off default risk while still keeping the loan in its portfolio. The downside to this hedge is that without default risk, a bank may have no motivation to actively monitor the loan and the counterparty has no relationship to the borrower.

Another kind of hedge is against concentration risk. A bank's risk management team may advise that the bank is overly concentrated with a particular borrower or industry. The bank can lay off some of this risk by buying a CDS. Because the borrower—the reference entity—is not a party to a credit default swap, entering into a CDS allows the bank to achieve its diversity objectives without impacting its loan portfolio or customer relations. Similarly, a bank selling a CDS can diversify its portfolio by gaining exposure to an industry in which the selling bank has no customer base.

A bank buying protection can also use a CDS to free regulatory capital. By offloading a particular credit risk, a bank is not required to hold as much capital in reserve against the risk of default (traditionally 8% of the total loan under Basel I). This frees resources the bank can use to make other loans to the same key customer or to other borrowers.

Hedging risk is not limited to banks as lenders. Holders of corporate bonds, such as banks, pension funds or insurance companies, may buy a CDS as a hedge for similar reasons. Pension fund example: A pension fund owns five-year bonds issued by Risky Corp with par value of $10 million. To manage the risk of losing money if Risky Corp defaults on its debt, the pension fund buys a CDS from Derivative Bank in a notional amount of $10 million. The CDS trades at 200 basis points (200 basis points = 2.00 percent). In return for this credit protection, the pension fund pays 2% of $10 million ($200,000) per annum in quarterly installments of $50,000 to Derivative Bank.

- If Risky Corporation does not default on its bond payments, the pension fund makes quarterly payments to Derivative Bank for 5 years and receives its $10 million back after five years from Risky Corp. Though the protection payments totaling $1 million reduce investment returns for the pension fund, its risk of loss due to Risky Corp defaulting on the bond is eliminated.

- If Risky Corporation defaults on its debt three years into the CDS contract, the pension fund would stop paying the quarterly premium, and Derivative Bank would ensure that the pension fund is refunded for its loss of $10 million minus recovery. The pension fund still loses the $600,000 it has paid over three years, but without the CDS contract it would have lost the entire $10 million minus recovery.

In addition to financial institutions, large suppliers can use a credit default swap on a public bond issue or a basket of similar risks as a proxy for its own credit risk exposure on receivables.

Although credit default swaps have been highly criticized for their role in the recent financial crisis, most observers conclude that using credit default swaps as a hedging device has a useful purpose.

Arbitrage

Capital Structure Arbitrage is an example of an arbitrage strategy that uses CDS transactions. This technique relies on the fact that a company's stock price and its CDS spread should exhibit negative correlation; i.e., if the outlook for a company improves then its share price should go up and its CDS spread should tighten, since it is less likely to default on its debt. However, if its outlook worsens then its CDS spread should widen and its stock price should fall.

Techniques reliant on this are known as capital structure arbitrage because they exploit market inefficiencies between different parts of the same company's capital structure; i.e., mis-pricings between a company's debt and equity. An arbitrageur attempts to exploit the *spread* between a company's CDS and its equity in certain situations.

For example, if a company has announced some bad news and its share price has dropped by 25%, but its CDS spread has remained unchanged, then an investor might expect the CDS spread to increase relative to the share price. Therefore, a basic strategy would be to go long on the CDS spread (by buying CDS protection) while simultaneously hedging oneself by buying the underlying stock. This technique would benefit in the event of the CDS spread widening relative to the equity price, but would lose money if the company's CDS spread tightened relative to its equity.

An interesting situation in which the inverse correlation between a company's stock price and CDS spread breaks down is during a Leveraged buyout (LBO). Frequently this leads to the company's CDS spread widening due to the extra debt that will soon be put on the company's books, but also an *increase* in its share price, since buyers of a company usually end up paying a premium.

Another common arbitrage strategy aims to exploit the fact that the swap-adjusted spread of a CDS should trade closely with that of the underlying cash bond issued by the reference entity. Misalignments in spreads may occur due to technical reasons such as:

- Specific settlement differences
- Shortages in a particular underlying instrument
- The cost of funding a position
- Existence of buyers constrained from buying exotic derivatives.

The difference between CDS spreads and asset swap spreads is called the *basis* and should theoretically be close to zero. Basis trades can aim to exploit any differences to make risk-free profit.

History

Conception

Forms of credit default swaps had been in existence from at least the early 1990s, with early trades carried out by Bankers Trust in 1991. J.P. Morgan & Co. is widely credited with creating the modern credit default swap in 1994. In that instance, J.P. Morgan had extended a $4.8 billion credit line to Exxon, which faced the threat of $5 billion in punitive damages for the Exxon Valdez oil spill. A team of J.P. Morgan bankers led by Blythe Masters then sold the credit risk from the credit line to the European Bank of Reconstruction and Development in order to cut the reserves that J.P. Morgan was required to hold against Exxon's default, thus improving its own balance sheet.

In 1997, JPMorgan developed a proprietary product called BISTRO (Broad Index Securitized Trust Offering) that used CDS to clean up a bank's balance sheet. The advantage of BISTRO was that it used securitization to split up the credit risk into little pieces that smaller investors found more digestible, since most investors lacked EBRD's capability to accept $4.8 billion in credit risk all at once. BISTRO was the first example of what later became known as synthetic collateralized debt obligations (CDOs).

Mindful of the concentration of default risk as one of the causes of the S&L crisis, regulators initially found CDS's ability to disperse default risk attractive. In 2000, credit default swaps became largely exempt from regulation by both the U.S. Securities and Exchange Commission (SEC) and the Commodity Futures Trading Commission (CFTC). The Commodity Futures Modernization Act of 2000, which was also responsible for the Enron loophole, specifically stated that CDSs are neither futures nor securities and so are outside the remit of the SEC and CFTC.

Market Growth

At first, banks were the dominant players in the market, as CDS were primarily used to hedge risk in connection with its lending activities. Banks also saw an opportunity to free up regulatory capital. By March 1998, the global market for CDS was estimated at about $300 billion, with JP Morgan alone accounting for about $50 billion of this.

The high market share enjoyed by the banks was soon eroded as more and more asset managers and hedge funds saw trading opportunities in credit default swaps. By 2002, investors as speculators, rather than banks as hedgers, dominated the market. National banks in the USA used credit default swaps as early as 1996. In that year, the Office of the Comptroller of the Currency measured the size of the market as tens of billions of dollars. Six years later, by year-end 2002, the outstanding amount was over $2 trillion.

Although speculators fueled the exponential growth, other factors also played a part. An extended market could not emerge until 1999, when ISDA standardized the documentation for credit default swaps. Also, the 1997 Asian Financial Crisis spurred a market for CDS in emerging market sovereign debt. In addition, in 2004, index trading began on a large scale and grew rapidly.

The market size for Credit Default Swaps more than doubled in size each year from $3.7 trillion in 2003. By the end of 2007, the CDS market had a notional value of $62.2 trillion. But notional amount fell during 2008 as a result of dealer "portfolio compression" efforts (replacing offsetting redundant contracts), and by the end of 2008 notional amount outstanding had fallen 38 percent to $38.6 trillion.

Explosive growth was not without operational headaches. On September 15, 2005, the New York Fed summoned 14 banks to its offices. Billions of dollars of CDS were traded daily but the record keeping was more than two weeks behind. This created severe risk management issues, as counterparties were in legal and financial limbo. U.K. authorities expressed the same concerns.

Market as of 2008

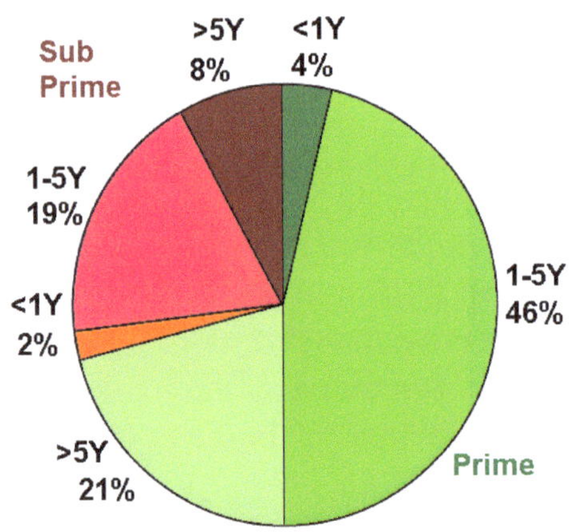

Composition of the United States 15.5 trillion US dollar CDS market at the end of 2008 Q2. Green tints show Prime asset CDSs, reddish tints show sub-prime asset CDSs. Numbers followed by "Y" indicate years until maturity.

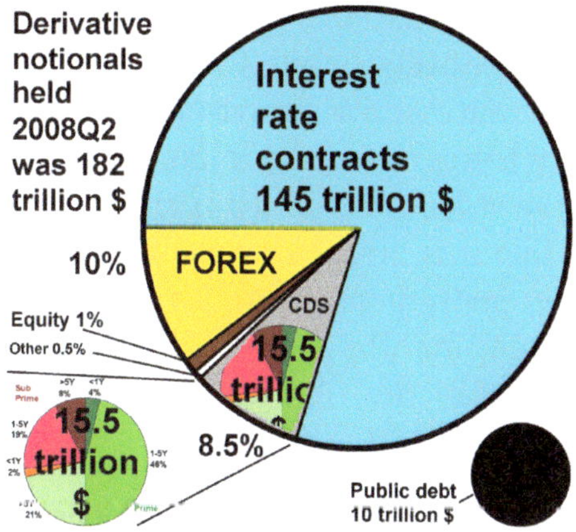

Proportion of CDSs nominals (lower left) held by United States banks compared to all derivatives, in 2008Q2. The black disc represents the 2008 public debt.

Since default is a relatively rare occurrence (historically around 0.2% of investment grade companies default in any one year), in most CDS contracts the only payments are the premium payments from buyer to seller. Thus, although the above figures for outstanding notionals are very large, in the absence of default the net cash flows are only a small fraction of this total: for a 100 bp = 1% spread, the annual cash flows are only 1% of the notional amount.

Regulatory concerns over CDS

The market for Credit Default Swaps attracted considerable concern from regulators after a number of large scale incidents in 2008, starting with the collapse of Bear Stearns.

In the days and weeks leading up to Bear's collapse, the bank's CDS spread widened dramatically, indicating a surge of buyers taking out protection on the bank. It has been suggested that this widening was responsible for the perception that Bear Stearns was vulnerable, and therefore restricted its access to wholesale capital, which eventually led to its forced sale to JP Morgan in March. An alternative view is that this surge in CDS protection buyers was a *symptom* rather than a *cause* of Bear's collapse; i.e., investors saw that Bear was in trouble, and sought to hedge any naked exposure to the bank, or speculate on its collapse.

In September, the bankruptcy of Lehman Brothers caused a total close to $400 billion to become payable to the buyers of CDS protection referenced against the insolvent bank. However the net amount that changed hands was around $7.2 billion. (The given citation does not support either of the two purported facts stated in previous two sentences.). This difference is due to the process of 'netting'. Market participants co-operated so that CDS sellers were allowed to deduct from their payouts the inbound funds due to them from their hedging positions. Dealers generally attempt to remain risk-neutral, so that their losses and gains after big events offset each other.

Also in September American International Group (AIG) required a $85 billion federal loan because it had been excessively selling CDS protection without hedging against the possibility that the reference entities might decline in value, which exposed the insurance giant to potential losses over $100 billion. The CDS on Lehman were settled smoothly, as was largely the case for the other 11 credit events occurring in 2008 that triggered payouts. And while it is arguable that other incidents would have been as bad or worse if less efficient instruments than CDS had been used for speculation and insurance purposes, the closing months of 2008 saw regulators working hard to reduce the risk involved in CDS transactions.

In 2008 there was no centralized exchange or clearing house for CDS transactions; they were all done over the counter (OTC). This led to recent calls for the market to open up in terms of transparency and regulation.

In November 2008 the Depository Trust & Clearing Corporation (DTCC), which runs a warehouse for CDS trade confirmations accounting for around 90% of the total market, announced that it will release market data on the outstanding notional of CDS trades on a weekly basis. The data can be accessed on the DTCC's website here:

By 2010, Intercontinental Exchange, through its subsidiaries, ICE Trust in New York, launched in 2008, and ICE Clear Europe Limited in London, UK, launched in July 2009, clearing entities for credit default swaps (CDS) had cleared more than $10 trillion in credit default swaps (CDS) (Terhune Bloomberg Business Week 2010-07-29). Bloomberg's Terhune (2010) explained how investors seeking high-margin returns use Credit Default Swaps (CDS) to bet against financial instruments owned by other companies and countries. Intercontinental's clearing houses guarantee every transaction between buyer and seller providing a much-needed safety net reducing the impact of a default by spreading the risk. ICE collects on every trade.(Terhune Bloomberg Business Week 2010-07-29). Brookings senior research fellow, Robert E. Litan, cautioned however, "valuable pricing data will not be fully reported, leaving ICE's institutional partners with a huge informational advantage over other traders. He calls ICE Trust "a derivatives dealers' club" in which members make money at the expense of non-members (Terhune citing Litan in Bloomberg Business Week 2010-07-29). (Litan Derivatives Dealers' Club 2010)." Actually, Litan conceded that "some limited progress toward central clearing of CDS has been made in recent months, with CDS contracts between dealers now being cleared centrally primarily through one clearinghouse (ICE Trust) in which the dealers have a significant financial interest (Litan 2010:6)." However, "as long as ICE Trust has a monopoly in clearing, watch for the dealers to limit the expansion of the products that are centrally cleared, and to create barriers to electronic trading and smaller dealers making competitive markets in cleared products (Litan 2010:8)."

In 2009 the U.S. Securities and Exchange Commission granted an exemption for Intercontinental Exchange to begin guaranteeing credit-default swaps. The SEC exemption represented the last regulatory approval needed by Atlanta-based Intercontinental. A derivatives analyst at Morgan Stanley, one of the backers for IntercontinentalExchange's subsidiary, ICE Trust in New York, launched in 2008, claimed that the "clearinghouse, and changes to the contracts to standardize them, will probably boost activity". Intercontinental Exchange's subsidiary, ICE Trust's larger competitor, CME Group Inc., hasn't received an SEC exemption, and agency spokesman John Nester said he didn't know when a decision would be made.

Market as of 2009

The early months of 2009 saw several fundamental changes to the way CDSs operate, resulting from concerns over the instruments' safety after the events of the previous year. According to Deutsche Bank managing director Athanassios Diplas "the industry pushed through 10 years worth of changes in just a few months". By late 2008 processes had been introduced allowing CDSs that offset each other to be cancelled. Along with termination of contracts that have recently paid out such as those based on Lehmans, this had by March reduced the face value of the market down to an estimated $30 trillion.

The Bank for International Settlements estimates that outstanding derivatives total $708 trillion. U.S. and European regulators are developing separate plans to stabilize the derivatives market. Additionally there are some globally agreed standards falling into place in March 2009, administered by International Swaps and Derivatives Association (ISDA). Two of the key changes are:

1. The introduction of central clearing houses, one for the US and one for Europe. A clearing house acts as the central counterparty to both sides of a CDS transaction, thereby reducing the counterparty risk that both buyer and seller face.

2. The international standardization of CDS contracts, to prevent legal disputes in ambiguous cases where what the payout should be is unclear.

Speaking before the changes went live, Sivan Mahadevan, a derivatives analyst at Morgan Stanley, one of the backers for IntercontinentalExchange's subsidiary, ICE Trust in New York, launched in 2008, claimed that

> "A clearinghouse, and changes to the contracts to standardize them, will probably boost activity. ... Trading will be much easier.... We'll see new players come to the market because they'll like the idea of this being a better and more traded product. We also feel like over time we'll see the creation of different types of products (Mahadevan cited in Bloomberg 2009)."

In the U.S., central clearing operations began in March 2009, operated by Inter Continental Exchange (ICE). A key competitor also interested in entering the CDS clearing sector is CME Group.

In Europe, CDS Index clearing was launched by IntercontinentalExchange's European subsidiary ICE Clear Europe on July 31, 2009. It launched Single Name clearing in Dec 2009. By the end of 2009, it had cleared CDS contracts worth EUR 885 billion reducing the open interest down to EUR 75 billion

By the end of 2009, banks had reclaimed much of their market share; hedge funds had largely retreated from the market after the crises. According to an estimate by the Banque de France, by late 2009 the bank JP Morgan alone now had about 30% of the global CDS market.

Government Approvals relating to ICE and its Competitor CME

The SEC's approval for ICE Futures' request to be exempted from rules that would prevent it clearing CDSs was the third government action granted to Intercontinental in one week. On March 3, its proposed acquisition of Clearing Corp., a Chicago clearinghouse owned by eight of the largest dealers in the credit-default swap market, was approved by the Federal Trade Commission and the Justice Department. On March 5, 2009, the Federal Reserve Board, which oversees the clearinghouse, granted a request for ICE to begin clearing.

Clearing Corp. shareholders including JPMorgan Chase & Co., Goldman Sachs Group Inc. and UBS AG, received $39 million in cash from Intercontinental in the acquisition, as well as the Clearing Corp.'s cash on hand and a 50–50 profit-sharing agreement with Intercontinental on the revenue generated from processing the swaps.

SEC spokesperson John Nestor stated

> “For several months the SEC and our fellow regulators have worked closely with all of the firms wishing to establish central counterparties.... We believe that CME should be in a position soon to provide us with the information necessary to allow the commission to take action on its exemptive requests.”

Other proposals to clear credit-default swaps have been made by NYSE Euronext, Eurex AG and LCH.Clearnet Ltd. Only the NYSE effort is available now for clearing after starting on Dec. 22. As of Jan. 30, no swaps had been cleared by the NYSE's London- based derivatives exchange, according to NYSE Chief Executive Officer Duncan Niederauer.

Clearing House Member Requirements

Members of the Intercontinental clearinghouse ICE Trust (now ICE Clear Credit) in March 2009 would have to have a net worth of at least $5 billion and a credit rating of A or better to clear their credit-default swap trades. Intercontinental said in the statement today that all market participants such as hedge funds, banks or other institutions are open to become members of the clearinghouse as long as they meet these requirements.

A clearinghouse acts as the buyer to every seller and seller to every buyer, reducing the risk of counterparty defaulting on a transaction. In the over-the-counter market, where credit- default swaps are currently traded, participants are exposed to each other in case of a default. A clearinghouse also provides one location for regulators to view traders' positions and prices.

J.P. Morgan Losses

In April 2012, hedge fund insiders became aware that the market in credit default swaps was possibly being affected by the activities of Bruno Iksil, a trader for J.P. Morgan Chase & Co., referred to as "the London whale" in reference to the huge positions he was taking. Heavy opposing bets to his positions are known to have been made by traders, including another branch of J.P. Morgan, who purchased the derivatives offered by J.P. Morgan in such high volumc. Major losses, $2 billion, were reported by the firm in May 2012 in relationship to these trades. The disclosure, which resulted in headlines in the media, did not disclose the exact nature of the trading involved, which remains in progress. The item traded, possibly related to CDX IG 9, an index based on the default risk of major U.S. corporations, has been described as a "derivative of a derivative".

Terms of a Typical CDS Contract

A CDS contract is typically documented under a *confirmation* referencing the credit derivatives definitions as published by the International Swaps and Derivatives Association. The confirmation typically specifies a *reference entity*, a corporation or sovereign that generally, although not always, has debt outstanding, and a *reference obligation*, usually an unsubordinated corporate bond or government bond. The period over which default protection extends is defined by the contract *effective date* and *scheduled termination date*.

The confirmation also specifies a *calculation agent* who is responsible for making determinations as to *successors* and *substitute reference obligations* (for example necessary if the original reference obligation was a loan that is repaid before the expiry of the contract), and for performing various calculation and administrative functions in connection with the transaction. By market convention, in contracts between CDS dealers and end-users, the dealer is generally the calculation agent, and in contracts between CDS dealers, the protection seller is generally the calculation agent.

It is not the responsibility of the calculation agent to determine whether or not a credit event has occurred but rather a matter of fact that, pursuant to the terms of typical contracts, must be supported by *publicly available information* delivered along with a *credit event notice*. Typical CDS contracts do not provide an internal mechanism for challenging the occurrence or non-occurrence of a credit event and rather leave the matter to the courts if necessary, though actual instances of specific events being disputed are relatively rare.

CDS confirmations also specify the *credit events* that will give rise to payment obligations by the protection seller and delivery obligations by the protection buyer. Typical credit events include *bankruptcy* with respect to the reference entity and *failure to pay* with respect to its direct or guaranteed bond or loan debt. CDS written on North American investment grade corporate reference entities, European corporate reference entities and sovereigns generally also include *restructuring* as a credit event, whereas trades referencing North American high-yield corporate reference entities typically do not.

Finally, standard CDS contracts specify *deliverable obligation characteristics* that limit the range of obligations that a protection buyer may deliver upon a credit event. Trading conventions for deliverable obligation characteristics vary for different markets and CDS contract types. Typical limitations include that deliverable debt be a bond or loan, that it have a maximum maturity of 30 years, that it not be subordinated, that it not be subject to transfer restrictions (other than Rule 144A), that it be of a standard currency and that it not be subject to some contingency before becoming due.

The premium payments are generally quarterly, with maturity dates (and likewise premium payment dates) falling on March 20, June 20, September 20, and December 20. Due to the proximity to the IMM dates, which fall on the third Wednesday of these months, these CDS maturity dates are also referred to as "IMM dates".

Credit Default Swap and Sovereign Debt Crisis

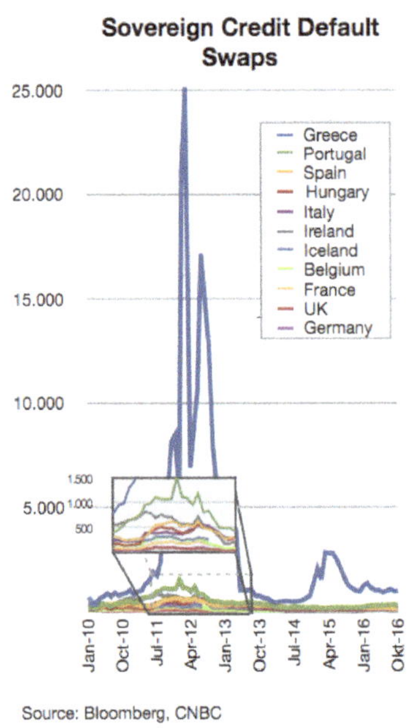

Sovereign credit default swap prices of selected European countries (2010-2011). The left axis is basis points, or 100ths of a percent; a level of 1,000 means it costs $1 million per year to protect $10 million of debt for five years.

The European sovereign debt crisis resulted from a combination of complex factors, including the globalisation of finance; easy credit conditions during the 2002–2008 period that encouraged high-risk lending and borrowing practices; the 2007–2012 global financial crisis; international trade imbalances; real-estate bubbles that have since burst; the 2008–2012 global recession; fiscal policy choices related to government revenues and expenses; and approaches used by nations to bail out troubled banking industries and private bondholders, assuming private debt burdens or socialising losses. The Credit default swap market also reveals the beginning of the sovereign crisis.

Since December 1, 2011 the European Parliament has banned naked Credit default swap (CDS) on the debt for sovereign nations.

The definition of restructuring is quite technical but is essentially intended to respond to circumstances where a reference entity, as a result of the deterioration of its credit, negotiates changes in the terms in its debt with its creditors as an alternative to formal insolvency proceedings (i.e. the debt is *restructured*). During the 2012 Greek sovereign debt crisis, one important issue was whether the restructuring would trigger Credit default swap (CDS) payments. European Central Bank and the International Monetary Fund negotiators avoided these triggers as they could have jeopardized the stability of major European banks who had been protection writers. An alternative could have been to create new CDS which clearly would pay in the event of debt restructuring. The market would have paid the spread between these and old (potentially more ambiguous) CDS. This practice is far more typical in jurisdictions that do not provide protective status to insolvent debtors similar to that provided by Chapter 11 of the United States Bankruptcy Code. In particular, concerns arising out of Conseco's restructuring in 2000 led to the credit event's removal from North American high yield trades.

Settlement

Physical or Cash

As described in an earlier section, if a credit event occurs then CDS contracts can either be *physically settled* or *cash settled*.

- Physical settlement: The protection seller pays the buyer par value, and in return takes delivery of a debt obligation of the reference entity. For example, a hedge fund has bought $5 million worth of protection from a bank on the senior debt of a company. In the event of a default, the bank pays the hedge fund $5 million cash, and the hedge fund must deliver $5 million face value of senior debt of the company (typically bonds or loans, which are typically worth very little given that the company is in default).
- Cash settlement: The protection seller pays the buyer the difference between par value and the market price of a debt obligation of the reference entity. For example, a hedge fund has bought $5 million worth of protection from a bank on the senior debt of a company. This company has now defaulted, and its se-

nior bonds are now trading at 25 (i.e., 25 cents on the dollar) since the market believes that senior bondholders will receive 25% of the money they are owed once the company is wound up. Therefore, the bank must pay the hedge fund \$5 million × (100% – 25%) = \$3.75 million.

The development and growth of the CDS market has meant that on many companies there is now a much larger outstanding notional of CDS contracts than the outstanding notional value of its debt obligations. (This is because many parties made CDS contracts for speculative purposes, without actually owning any debt that they wanted to insure against default.) For example, at the time it filed for bankruptcy on September 14, 2008, Lehman Brothers had approximately \$155 billion of outstanding debt but around \$400 billion notional value of CDS contracts had been written that referenced this debt. Clearly not all of these contracts could be physically settled, since there was not enough outstanding Lehman Brothers debt to fulfill all of the contracts, demonstrating the necessity for cash settled CDS trades. The trade confirmation produced when a CDS is traded states whether the contract is to be physically or cash settled.

Auctions

When a credit event occurs on a major company on which a lot of CDS contracts are written, an auction (also known as a *credit-fixing event*) may be held to facilitate settlement of a large number of contracts at once, at a fixed cash settlement price. During the auction process participating dealers (e.g., the big investment banks) submit prices at which they would buy and sell the reference entity's debt obligations, as well as net requests for physical settlement against par. A second stage Dutch auction is held following the publication of the initial midpoint of the dealer markets and what is the net open interest to deliver or be delivered actual bonds or loans. The final clearing point of this auction sets the final price for cash settlement of all CDS contracts and all physical settlement requests as well as matched limit offers resulting from the auction are actually settled. According to the International Swaps and Derivatives Association (ISDA), who organised them, auctions have recently proved an effective way of settling the very large volume of outstanding CDS contracts written on companies such as Lehman Brothers and Washington Mutual. Commentator Felix Salmon, however, has questioned in advance ISDA's ability to structure an auction, as defined to date, to set compensation associated with a 2012 bond swap in Greek government debt. For its part, ISDA in the leadup to a 50% or greater "haircut" for Greek bondholders, issued an opinion that the bond swap would not constitute a default event.

Pricing and Valuation

There are two competing theories usually advanced for the pricing of credit default swaps. The first, referred to herein as the 'probability model', takes the present value of a series of cashflows weighted by their probability of non-default. This method suggests that credit default swaps should trade at a considerably lower spread than corporate bonds.

The second model, proposed by Darrell Duffie, but also by John Hull and Alan White, uses a no-arbitrage approach.

Probability Model

Under the probability model, a credit default swap is priced using a model that takes four inputs; this is similar to the rNPV (risk-adjusted NPV) model used in drug development:

- the "issue premium",
- the recovery rate (percentage of notional repaid in event of default),
- the "credit curve" for the reference entity and
- the "LIBOR curve".

If default events never occurred the price of a CDS would simply be the sum of the discounted premium payments. So CDS pricing models have to take into account the possibility of a default occurring some time between the effective date and maturity date of the CDS contract. For the purpose of explanation we can imagine the case of a one-year CDS with effective date t_0 with four quarterly premium payments occurring at times t_1, t_2, t_3, and t_4. If the nominal for the CDS is N and the issue premium is c then the size of the quarterly premium payments is $Nc/4$. If we assume for simplicity that defaults can only occur on one of the payment dates then there are five ways the contract could end:

- either it does not have any default at all, so the four premium payments are made and the contract survives until the maturity date, or
- a default occurs on the first, second, third or fourth payment date.

To price the CDS we now need to assign probabilities to the five possible outcomes, then calculate the present value of the payoff for each outcome. The present value of the CDS is then simply the present value of the five payoffs multiplied by their probability of occurring.

This is illustrated in the following tree diagram where at each payment date either the contract has a default event, in which case it ends with a payment of $N(1-R)$ shown in red, where R is the recovery rate, or it survives without a default being triggered, in which case a premium payment of $Nc/4$ is made, shown in blue. At either side of the diagram are the cashflows up to that point in time with premium payments in blue and default payments in red. If the contract is terminated the square is shown with solid shading.

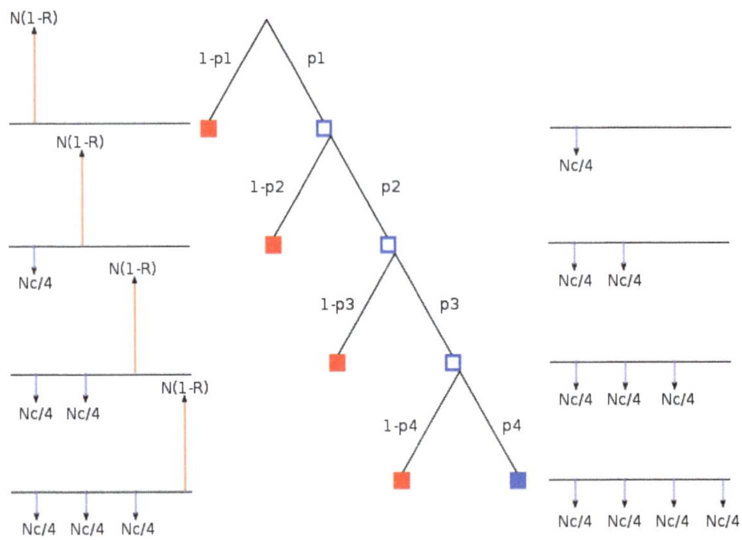

The probability of surviving over the interval t_{i-1} to t_i without a default payment is p_i and the probability of a default being triggered is $1-p_i$. The calculation of present value, given discount factor of δ_1 to δ_4 is then

Description	Premium Payment PV	Default Payment PV	Probability
Default at time t_1	0	$N(1-R)\delta_1$	$1-p_1$
Default at time t_2	$-\frac{Nc}{4}\delta_1$	$N(1-R)\delta_2$	$p_1(1-p_2)$
Default at time t_3	$-\frac{Nc}{4}(\delta_1+\delta_2)$	$N(1-R)\delta_3$	$p_1p_2(1-p_3)$
Default at time t_4	$-\frac{Nc}{4}(\delta_1+\delta_2+\delta_3)$	$N(1-R)\delta_4$	$p_1p_2p_3(1-p_4)$
No defaults	$-\frac{Nc}{4}(\delta_1+\delta_2+\delta_3+\delta_4)$	0	$p_1\times p_2\times p_3\times p_4$

The probabilities p_1, p_2, p_3, p_4 can be calculated using the credit spread curve. The probability of no default occurring over a time period from to $t+\Delta t$ decays exponentially with a time-constant determined by the credit spread, or mathematically $p=\exp(-s(t)\Delta t/(1-R))$ where $s(t)$ is the credit spread zero curve at time t. The riskier the reference entity the greater the spread and the more rapidly the survival probability decays with time.

To get the total present value of the credit default swap we multiply the probability of each outcome by its present value to give

$$\begin{aligned}PV &= (1-p_1)N(1-R)\delta_1\\ &+ p_1(1-p_2)[N(1-R)\delta_2 - \frac{Nc}{4}\delta_1]\\ &+ p_1p_2(1-p_3)[N(1-R)\delta_3 - \frac{Nc}{4}(\delta_1+\delta_2)]\\ &+ p_1p_2p_3(1-p_4)[N(1-R)\delta_4 - \frac{Nc}{4}(\delta_1+\delta_2+\delta_3)]\\ &- p_1p_2p_3p_4(\delta_1+\delta_2+\delta_3+\delta_4)\frac{Nc}{4}\end{aligned}$$

No-arbitrage Model

In the 'no-arbitrage' model proposed by both Duffie, and Hull-White, it is assumed that there is no risk free arbitrage. Duffie uses the LIBOR as the risk free rate, whereas Hull and White use US Treasuries as the risk free rate. Both analyses make simplifying assumptions (such as the assumption that there is zero cost of unwinding the fixed leg of the swap on default), which may invalidate the no-arbitrage assumption. However the Duffie approach is frequently used by the market to determine theoretical prices.

Under the Duffie construct, the price of a credit default swap can also be derived by calculating the asset swap spread of a bond. If a bond has a spread of 100, and the swap spread is 70 basis points, then a CDS contract should trade at 30. However, there are sometimes technical reasons why this will not be the case, and this may or may not present an arbitrage opportunity for the canny investor. The difference between the theoretical model and the actual price of a credit default swap is known as the basis.

Criticisms

Critics of the huge credit default swap market have claimed that it has been allowed to become too large without proper regulation and that, because all contracts are privately negotiated, the market has no transparency. Furthermore, there have been claims that CDSs exacerbated the 2008 global financial crisis by hastening the demise of companies such as Lehman Brothers and AIG.

In the case of Lehman Brothers, it is claimed that the widening of the bank's CDS spread reduced confidence in the bank and ultimately gave it further problems that it was not able to overcome. However, proponents of the CDS market argue that this confuses cause and effect; CDS spreads simply reflected the reality that the company was in serious trouble. Furthermore, they claim that the CDS market allowed investors who had counterparty risk with Lehman Brothers to reduce their exposure in the case of their default.

Credit default swaps have also faced criticism that they contributed to a breakdown in negotiations during the 2009 General Motors Chapter 11 reorganization, because certain bondholders might benefit from the credit event of a GM bankruptcy due to their holding of CDSs. Critics speculate that these creditors had an incentive to push for the company to enter bankruptcy protection. Due to a lack of transparency, there was no way to identify the protection buyers and protection writers.

It was also feared at the time of Lehman's bankruptcy that the $400 billion notional of CDS protection which had been written on the bank could lead to a net payout of $366 billion from protection sellers to buyers (given the cash-settlement auction settled at a final price of 8.625%) and that these large payouts could lead to further bankruptcies of firms without enough cash to settle their contracts. However, industry estimates after the auction suggest that net cashflows were only in the region of $7 billion. because many parties held offsetting positions. Furthermore, CDS deals are marked-to-market frequently. This would have led to margin calls from buyers to sellers as Lehman's CDS spread widened, reducing the net cashflows on the days after the auction.

Senior bankers have argued that not only has the CDS market functioned remarkably well during the financial crisis; that CDS contracts have been acting to distribute risk just as was intended; and that it is not CDSs themselves that need further regulation but the parties who trade them.

Some general criticism of financial derivatives is also relevant to credit derivatives. Warren Buffett famously described derivatives bought speculatively as "financial weapons of mass destruction." In Berkshire Hathaway's annual report to shareholders in 2002, he said, "Unless derivatives contracts are collateralized or guaranteed, their ultimate value also depends on the creditworthiness of the counterparties to them. In the meantime, though, before a contract is settled, the counterparties record profits and losses—often huge in amount—in their current earnings statements without so much as a penny changing hands. The range of derivatives contracts is limited only by the imagination of man (or sometimes, so it seems, madmen)."

To hedge the counterparty risk of entering a CDS transaction, one practice is to buy CDS protection on one's counterparty. The positions are marked-to-market daily and collateral pass from buyer to seller or vice versa to protect both parties against counterparty default, but money does not always change hands due to the offset of gains and losses by those who had both bought and sold protection. Depository Trust & Clearing Corporation, the clearinghouse for the majority of trades in the US over-the-counter market, stated in October 2008 that once offsetting trades were considered, only an estimated $6 billion would change hands on October 21, during the settlement of the CDS contracts issued on Lehman Brothers' debt, which amounted to somewhere between $150 to $360 billion.

Despite Buffett's criticism on derivatives, in October 2008 Berkshire Hathaway revealed to regulators that it has entered into at least $4.85 billion in derivative transactions. Buffett stated in his 2008 letter to shareholders that Berkshire Hathaway has no counterparty risk in its derivative dealings because Berkshire require counterparties to make payments when contracts are initiated, so that Berkshire always holds the money. Berkshire Hathaway was a large owner of Moody's stock during the period that it was one of two primary rating agencies for subprime CDOs, a form of mortgage security derivative dependent on the use of credit default swaps.

The monoline insurance companies got involved with writing credit default swaps on mortgage-backed CDOs. Some media reports have claimed this was a contributing factor to the downfall of some of the monolines. In 2009 one of the monolines, MBIA, sued Merrill Lynch, claiming that Merrill had misrepresented some of its CDOs to MBIA in order to persuade MBIA to write CDS protection for those CDOs.

Systemic Risk

During the 2008 financial crisis, counterparties became subject to a risk of default, amplified with the involvement of Lehman Brothers and AIG in a very large number of CDS transactions. This is an example of systemic risk, risk which threatens an entire market, and a number of commentators have argued that size and deregulation of the CDS market have increased this risk.

For example, imagine if a hypothetical mutual fund had bought some Washington Mutual corporate bonds in 2005 and decided to hedge their exposure by buying CDS protection from Lehman Brothers. After Lehman's default, this protection was no longer active, and Washington Mutual's sudden default only days later would have led to a massive loss on the bonds, a loss that should have been insured by the CDS. There was also fear that Lehman Brothers and AIG's inability to pay out on CDS contracts would lead to the unraveling of complex interlinked chain of CDS transactions between financial institutions. So far this does not appear to have happened, although some commentators have noted that because the total CDS exposure of a bank is not public knowledge, the fear that one could face large losses or possibly even default themselves was a contributing factor to the massive decrease in lending liquidity during September/October 2008.

Chains of CDS transactions can arise from a practice known as "netting". Here, company B may buy a CDS from company A with a certain annual *premium*, say 2%. If the condition of the reference company worsens, the risk premium rises, so company B can sell a CDS to company C with a premium of say, 5%, and pocket the 3% difference. However, if the reference company defaults, company B might not have the assets on hand to make good on the contract. It depends on its contract with company A to provide a large payout, which it then passes along to company C.

The problem lies if one of the companies in the chain fails, creating a "domino effect" of losses. For example, if company A fails, company B will default on its CDS contract to company C, possibly resulting in bankruptcy, and company C will potentially experience a large loss due to the failure to receive compensation for the bad debt it held from the reference company. Even worse, because CDS contracts are private, company C will not know that its fate is tied to company A; it is only doing business with company B.

As described above, the establishment of a central exchange or clearing house for CDS trades would help to solve the "domino effect" problem, since it would mean that all trades faced a central counterparty guaranteed by a consortium of dealers.

Tax and Accounting Issues

The U.S federal income tax treatment of CDS is uncertain (Nirenberg and Kopp 1997:1, Peaslee & Nirenberg 2008-07-21:129 and Brandes 2008). Commentators have suggested that, depending on how they are drafted, they are either notional principal contracts or options for tax purposes,(Peaslee & Nirenberg 2008-07-21:129). but this is not certain. There is a risk of having CDS recharacterized as different types of financial instruments because they resemble put options and credit guarantees. In particular, the degree of risk depends on the type of settlement (physical/cash and binary/FMV) and trigger (default only/any credit event) (Nirenberg & Kopp 1997:8). And, as noted below, the appropriate treatment for Naked CDS may be entirely different.

If a CDS is a notional principal contract, pre-default periodic and nonperiodic payments on the swap are deductible and included in ordinary income. If a payment is a termination payment, or a payment received on a sale of the swap to a third party, however, its tax treatment is an open question. In 2004, the Internal Revenue Service announced that it was studying the characterization of CDS in response to taxpayer confusion. As the outcome of its study, the IRS issued proposed regulations in 2011 specifically classifying CDS as notional principal contracts, and thereby qualifying such termination and sale payments for favorable capital gains tax treatment. These proposed regulations—which are yet to be finalized—have already been subject to criticism at a public hearing held by the IRS in January 2012, as well as in the academic press, insofar as that classification would apply to Naked CDS.

The thrust of this criticism is that Naked CDS are indistinguishable from gambling wagers, and thus give rise in all instances to ordinary income, including to hedge fund managers on their so-called carried interests, and that the IRS exceeded its authority with the proposed regulations. This is evidenced by the fact that Congress confirmed that certain derivatives, including CDS, do constitute gambling when, in 2000, to allay industry fears that they were illegal gambling, it exempted them from "any State or local law that prohibits or regulates gaming." While this decriminalized Naked CDS, it did not grant them relief under the federal gambling tax provisions.

The accounting treatment of CDS used for hedging may not parallel the economic effects and instead, increase volatility. For example, GAAP generally require that CDS be reported on a mark to market basis. In contrast, assets that are held for investment, such as a commercial loan or bonds, are reported at cost, unless a probable and significant loss is expected. Thus, hedging a commercial loan using a CDS can induce considerable volatility into the income statement and balance sheet as the CDS changes value over its life due to market conditions and due to the tendency for shorter dated CDS to sell at lower prices than longer dated CDS. One can try to account for the CDS as a hedge under FASB 133 but in practice that can prove very difficult unless the risky asset owned by the bank or corporation is exactly the same as the Reference Obligation used for the particular CDS that was bought.

LCDS

A new type of default swap is the "loan only" credit default swap (LCDS). This is conceptually very similar to a standard CDS, but unlike "vanilla" CDS, the underlying protection is sold on syndicated secured loans of the Reference Entity rather than the broader category of "Bond or Loan". Also, as of May 22, 2007, for the most widely traded LCDS form, which governs North American single name and index trades, the default settlement method for LCDS shifted to auction settlement rather than physical settlement. The auction method is essentially the same that has been used in the various ISDA cash settlement auction protocols, but does not require parties to take any additional steps following a credit event (i.e., adherence to a protocol) to elect cash settlement. On October 23, 2007, the first ever LCDS auction was held for Movie Gallery.

Because LCDS trades are linked to secured obligations with much higher recovery values than the unsecured bond obligations that are typically assumed the cheapest to deliver in respect of vanilla CDS, LCDS spreads are generally much tighter than CDS trades on the same name.

References

- "Media Statement: DTCC Policy for Releasing CDS Data to Global Regulators". Depository Trust & Clearing Corporation. March 23, 2010. Retrieved April 22, 2010
- Berger, Allen N., and Gregory F. Udell. "Collateral, loan quality and bank risk."Journal of Monetary Economics 25.1 (1990): 21-42
- Cornett, Marcia Millon; Saunders, Anthony (2006). Financial Institutions Management: A Risk Management Approach, 5th Edition. McGraw-Hill. ISBN 978-0-07-304667-9
- Federal Reserve Banks of, New York; et al. (March 2016). "2015 Small Business Credit Survey Employer Firms". Newyorkfed. Retrieved April 10, 2017
- Altman, Edward I., and Anthony Saunders. "Credit risk measurement: Developments over the last 20 years." Journal of Banking & Finance 21.11 (1997): 1721-1742
- Goetz; Gupta (1996). "Who takes the credit?Gender, Power, Control over loan use in Rural credit program in Bangladesh" (PDF). World Development. 24 (1): 45–63. doi:10.1016/0305-750x(95)00124

- Jonnard, Claude (1997-12-29). International Business and TradeTheory, Practice, and Policy. CRC Press. ISBN 9781574441550
- Brainard, Lael (September 30, 2015). "Community Banks, Small Business Credit and Online Lending". Federal Reserve. Retrieved April 7, 2017
- Soros, George (March 24, 2009). "Opinion: One Way to Stop Bear Raids". Wall Street Journal. Retrieved April 24, 2010
- Aryya, Gangopadhyay (2001-07-01). Managing Business with Electronic Commerce: Issues and Trends: Issues and Trends. Idea Group Inc (IGI). ISBN 9781591400073
- Banerjee, Abhijit; Esther Duflo; Rachel Glennester; Cynthia Kinnan. "The miracle of microfinance? Evidence from a randomized evaluation". Retrieved 17 April 2012
- Smithson, Charles; David Mengle (Fall 2006). "The Promise of Credit Derivatives in Nonfinancial Corporations (and Why It's Failed to Materialize)" (PDF). Journal of Applied Corporate Finance. 18 (4): 54–60. doi:10.1111/j.1745-6622.2006.00111.x. Retrieved April 8, 2010
- Lucas, Douglas; Laurie S. Goodman; Frank J. Fabozzi (May 5, 2006). Collateralized Debt Obligations: Structures and Analysis, 2nd Edition. John Wiley & Sons Inc. p. 221. ISBN 978-0-471-71887-1
- Spooner, Lysander (1846). "Poverty: Its illegal causes and legal cure.". Boston. Archived from the original on 25 October 2012. Retrieved 30 January 2012
- Tett, Gillian (2009). Fool's Gold: How Unrestrained Greed Corrupted a Dream, Shattered Global Markets and Unleashed a Catastrophe. Little Brown. pp. 48–67, 87, 303. ISBN 978-0-349-12189-5
- "Teaching entrepreneurship: Venezuela's BOD backs micro-business funding". World Finance. 24 August 2015. Retrieved 14 October 2015
- Jarrow, R. A.; Lando, D.; Turnbull, S. M. (1997). "A Markov Model for the Term Structure of Credit Risk Spreads". Review of Financial Studies. 10 (2): 481–523. ISSN 0893-9454. doi:10.1093/rfs/10.2.481
- "Chart; ISDA Market Survey; Notional amounts outstanding at year-end, all surveyed contracts, 1987–present" (PDF). International Swaps and Derivatives Association (ISDA). Retrieved April 8, 2010

4

Operational Risk Management

Operational risk is the risk that is incurred by and is inherent in, the institutional structure, staff and internal processes of any recognized company or organization. Operational risk is unavoidable and is suffered unwillingly. Bank management is best understood in confluence with the major topics listed in the following chapter.

Operational Risk

Risk of direct or indirect loss resulting from inadequate or failed internal processes, people and systems. The failure may be due to external events also. Excludes "Business Risk" and "Strategic Risk".

Operational risk is "the risk of a change in value caused by the fact that actual losses, incurred for inadequate or failed internal processes, people and systems, or from external events (including legal risk), differ from the expected losses". This definition, adopted by the European union Solvency II Directive for insurers, is a variation from that adopted in the Basel II regulations for banks. In October 2014, the Basel Committee on Banking Supervision proposed a revision to its operational risk capital framework that sets out a new standardized approach to replace the basic indicator approach and the standardized approach for calculating operational risk capital.

It can also include other classes of risk, such as fraud, security, privacy protection, legal risks, physical (e.g. infrastructure shutdown) or environmental risks.

Operational risk is a broad discipline, close to good management and quality management.

In similar fashion, operational risks affect client satisfaction, reputation and shareholder value, all while increasing business volatility.

Contrary to other risks (e.g. credit risk, market risk, insurance risk) operational risks are usually not willingly incurred nor are they revenue driven. Moreover, they are not diversifiable and cannot be laid off, meaning that, as long as people, systems and processes remain imperfect, operational risk cannot be fully eliminated.

Operational risk is, nonetheless, manageable as to keep losses within some level of risk tolerance (i.e. the amount of risk one is prepared to accept in pursuit of his objectives), determined by balancing the costs of improvement against the expected benefits.

Wider trends such as globalization, the expansion of the internet and the rise of social media, as well as the increasing demands for greater corporate accountability worldwide, reinforce the need for proper operational risk management.

Background

Until Basel II reforms to banking supervision, operational risk was a residual category reserved for risks and uncertainties which were difficult to quantify and manage in traditional ways – the "other risks" basket.

Such regulations institutionalized operational risk as a category of regulatory and managerial attention and connected operational risk management with good corporate governance.

Of course, businesses in general, and other institutions such as the military, have been aware, for many years, of hazards arising from operational factors, internal or external. The primary goal of the military is to fight and win wars in quick and decisive fashion, and with minimal losses. For the military, and the businesses of the world alike, operational risk management is an effective process for preserving resources by anticipation.

Two decades (from 1980 to the early 2000s) of globalization and deregulation (e.g. Big Bang (financial markets)), combined with the increased sophistication of financial services around the world, have introduced additional complexities into the activities of banks, insurers and firms in general and therefore their risk profiles.

Since the mid-1990s, the topics of market risk and credit risk have been the subject of much debate and research, with the result that financial institutions have made significant progress in the identification, measurement and management of both these forms of risk.

However, the near collapse of the U.S. financial system in September 2008 is an indication that our ability to measure market and credit risk is far from perfect and eventually led to introduction of new regulatory requirements worldwide, including Basel III regulations for banks and Solvency II regulations for insurers.

Events such as the September 11 terrorist attacks, rogue trading losses at Société Générale, Barings, AIB, UBS and National Australia Bank serve to highlight the fact that the scope of risk management extends beyond merely market and credit risk.

These reasons underscore banks' and supervisors' growing focus upon the identification and measurement of operational risk.

The list of risks (and, more importantly, the scale of these risks) faced by banks today includes fraud, system failures, terrorism and employee compensation claims. These types of risk are generally classified under the term 'operational risk'.

The identification and measurement of operational risk is a real and live issue for modern-day banks, particularly since the decision by the Basel Committee on Banking Supervision (BCBS) to introduce a capital charge for this risk as part of the new capital adequacy framework (Basel II).

Definition

The Basel II Committee defines operational risk as:

"The risk of loss resulting from inadequate or failed internal processes, people and systems or from external events."

However, the Basel Committee recognizes that operational risk is a term that has a variety of meanings and therefore, for internal purposes, banks are permitted to adopt their own definitions of operational risk, provided that the minimum elements in the Committee's definition are included.

Scope Exclusions

The Basel II definition of operational risk excludes, for example, strategic risk – the risk of a loss arising from a poor strategic business decision.

Other risk terms are seen as potential consequences of operational risk events. For example, reputational risk (damage to an organization through loss of its reputation or standing) can arise as a consequence (or impact) of operational failures – as well as from other events.

Basel II Seven Event Type Categories

The following lists the official Basel II defines the seven event types with some examples for each category:

1. Internal Fraud – misappropriation of assets, tax evasion, intentional mismarking of positions, bribery
2. External Fraud – theft of information, hacking damage, third-party theft and forgery
3. Employment Practices and Workplace Safety – discrimination, workers compensation, employee health and safety
4. Clients, Products, and Business Practice – market manipulation, antitrust, improper trade, product defects, fiduciary breaches, account churning

5. Damage to Physical Assets – natural disasters, terrorism, vandalism
6. Business Disruption and Systems Failures – utility disruptions, software failures, hardware failures
7. Execution, Delivery, and Process Management – data entry errors, accounting errors, failed mandatory reporting, negligent loss of client assets

Difficulties

It is relatively straightforward for an organization to set and observe specific, measurable levels of market risk and credit risk because models exist which attempt to predict the potential impact of market movements, or changes in the cost of credit. It should be noted however that these models are only as good as the underlying assumptions, and a large part of the recent financial crisis arose because the valuations generated by these models for particular types of investments were based on incorrect assumptions.

By contrast it is relatively difficult to identify or assess levels of operational risk and its many sources. Historically organizations have accepted operational risk as an unavoidable cost of doing business. Many now though collect data on operational losses – for example through system failure or fraud – and are using this data to model operational risk and to calculate a capital reserve against future operational losses. In addition to the Basel II requirement for banks, this is now a requirement for European insurance firms who are in the process of implementing Solvency II, the equivalent of Basel II for the banking sector.

Methods of operational risk management

Basel II and various Supervisory bodies of the countries have prescribed various soundness standards for Operational Risk Management for Banks and similar Financial Institutions. To complement these standards, Basel II has given guidance to 3 broad methods of Capital calculation for Operational Risk

- Basic Indicator Approach – based on annual revenue of the Financial Institution
- Standardized Approach – based on annual revenue of each of the broad business lines of the Financial Institution
- Advanced Measurement Approaches – based on the internally developed risk measurement framework of the bank adhering to the standards prescribed (methods include IMA, LDA, Scenario-based, Scorecard etc.)

The Operational Risk Management framework should include identification, measurement, monitoring, reporting, control and mitigation frameworks for Operational Risk.

Basic Indicator Approach

The basic approach or basic indicator approach is a set of operational risk measurement techniques proposed under Basel II capital adequacy rules for banking institutions.

Basel II requires all banking institutions to set aside capital for operational risk. Basic indicator approach is much simpler compared to the alternative approaches (i.e. standardized approach (operational risk) and advanced measurement approach) and thus has been recommended for banks without significant international operations.

Based on the original Basel Accord, banks using the basic indicator approach must hold capital for operational risk equal to the average over the previous three years of a fixed percentage of positive annual gross income. Figures for any year in which annual gross income is negative or zero should be excluded from both the numerator and denominator when calculating the average. A standard deviation is commonly also taken.

The fixed percentage 'alpha' is typically 15 percent of annual gross income.

Standardized Approach (Operational Risk)

In the context of operational risk, the standardized approach or standardised approach is a set of operational risk measurement techniques proposed under Basel II capital adequacy rules for banking institutions.

Basel II requires all banking institutions to set aside capital for operational risk. Standardized approach falls between basic indicator approach and advanced measurement approach in terms of degree of complexity.

Based on the original Basel Accord, under the Standardised Approach, banks' activities are divided into eight business lines: corporate finance, trading & sales, retail banking, commercial banking, payment & settlement, agency services, asset management, and retail brokerage. Within each business line, gross income is a broad indicator that serves as a proxy for the scale of business operations and thus the likely scale of operational risk exposure within each of these business lines. The capital charge for each business line is calculated by multiplying gross income by a factor (denoted beta) assigned to that business line. Beta serves as a proxy for the industry-wide relationship between the operational risk loss experience for a given business line and the aggregate level of gross income for that business line.

Business Line	Beta Factor
Corporate finance	18%
Trading and sales	18%
Retail banking	12%
Commercial banking	15%
Payment and settlement	18%

Agency services	15%
Asset Management	12%
Retail Brokerage	12%

The total capital charge is calculated as the three-year average of the simple summation of the regulatory capital charges across each of the business lines in each year. In any given year, negative capital charges (resulting from negative gross income) in any business line may offset positive capital charges in other business lines without limit.

In order to qualify for use of the standardised approach, a bank must satisfy its regulator that, at a minimum:

- Its board of directors and senior management, as appropriate, are actively involved in the oversight of the operational risk management framework;
- It has an operational risk management system that is conceptually sound and is implemented with integrity; and
- It has sufficient resources in the use of the approach in the major business lines as well as the control and audit areas.

On March 4, 2016, the Basel Committee on Banking Supervision finally updated its proposal for calculating operational risk capital, introducing the Standardized Measurement Approach ("SMA"). Building upon its 2014 version, the SMA would not only replace the existing standardized approaches, but also the Advanced Measurement Approach. Under the SMA, regulatory capital levels will be determined using a simple formulaic method which facilitates comparability across the industry.

Advanced Measurement Approach

Advanced Measurement Approaches (AMA) is one of three possible operational risk methods that can be used under Basel II by a bank or other financial institution. The other two are the Basic Indicator Approach and the Standardised Approach. The methods (or approaches) increase in sophistication and risk sensitivity with AMA being the most advanced of the three.

Under AMA the banks are allowed to develop their own empirical model to quantify required capital for operational risk. Banks can use this approach only subject to approval from their local regulators. Once a bank has been approved to adopt AMA, it cannot revert to a simpler approach without supervisory approval.

Also, according to section 664 of original Basel Accord, in order to qualify for use of the AMA a bank must satisfy its supervisor that, at a minimum:

- Its board of directors and senior management, as appropriate, are actively involved in the oversight of the operational risk management framework;

- It has an operational risk management system that is conceptually sound and is implemented with integrity; and
- It has sufficient resources in the use of the approach in the major business lines as well as the control and audit areas.

The Four Data Elements

According to the BCBS Supervisory Guidelines, an AMA framework must include the use of four data elements: (i) Internal loss data (ILD), (ii) External data (ED), (iii) Scenario analysis (SBA), and (iv) Business environment and internal control factors (BEICFs).

Loss Distribution Approach

While AMA does not specify the use of any particular modeling technique, one common approach taken in the banking industry is the Loss Distribution Approach (LDA). With LDA, a bank first segments operational losses into homogeneous segments, called units of measure (UoMs). For each unit of measure, the bank then constructs a loss distribution that represents its expectation of total losses that can materialize in a one-year horizon. Given that data sufficiency is a major challenge for the industry, annual loss distribution cannot be built directly using annual loss figures. Instead, a bank will develop a frequency distribution that describes the number of loss events in a given year, and a severity distribution that describes the loss amount of a single loss event. The frequency and severity distributions are assumed to be independent. The convolution of these two distributions then give rise to the (annual) loss distribution.

Measurement of Operational Risk

Proposed Operational Risk Capital Requirements

Reduced from 20% to 12% of a Bank's Total Regulatory Capital Requirement (November, 2001)

Based on a Bank's choice:

(a) Basic Indicator Approach which levies a single operational risk charge for the entire bank

or

(b) Standardized Approach which divides a bank's different lines of business, each with its own operational risk charge

or

(c) Advanced Management Approach which uses the bank's own internal models of operational risk measurement to assess a capital requirement

Basel I

- Two minimum standards

  – Asset to capital multiple

  – Risk based capital ratio

- Scope is limited

  – Portfolio effects missing: a well diversified portfolio is much less likely to suffer

  – massive losses

  – Netting is absent

- No market or operational risk

Operational Risk Policy

Risk Management Policy

- Planning of operational risk management.
- Identification of business lines.
- Mapping of business lines.
- Determine sources of external loss data.
- Identify process of inferring external loss data.
- Classification of loss events.
- Consolidation of loss events.
- Reporting procedure for loss events.
- Mapping Business Events

Mapping Business Events

- Business units
- Business lines
- Activity groups

Monetary Policy

Monetary policy is the process by which the monetary authority of a country, like the central bank or currency board, controls the supply of money, often targeting an inflation rate or interest rate to ensure price stability and general trust in the currency.

Further goals of a monetary policy are usually to contribute to economic growth and stability, to lower unemployment, and to maintain predictable exchange rates with other currencies.

Monetary economics provides insight into how to craft an optimal monetary policy. Since the 1970s, monetary policy has generally been formed separately from fiscal policy, which refers to taxation, government spending, and associated borrowing.

Monetary policy is referred to as either being expansionary or contractionary. Expansionary policy is when a monetary authority uses its tools to stimulate the economy. An expansionary policy increases the total supply of money in the economy more rapidly than usual. It is traditionally used to try to combat unemployment in a recession by lowering interest rates in the hope that easy credit will entice businesses into expanding. Also, this increases the aggregate demand (the overall demand for all goods and services in an economy), which boosts growth as measured by gross domestic product (GDP). Expansionary monetary policy usually diminishes the value of the currency, thereby decreasing the exchange rate.

The opposite of expansionary monetary policy is contractionary monetary policy, which slows the rate of growth in the money supply or even shrinks it. This slows economic growth to prevent inflation. Contractionary monetary policy can lead to increased unemployment and depressed borrowing and spending by consumers and businesses, which can eventually result in an economic recession; it should hence be well managed and conducted with care.

History

Monetary policy is associated with interest rates and availability of credit. Instruments of monetary policy have included short-term interest rates and bank reserves through the monetary base. For many centuries there were only two forms of monetary policy: (i) Decisions about coinage; (ii) Decisions to print paper money to create credit. Interest rates, while now thought of as part of monetary authority, were not generally coordinated with the other forms of monetary policy during this time. Monetary policy was seen as an executive decision, and was generally in the hands of the authority with seigniorage, or the power to coin. With the advent of larger trading networks came the ability to set the price between gold and silver, and the price of the local currency to foreign currencies. This official price could be enforced by law, even if it varied from the market price.

Paper money called "jiaozi" originated from promissory notes in 7th century China. Jiaozi did not replace metallic currency, and were used alongside the copper coins. The successive Yuan Dynasty was the first government to use paper currency as the predominant circulating medium. In the later course of the dynasty, facing massive shortages of specie to fund war and their rule in China, they began printing paper money without restrictions, resulting in hyperinflation.

With the creation of the Bank of England in 1694, which acquired the responsibility to print notes and back them with gold, the idea of monetary policy as independent of executive action began to be established. The goal of monetary policy was to maintain the value of the coinage, print notes which would trade at par to specie, and prevent coins from leaving circulation. The establishment of central banks by industrializing nations was associated then with the desire to maintain the nation's peg to the gold standard, and to trade in a narrow band with other gold-backed currencies. To accomplish this end, central banks as part of the gold standard began setting the interest rates that they charged, both their own borrowers, and other banks who required liquidity. The maintenance of a gold standard required almost monthly adjustments of interest rates. The gold standard is a system under which the price of the national currency is measured in units of gold bars and is kept constant by the government's promise to buy or sell gold at a fixed price in terms of the base currency. The gold standard might be regarded as a special case of "fixed exchange rate" policy, or as a special type of commodity price level targeting. Nowadays this type of monetary policy is no longer used by any country.

During the period 1870–1920, the industrialized nations set up central banking systems, with one of the last being the Federal Reserve in 1913. By this point the role of the central bank as the "lender of last resort" was understood. It was also increasingly understood that interest rates had an effect on the entire economy, in no small part because of the marginal revolution in economics, which demonstrated how people would change a decision based on a change in the economic trade-offs.

Monetarist economists long contended that the money-supply growth could affect the macroeconomy. These included Milton Friedman who early in his career advocated that government budget deficits during recessions be financed in equal amount by money creation to help to stimulate aggregate demand for output. Later he advocated simply increasing the monetary supply at a low, constant rate, as the best way of maintaining low inflation and stable output growth. However, when U.S. Federal Reserve Chairman Paul Volcker tried this policy, starting in October 1979, it was found to be impractical, because of the highly unstable relationship between monetary aggregates and other macroeconomic variables. Even Milton Friedman later acknowledged that direct money supply targeting was less successful than he had hoped.

Therefore, monetary decisions today take into account a wider range of factors, such as:

- short-term interest rates;

- long-term interest rates;
- velocity of money through the economy;
- exchange rates;
- credit quality;
- bonds and equities (corporate ownership and debt);
- government versus private sector spending/savings;
- international capital flows of money on large scales;
- financial derivatives such as options, swaps, futures contracts, etc.

Tools

Traditional Tools

The central bank influences interest rates by expanding or contracting the monetary base, which consists of currency in circulation and banks' reserves on deposit at the central bank. Central banks have three main tools of monetary policy: open market operations, the discount rate and the reserve requirements.

The most commonly used tool by which the central bank can affect the monetary base is by open market operations. This entails managing the quantity of money in circulation through the buying and selling of various financial instruments, such as treasury bills, company bonds, or foreign currencies, in exchange for money on deposit at the central bank. Those deposits are convertible to currency, so all of these purchases or sales result in more or less base currency entering or leaving market circulation. For example, if the central bank wishes to lower interest rates (executing expansionary monetary policy), it purchases government debt, thereby increasing the amount of cash in circulation or crediting banks' reserve accounts. Commercial banks then have more money to lend, so they reduce lending rates, making loans less expensive. Cheaper credit card interest rates boost consumer spending. Additionally, when business loans are more affordable, companies can expand to keep up with consumer demand. They ultimately hire more workers, whose incomes rise, which in its turn also increases the demand. This tool is usually enough to stimulate demand and drive economic growth to a healthy rate. Usually, the short-term goal of open market operations is to achieve a specific short-term interest rate target. In other instances, monetary policy might instead entail the targeting of a specific exchange rate relative to some foreign currency or else relative to gold. For example, in the case of the USA the Federal Reserve targets the federal funds rate, the rate at which member banks lend to one another overnight; however, the monetary policy of China is to target the exchange rate between the Chinese renminbi and a basket of foreign currencies.

If the open market operations do not lead to the desired effects, a second tool can be used: the central bank can lower the interest rate it charges on discounts or overdrafts. If the interest rate on such transactions is sufficiently low, commercial banks can borrow from the central bank to meet reserve requirements and use the additional liquidity to expand their balance sheets, increasing the credit available to the economy.

A third alternative is to change the reserve requirements. The reserve requirement refers to the proportion of total assets that banks must keep on hand overnight, either in its vaults or at the central bank. Banks only maintain a small portion of their assets as cash available for immediate withdrawal; the rest is invested in illiquid assets like mortgages and loans. Lowering the reserve requirement frees up funds for banks to increase loans or buy other profitable assets. This is expansionary because it creates credit. However, even though this tool immediately increases liquidity, central banks rarely change the reserve requirement because it is expensive and requires a lot of new policies and procedures, disrupting member banks. The use of open market operations is therefore preferred.

Other: Unconventional Monetary Policy at the Zero Bound

Other forms of monetary policy, particularly used when interest rates are at or near 0% and there are concerns about deflation or deflation is occurring, are referred to as unconventional monetary policy. These include credit easing, quantitative easing, forward guidance, and signaling. In credit easing, a central bank purchases private sector assets to improve liquidity and improve access to credit. Signaling can be used to lower market expectations for lower interest rates in the future. For example, during the credit crisis of 2008, the US Federal Reserve indicated rates would be low for an "extended period", and the Bank of Canada made a "conditional commitment" to keep rates at the lower bound of 25 basis points (0.25%) until the end of the second quarter of 2010.

Further heterodox monetary policy proposals include the idea of helicopter money whereby central banks would create money without assets as counterpart in their balance sheet. The money created could be distributed directly to the population as a citizen's dividend. This option has been increasingly discussed since March 2016 after the ECB's president Mario Draghi said he found the concept "very interesting".

Nominal Anchors

A nominal anchor for monetary policy is a single variable or device which the central bank uses to pin down expectations of private agents about the nominal price level or its path or about what the central bank might do with respect to achieving that path. Monetary regimes combine long-run nominal anchoring with flexibility in the short run. Nominal variables used as anchors primarily include exchange rate targets, money supply targets, and inflation targets with interest rate policy.

Types

In practice, to implement any type of monetary policy the main tool used is modifying the amount of base money in circulation. The monetary authority does this by buying or selling financial assets (usually government obligations). These open market operations change either the amount of money or its liquidity (if less liquid forms of money are bought or sold). The multiplier effect of fractional reserve banking amplifies the effects of these actions.

Constant market transactions by the monetary authority modify the supply of currency and this impacts other market variables such as short-term interest rates and the exchange rate.

The distinction between the various types of monetary policy lies primarily with the set of instruments and target variables that are used by the monetary authority to achieve their goals.

Monetary Policy:	Target Market Variable:	Long Term Objective:
Inflation Targeting	Interest rate on overnight debt	A given rate of change in the CPI
Price Level Targeting	Interest rate on overnight debt	A specific CPI number
Monetary Aggregates	The growth in money supply	A given rate of change in the CPI
Fixed Exchange Rate	The spot price of the currency	The spot price of the currency
Gold Standard	The spot price of gold	Low inflation as measured by the gold price
Mixed Policy	Usually interest rates	Usually unemployment + CPI change

The different types of policy are also called monetary regimes, in parallel to exchange-rate regimes. A fixed exchange rate is also an exchange-rate regime; The Gold standard results in a relatively fixed regime towards the currency of other countries on the gold standard and a floating regime towards those that are not. Targeting inflation, the price level or other monetary aggregates implies floating exchange rate unless the management of the relevant foreign currencies is tracking exactly the same variables (such as a harmonized consumer price index).

In economics, an expansionary fiscal policy includes higher spending and tax cuts, that encourage economic growth. In turn, an expansionary monetary policy is one that seeks to increase the size of the money supply. As usual, inciting of money supply is aimed at lowering the interest rates on purpose to achieve economic growth by increase of economic activity. Conversely, contractionary monetary policy seeks to reduce the size of the money supply. In most nations, monetary policy is controlled by either a central bank or a finance ministry. Neoclassical and Keynesian economics significantly differ on the effects and effectiveness of monetary policy on influencing the **real** economy; there is no clear consensus on how monetary policy affects real economic variables (aggregate output or income, employment). Both economic schools accept that monetary policy affects monetary variables (price levels, interest rates).

Inflation Targeting/inflation and Interest Rate Targets

Under this policy approach the target is to keep inflation, under a particular definition such as Consumer Price Index, within a desired range.

The inflation target is achieved through periodic adjustments to the Central Bank interest rate target. The interest rate used is generally the overnight rate at which banks lend to each other overnight for cash flow purposes. Depending on the country this particular interest rate might be called the cash rate or something similar.

As the Fisher Effect model explains, the equation linking inflation with interest rates (both foreign and abroad) is the following:

$$\Pi = i - r$$

Where π is the inflation at home, i is the home interest rate set by the central bank, and r is the real world interest rate. Using i as an anchor, central banks can influence π. However, a necessary assumption for this equation to hold, is that the world real interest rate is constant. Central banks can choose to maintain a fixed interest rates at all times, or to keep a constant interest rate until the real world interest rate changes. The duration of this policy varies, because of the simplicity associated with changing the nominal interest rate.

The interest rate target is maintained for a specific duration using open market operations. Typically the duration that the interest rate target is kept constant will vary between months and years. This interest rate target is usually reviewed on a monthly or quarterly basis by a policy committee.

Changes to the interest rate target are made in response to various market indicators in an attempt to forecast economic trends and in so doing keep the market on track towards achieving the defined inflation target. For example, one simple method of inflation targeting called the Taylor rule adjusts the interest rate in response to changes in the inflation rate and the output gap. The rule was proposed by John B. Taylor of Stanford University.

The inflation targeting approach to monetary policy approach was pioneered in New Zealand. It has been used in Australia, Brazil, Canada, Chile, Colombia, the Czech Republic, Hungary, New Zealand, Norway, Iceland, India, Philippines, Poland, Sweden, South Africa, Turkey, and the United Kingdom.

Price Level Targeting

Price level targeting is a monetary policy that is similar to inflation targeting except that CPI growth in one year over or under the long term price level target is offset in subsequent years such that a targeted price-level is reached over time, e.g. five years, giving more certainty about future price increases to consumers. Under inflation targeting what happened in the immediate past years is not taken into account or adjusted for in the current and future years.

Uncertainty in price levels can create uncertainty around price and wage setting activity for firms and workers, and undermines any information that can be gained from relative prices, as it is more difficult for firms to determine if a change in the price of a good or service is because of inflation or other factors, such as an increase in the efficiency of factors of production, if inflation is high and volatile. An increase in inflation also leads to a decrease in the demand for money, as it reduces the incentive to hold money and increases transaction costs and shoe leather costs.

Monetary Aggregates/money Supply Targeting

In the 1980s, several countries used an approach based on a constant growth in the money supply. This approach was refined to include different classes of money and credit (M0, M1 etc.). In the US this approach to monetary policy was discontinued with the selection of Alan Greenspan as Fed Chairman.

This approach is also sometimes called monetarism.

Central banks might choose to set a money supply growth target as a nominal anchor to keep prices stable in the long term. The quantity theory, is a long run model, which links price levels to money supply and demand. Using this equation, we can rearrange to see the following:

$$\Pi = \mu - g$$

Where π is the inflation, μ is the money supply growth rate and g is the real output growth. This equation suggests that controlling the money supply's growth rate can ultimately lead to price stability in the long run. To use this nominal anchor, a central bank would need to set μ equal to a constant and commit to maintaining this target.

However, the money supply growth rate is considered a weak policy, because there is no way to target real output growth, As a result, a higher output growth rate will result in a too low level of inflation. A low output growth rate will result in inflation that would be higher than the desired level.

While monetary policy typically focuses on a price signal of one form or another, this approach is focused on monetary quantities. As these quantities could have a role on the economy and business cycles depending on the households' risk aversion level, money is sometimes explicitly added in the central bank's reaction function. Recently, however, central banks are shifting away from policies that focus on money supply targeting, because of the uncertainty that real output growth introduces. Some central banks, like the ECB, are choosing to combine money supply anchor with other targets.

Fixed Exchange Rate Targeting

This policy is based on maintaining a fixed exchange rate with a foreign currency. There are varying degrees of fixed exchange rates, which can be ranked in relation to how rigid the fixed exchange rate is with the anchor nation.

Under a system of fiat fixed rates, the local government or monetary authority declares a fixed exchange rate but does not actively buy or sell currency to maintain the rate. Instead, the rate is enforced by non-convertibility measures (e.g. capital controls, import/export licenses, etc.). In this case there is a black market exchange rate where the currency trades at its market/unofficial rate.

Under a system of fixed-convertibility, currency is bought and sold by the central bank or monetary authority on a daily basis to achieve the target exchange rate. This target rate may be a fixed level or a fixed band within which the exchange rate may fluctuate until the monetary authority intervenes to buy or sell as necessary to maintain the exchange rate within the band. (In this case, the fixed exchange rate with a fixed level can be seen as a special case of the fixed exchange rate with bands where the bands are set to zero.)

Under a system of fixed exchange rates maintained by a currency board every unit of local currency must be backed by a unit of foreign currency (correcting for the exchange rate). This ensures that the local monetary base does not inflate without being backed by hard currency and eliminates any worries about a run on the local currency by those wishing to convert the local currency to the hard (anchor) currency.

Under dollarization, foreign currency (usually the US dollar, hence the term "dollarization") is used freely as the medium of exchange either exclusively or in parallel with local currency. This outcome can come about because the local population has lost all faith in the local currency, or it may also be a policy of the government (usually to rein in inflation and import credible monetary policy).

Theoretically, using Relative PPP, the rate of depreciation must equal the inflation differential.

$$(E_{(H/F)}))/(E_{H/F}) = \Pi_H + \Pi_F$$

which implies that:

$$\Pi_H = (E_{(H/F)}))/(E_{H/F}) + \Pi_F$$

where the subscript "H" denotes the home country and "F" indicates the foreign country. The anchor variable is the rate of depreciation, (E(H/F))/ (EH/F) . Therefore, the rate of inflation at home must equal the rate of inflation in the foreign country plus the rate of depreciation of the exchange rate of home's currency, relative to the other.

With a strict fixed exchange rate or a peg, the rate of depreciation of the exchange rate is set equal to zero, such as in currency unions. In the case of a crawling peg, the rate is set equal to constant. With a limited flexible band, the rate of depreciation is allowed to fluctuate within a given range.

By fixing the rate of depreciation, PPP theory concludes that the home country's inflation rate must depend on the foreign country. For example, a two percent increase in inflation at home raises the foreign country's inflation by two percent. Countries may decide to use a fixed exchange rate monetary regime in order to take advantage of price stability and control inflation. In practice, more than half of nation's monetary regimes use fixed exchange rate anchoring.

These policies often abdicate monetary policy to the foreign monetary authority or government as monetary policy in the pegging nation must align with monetary policy in the anchor nation to maintain the exchange rate. The degree to which local monetary policy becomes dependent on the anchor nation depends on factors such as capital mobility, openness, credit channels and other economic factors.

In Practice

Nominal anchors are possible with various exchange rate regimes.

Type of Nominal Anchor	Compatible Exchange Rate Regimes
Exchange Rate Target	Currency Union/Countries without own currency, Pegs/ Bands/Crawls, Managed Floating
Money Supply Target	Managed Floating, Freely Floating
Inflation Target (+ Interest Rate Policy)	Managed Floating, Freely Floating

Following the collapse of Bretton Woods, nominal anchoring has grown in importance for monetary policy makers and inflation reduction. Particularly, governments sought to use anchoring in order to curtail rapid and high inflation during the 1970s and 1980s. By the 1990s, countries began to explicitly set credible nominal anchors. In addition, many countries chose a mix of more than one target, as well as implicit targets. As a result, global inflation rates have, on average, decreased gradually since the 1970s and central banks have gained credibility and increasing independence.

The Global Financial Crisis of 2008 has sparked controversy over the use and flexibility of inflation nominal anchoring. Many economists argue that inflation targets are currently set too low by many monetary regimes. During the crisis, many inflation anchoring countries reached the lower bound of zero rates, resulting in inflation rates decreasing to almost zero or even deflation.

Implications

The anchors discussed in this section suggest that keeping inflation at the desired level is feasible by setting a target interest rate, money supply growth rate, price level, or rate of depreciation. However, these anchors are only valid if a central bank commits to maintaining them. This, in turn, requires that the central bank abandons their monetary policy autonomy in the long run. Should a central bank use one of these anchors to maintain a target inflation rate, they would have to forfeit using other policies. On that note, it is important to mention that using these anchors may prove more complicated for certain exchange rate regimes. Freely floating or managed floating regimes, have more options to affect their inflation, because they enjoy more flexibility than a pegged currency or a country without a currency. The latter regimes would have to implement an exchange rate target to influence their inflation, as none of the other instruments are available to them.

Credibility

The short-term effects of monetary policy can be influenced by the degree to which announcements of new policy are deemed credible. In particular, when an anti-inflation policy is announced by a central bank, in the absence of credibility in the eyes of the public inflationary expectations will not drop, and the short-run effect of the announcement and a subsequent sustained anti-inflation policy is likely to be a combination of somewhat lower inflation and higher unemployment. But if the policy announcement is deemed credible, inflationary expectations will drop commensurately with the announced policy intent, and inflation is likely to come down more quickly and without so much of a cost in terms of unemployment.

Thus there can be an advantage to having the central bank be independent of the political authority, to shield it from the prospect of political pressure to reverse the direction of the policy. But even with a seemingly independent central bank, a central bank whose hands are not tied to the anti-inflation policy might be deemed as not fully credible; in this case there is an advantage to be had by the central bank being in some way bound to follow through on its policy pronouncements, lending it credibility.

Contexts

In International Economics

Optimal monetary policy in international economics is concerned with the question of how monetary policy should be conducted in interdependent open economies. The classical view holds that international macroeconomic interdependence is only relevant if it affects domestic output gaps and inflation, and monetary policy prescriptions can abstract from openness without harm. This view rests on two implicit assumptions: a high responsiveness of import prices to the exchange rate, i.e. producer currency pricing (PCP), and frictionless international financial markets supporting the efficiency of flexible price allocation. The violation or distortion of these assumptions found in empirical research is the subject of a substantial part of the international optimal monetary policy literature. The policy trade-offs specific to this international perspective are threefold:

First, research suggests only a weak reflection of exchange rate movements in import prices, lending credibility to the opposed theory of local currency pricing (LCP). The consequence is a departure from the classical view in the form of a trade-off between output gaps and misalignments in international relative prices, shifting monetary policy to CPI inflation control and real exchange rate stabilization.

Second, another specificity of international optimal monetary policy is the issue of strategic interactions and competitive devaluations, which is due to cross-border spillovers in quantities and prices. Therein, the national authorities of different countries face incentives to manipulate the terms of trade to increase national welfare in the absence of international policy coordination. Even though the gains of international policy coordination might be small, such gains may become very relevant if balanced against incentives for international noncooperation.

Third, open economies face policy trade-offs if asset market distortions prevent global efficient allocation. Even though the real exchange rate absorbs shocks in current and expected fundamentals, its adjustment does not necessarily result in a desirable allocation and may even exacerbate the misallocation of consumption and employment at both the domestic and global level. This is because, relative to the case of complete markets, both the Phillips curve and the loss function include a welfare-relevant measure of cross-country imbalances. Consequently, this results in domestic goals, e.g. output gaps or inflation, being traded-off against the stabilization of external variables such as the terms of trade or the demand gap. Hence, the optimal monetary policy in this case consists of redressing demand imbalances and/or correcting international relative prices at the cost of some inflation.

Corsetti, Dedola and Leduc (2011) summarize the status quo of research on international monetary policy prescriptions: "Optimal monetary policy thus should target a combination of inward-looking variables such as output gap and inflation, with currency misalignment and cross-country demand misallocation, by leaning against the wind of misaligned exchange rates and international imbalances." This is main factor in country money status.

In Developing Countries

Developing countries may have problems establishing an effective operating monetary policy. The primary difficulty is that few developing countries have deep markets in government debt. The matter is further complicated by the difficulties in forecasting money demand and fiscal pressure to levy the inflation tax by expanding the base rapidly. In general, the central banks in many developing countries have poor records in managing monetary policy. This is often because the monetary authority in developing countries are mostly not independent of the government, so good monetary policy takes a backseat to the political desires of the government or are used to pursue other non-monetary goals. For this and other reasons, developing countries that want to establish credible monetary policy may institute a currency board or adopt dollarization.

This can avoid interference from the government and may lead to the adoption of monetary policy as carried out in the anchor nation. Recent attempts at liberalizing and reform of financial markets (particularly the recapitalization of banks and other financial institutions in Nigeria and elsewhere) are gradually providing the latitude required to implement monetary policy frameworks by the relevant central banks.

Trends

Transparency

Beginning with New Zealand in 1990, central banks began adopting formal, public inflation targets with the goal of making the outcomes, if not the process, of monetary policy more transparent. In other words, a central bank may have an inflation target of 2% for a given year, and if inflation turns out to be 5%, then the central bank will typically have to submit an explanation. The Bank of England exemplifies both these trends. It became independent of government through the Bank of England Act 1998 and adopted an inflation target of 2.5% RPI, revised to 2% of CPI in 2003. The European Central Bank adopted, in 1998, a definition of price stability within the Eurozone as inflation of under 2% HICP. In 2003, this was revised to inflation below, but close to, 2% over the medium term. Since then, the target of 2% has become common for other major central banks, including the Federal Reserve (since January 2012) and Bank of Japan (since January 2013).

Effect on Business Cycles

There continues to be some debate about whether monetary policy can (or should) smooth business cycles. A central conjecture of Keynesian economics is that the central bank can stimulate aggregate demand in the short run, because a significant number of prices in the economy are fixed in the short run and firms will produce as many goods and services as are demanded (in the long run, however, money is neutral, as in the neoclassical model). However, some economists from the new classical school contend that central banks cannot affect business cycles.

Behavioral Monetary Policy

Conventional macroeconomic models assume that all agents in an economy are fully rational. A rational agent has clear preferences, models uncertainty via expected values of variables or functions of variables, and always chooses to perform the action with the optimal expected outcome for itself among all feasible actions – they maximize their utility. Monetary policy analysis and decisions hence traditionally rely on this New Classical approach. However, as studied by the field of behavioral economics that takes into account the concept of bounded rationality, people often deviate from the way that these neoclassical theories assume. Humans are generally not able to react fully rational to the world around them – they do not make decisions in the rational way commonly envisioned in standard macroeconomic models. People have time limitations, cognitive biases, care about issues like fairness and equity and follow rules of thumb (heuristics).

This has implications for the conduct of monetary policy. Monetary policy is the final outcome of a complex interaction between monetary institutions, central banker preferences and policy rules, and hence human decision-making plays an important role. It is more and more recognized that the standard rational approach does not provide an optimal foundation for monetary policy actions. These models fail to address important human anomalies and behavioral drivers that explain monetary policy decisions.

An example of a behavioral bias that characterizes the behavior of central bankers is loss aversion: for every monetary policy choice, losses loom larger than gains, and both are evaluated with respect to the status quo. One result of loss aversion is that when gains and losses are symmetric or nearly so, risk aversion may set in. Loss aversion can be found in multiple contexts in monetary policy. The "hard fought" battle against the Great Inflation, for instance, might cause a bias against policies that risk greater inflation. Another common finding in behavioral studies is that individuals regularly offer estimates of their own ability, competence, or judgments that far exceed an objective assessment: they are overconfident. Central bank policymakers may fall victim to overconfidence in managing the macroeconomy in terms of timing, magnitude, and even the qualitative impact of interventions. Overconfidence can result in actions of the central bank that are either "too little" or "too much". When policymakers believe their actions will have larger effects than objective analysis would indicate, this results in too little intervention. Overconfidence can, for instance, cause problems when relying on interest rates to gauge the stance of monetary policy: low rates might mean that policy is easy, but they could also signal a weak economy.

These are examples of how behavioral phenomena may have a substantial influence on monetary policy. Monetary policy analyses should thus account for the fact that policymakers (or central bankers) are individuals and prone to biases and temptations that can sensibly influence their ultimate choices in the setting of macroeconomic and/or interest rate targets.

Management of Operational Risk

Operational Risk Management

The term Operational Risk Management (ORM) is defined as a continual cyclic process which includes risk assessment, risk decision making, and implementation of risk controls, which results in acceptance, mitigation, or avoidance of risk. ORM is the oversight of operational risk, including the risk of loss resulting from inadequate or failed internal processes and systems; human factors; or external events.

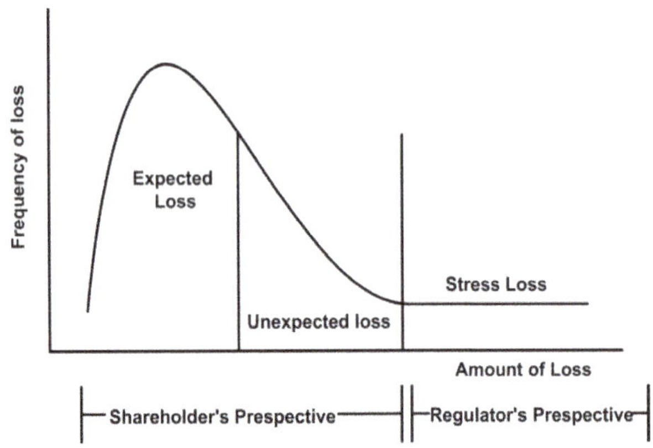

Four Principles of ORM

The U.S. Department of Defense summarizes the principles of ORM as follows:

- Accept risk when benefits outweigh the cost.
- Accept no unnecessary risk.
- Anticipate and manage risk by planning.
- Make risk decisions at the right level.

Three Levels of ORM

In Depth

In depth risk management is used before a project is implemented, when there is plenty of time to plan and prepare. Examples of in depth methods include training, drafting instructions and requirements, and acquiring personal protective equipment.

Deliberate

Deliberate risk management is used at routine periods through the implementation of a project or process. Examples include quality assurance, on-the-job training, safety briefs, performance reviews, and safety checks.

Time Critical

Time critical risk management is used during operational exercises or execution of tasks. It is defined as the effective use of all available resources by individuals, crews, and teams to safely and effectively accomplish the mission or task using risk management concepts when time and resources are limited. Examples of tools used includes execution check-lists and change management. This requires a high degree of situational awareness.

ORM Process

In Depth

The International Organization for Standardization defines the risk management process in a four-step model:

1. Establish context
2. Risk assessment
    - Risk identification
    - Risk analysis
    - Risk evaluation
3. Risk treatment
4. Monitor and review

This process is cyclic as any changes to the situation (such as operating environment or needs of the unit) requires re-evaluation per step one.

Deliberate

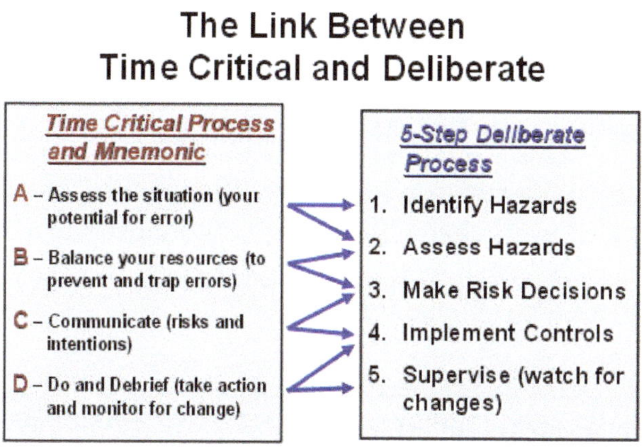

The U.S. Department of Defense summarizes the deliberate level of ORM process in a five-step model:

1. Identify hazards
2. Assess hazards
3. Make risk decisions
4. Implement controls
5. Supervise (and watch for changes)

Time Critical

The U.S. Navy summarizes the time-critical risk management process in a four-step model:

1. Assess the situation.

The three conditions of the Assess step are task loading, additive conditions, and human factors.

- Task loading refers to the negative effect of increased tasking on performance of the tasks.
- Additive factors refers to having a situational awareness of the cumulative effect of variables (conditions, etc.).
- Human factors refers to the limitations of the ability of the human body and mind to adapt to the work environment (e.g. stress, fatigue, impairment, lapses of attention, confusion, and willful violations of regulations).

2. Balance your resources.

This refers to balancing resources in three different ways:

- Balancing resources and options available. This means evaluating and leveraging all the informational, labor, equipment, and material resources available.
- Balancing Resources verses hazards. This means estimating how well prepared you are to safely accomplish a task and making a judgement call.
- Balancing individual verses team effort. This means observing individual risk warning signs. It also means observing how well the team is communicating, knows the roles that each member is supposed to play, and the stress level and participation level of each team member.

3. Communicate risks and intentions.

- Communicate hazards and intentions.
- Communicate to the right people.
- Use the right communication style. Asking questions is a technique to opening the lines of communication. A direct and forceful style of communication gets a specific result from a specific situation.

4. Do and debrief. (Take action and monitor for change.)

This is accomplished in three different phases:

- Mission Completion is a point where the exercise can be evaluated and reviewed in full.

- Execute and Gauge Risk involves managing change and risk while an exercise is in progress.
- Future Performance Improvements refers to preparing a "lessons learned" for the next team that plans or executes a task.

Benefits of ORM

1. Reduction of operational loss.
2. Lower compliance/auditing costs.
3. Early detection of unlawful activities.
4. Reduced exposure to future risks.

Chief Operational Risk Officer

The role of the Chief Operational Risk Officer (CORO) continues to evolve and gain importance. In addition to being responsible for setting up a robust Operational Risk Management function at companies, the role also plays an important part in increasing awareness of the benefits of sound operational risk management.

Most complex financial institutions have a Chief Operational Risk Officer. The position is also required for Banks that fall into the Basel II Advanced Measurement Approach "mandatory" category.

ORM Software

The impact of the Enron failure and the implementation of the Sarbanes–Oxley Act has caused several software development companies to create enterprise-wide software packages to manage risk. These software systems allow the financial audit to be executed at lower cost.

Forrester Research has identified 115 Governance, Risk and Compliance vendors that cover operational risk management projects. Active Agenda is an open source project dedicated to operational risk management.

References

- Guégan, D.; Hassani, B.K. (2012). "Operational risk: A Basel II++ step before Basel III". Journal of Risk Management in Financial Institutions. 6: 37–53
- O'Sullivan, Arthur; Sheffrin, Steven M. (2003). Economics: Principles in Action. Upper Saddle River, New Jersey: Pearson Prentice Hall. p. 551. ISBN 0-13-063085-3
- Cuthbertson, K., Nitzsche, D. and Hyde, S.(2008). Monetary policy and behavioral finance. Journal of Economic Surveys, 21(5), pp. 935-969

- "Operational Risks in Financial Services: An Old Challenge in a New Environment" (PDF). Credit Suisse Group. Retrieved 2014-04-29
- Frachot, A.; Georges, P.; Roncalli, T. (2001). "Loss Distribution Approach for Operational Risk". GRO, Crédit Lyonnais. doi:10.2139/ssrn.1032523
- Benchimol, J., Fourçans, A. (2012), Money and risk in a DSGE framework: A Bayesian application to the Eurozone, Journal of Macroeconomics, vol. 34, pp. 95–111
- Jahan, Sarwat. "Inflation Targeting: Holding the Line". International Monetary Funds, Finance & Development. Retrieved 28 December 2014
- Guégan, D.; Hassani, B.K. (2013). "Using a time series approach to correct serial correlation in Operational Risk capital calculation". Journal of Operational Risk. 8 (3): 31–56
- Noyer, Christian (12 January 2016). "Thoughts on the zero lower bound in relation with monetary and financial stability". Bank for International Settlements. Retrieved 18 January 2016

Permissions

All chapters in this book are published with permission under the Creative Commons Attribution Share Alike License or equivalent. Every chapter published in this book has been scrutinized by our experts. Their significance has been extensively debated. The topics covered herein carry significant information for a comprehensive understanding. They may even be implemented as practical applications or may be referred to as a beginning point for further studies.

We would like to thank the editorial team for lending their expertise to make the book truly unique. They have played a crucial role in the development of this book. Without their invaluable contributions this book wouldn't have been possible. They have made vital efforts to compile up to date information on the varied aspects of this subject to make this book a valuable addition to the collection of many professionals and students.

This book was conceptualized with the vision of imparting up-to-date and integrated information in this field. To ensure the same, a matchless editorial board was set up. Every individual on the board went through rigorous rounds of assessment to prove their worth. After which they invested a large part of their time researching and compiling the most relevant data for our readers.

The editorial board has been involved in producing this book since its inception. They have spent rigorous hours researching and exploring the diverse topics which have resulted in the successful publishing of this book. They have passed on their knowledge of decades through this book. To expedite this challenging task, the publisher supported the team at every step. A small team of assistant editors was also appointed to further simplify the editing procedure and attain best results for the readers.

Apart from the editorial board, the designing team has also invested a significant amount of their time in understanding the subject and creating the most relevant covers. They scrutinized every image to scout for the most suitable representation of the subject and create an appropriate cover for the book.

The publishing team has been an ardent support to the editorial, designing and production team. Their endless efforts to recruit the best for this project, has resulted in the accomplishment of this book. They are a veteran in the field of academics and their pool of knowledge is as vast as their experience in printing. Their expertise and guidance has proved useful at every step. Their uncompromising quality standards have made this book an exceptional effort. Their encouragement from time to time has been an inspiration for everyone.

The publisher and the editorial board hope that this book will prove to be a valuable piece of knowledge for students, practitioners and scholars across the globe.

Index